A NEW ERA?

TIMOR-LESTE AFTER THE UN

A NEW ERA?

TIMOR-LESTE AFTER THE UN

Edited by Sue Ingram, Lia Kent and Andrew McWilliam

PRESS

Published by ANU Press
The Australian National University
Acton ACT 2601, Australia
Email: anupress@anu.edu.au
This title is also available online at http://press.anu.edu.au

---

National Library of Australia Cataloguing-in-Publication entry

Title: A new era? : Timor-Leste after the UN / Lia Kent, Sue Ingram, Andrew McWilliam, editors.

ISBN: 9781925022506 (paperback) 9781925022513 (ebook)

Subjects: Timor-Leste--Politics and government .
Timor-Leste--Economic conditions--21st century.
Timor-Leste--Social conditions--21st century.

Other Creators/Contributors:
Kent, Lia, editor.
Ingram, Sue, editor.
McWilliam, Andrew, editor.

Dewey Number: 959.8704

All rights reserved. No part of this publication may be reproduced, stored in a retrieval system or transmitted in any form or by any means, electronic, mechanical, photocopying or otherwise, without the prior permission of the publisher.

Cover design and layout by ANU Press.

This edition © 2015 ANU Press

Contents

List of Illustrations vii
List of Contributors ix
Acknowledgements. xi
Acronyms and Initialisms xiii

1. Introduction: Building the Nation: Legacies and Challenges for Timor-Leste . . . 1
   Sue Ingram, Lia Kent and Andrew McWilliam

PART ONE: BUILDING A NATION-STATE IN THE SHADOW OF HISTORY

2. The Challenges of Nation-State Building 17
   Agio Pereira

3. Past, Present and Future: Why the Past Matters 31
   Fidelis Magalhães

4. The Politics of History in Timor-Leste. 41
   Michael Leach

5. Challenges to the Consolidation of Democracy 59
   Rui Graça Feijó

PART TWO: TRENDS IN ECONOMIC DEVELOPMENT

6. Can the Petroleum Fund Exorcise the Resource Curse from Timor-Leste? 73
   Charles Scheiner

7. Progress and Challenges of Infrastructure Spending in Timor-Leste 103
   Antonio Vitor

8. Securing a New Ordering of Power in Timor-Leste: The Role
   of Sub-national Spending 117
   Saku Akmeemana and Doug Porter

9. 'Empty Land'? The Politics of Land in Timor-Leste 141
    Meabh Cryan

PART THREE: STABILITY AND PEACE-BUILDING

10. After Xanana: Challenges for Stability 155
    Cillian Nolan

11. Rethinking Governance and Security in Timor-Leste 169
    Damian Grenfell

12. Building Social Cohesion from Below: Learning from the *Laletek* (Bridge)
    Project 2010–12 187
    Catharina Maria

PART FOUR: CITIZENS, INEQUALITIES AND MIGRATION

13. A Social Movement as an Antidote to Corruption 203
    Adérito de Jesus Soares

14. The Veterans' Valorisation Scheme: Marginalising Women's
    Contributions to the Resistance. 213
    Lia Kent and Naomi Kinsella

15. Rural–Urban Inequalities and Migration in Timor-Leste 225
    Andrew McWilliam

16. Assessing the Implementation and Impact of Timor-Leste's Cash
    Payment Schemes. 235
    Joanne Wallis

17. Displacement and Informal Repatriation in a Rural Timorese Village. 251
    Pyone Myat Thu

List of Illustrations

Figure 6.1 Sectoral contributions to Timor-Leste's 'non-oil' GDP per capita in 2013.....75
Figure 6.2 What do Timorese people do for work?.....77
Figure 6.3 Timor-Leste's petroleum revenue streams.....79
Figure 6.4 State revenues and expenditures.....80
Figure 6.5 Oil and gas income peaked in 2012 and continues to fall.....81
Figure 6.6 Budgeted, executed and recurrent spending year by year.....82
Figure 6.7 Allocation of the revised 2015 State Budget (US$1.570 billion).....83
Figure 6.8 Base case scenario from sustainability model.....91
Figure 7.1 National road upgrading project.....113
Figure 8.1 Major infrastructure spending FY 2004 – FY 2013 (US$ millions).....119
Figure 8.2 PR/PDD and PDL budgets (US$ millions).....121
Figure 8.3 PDD and PDL budget compared to public overall and capital spending (US$ millions).....124
Figure 8.4 Sub-national spending in Timor—a chronology.....126
Figure 8.5 Budget execution measures, 2009–12.....128
Figure 9.1 Prioritisation of community level land problems.....146
Figure 9.2 Explaining the significance of land, Tutuala, Lautem.....148
Figure 11.1 *Sorumutu*, Dili, 2006.....172
Figure 11.2 *Sorumutu* venue, Dili, 2006.....181
Figure 12.1 Liliana Amaral, Lalatek Technical Advisor, leading a mapping exercise in Fatuhada.....190

Figure 12.2 The four dimensions of a conflict transformation framework. 194

Figure 17.1 Map of Timor Island showing the districts in Timor-Leste and Kupang, the capital of West Timor. 253

List of Contributors

Saku Akmeemana is Senior Governance Specialist, World Bank.

Meabh Cryan is a PhD scholar in the State, Society and Governance in Melanesia program at The Australian National University. She previously worked for the *Rede ba Rai* (Land Network) and the Haburas Foundation *Matadalan ba Rai* program in Timor-Leste.

Rui Graça Feijó is Associate Researcher at the *CES-Centro de Estudos Sociais* (Centre for Social Studies), University of Coimbra, Portugal.

Damian Grenfell is Director of the Centre for Global Research, RMIT University.

Sue Ingram is a PhD scholar in the State, Society and Governance in Melanesia program at The Australian National University.

Lia Kent is a Research Fellow in the State, Society and Governance in Melanesia program at The Australian National University.

Naomi Kinsella is an independent human rights and law consultant currently resident in Myanmar.

Michael Leach is Associate Professor and Chair, Department of Education and Social Sciences, Faculty of Health, Arts and Design, Swinburne University of Technology.

Fidelis Magalhães is Presidential Chief of Staff, Presidency of the Republic of Timor-Leste.

Catharina Maria is an independent peace-building, gender and capacity strengthening consultant currently based in Bangkok.

Andrew McWilliam is Senior Fellow in Anthropology, College of Asia and the Pacific at The Australian National University.

Pyone Myat Thu is a Research Associate in the School of Anatomy, Physiology and Human Biology at The University of Western Australia. She was previously a Research Fellow in the State, Society and Governance of Melanesia program at ANU.

Cillian Nolan is Deputy Director of the Institute for Policy Analysis of Conflict (IPAC) in Jakarta.

Agio Pereira is Minister of State and of the Presidency of the Council of Ministers.

Doug Porter is Justice and Rule of Law Adviser, Governance Global Practice, the World Bank.

Charles Scheiner is a researcher at *La'o Hamutuk* (The Timor-Leste Institute for Development Monitoring and Analysis), Dili, Timor-Leste.

Adérito de Jesus Soares is a PhD scholar in the Regulatory Institutions Network at The Australian National University and the former Anti-corruption Commissioner in Timor-Leste.

Antonio Vitor is a consultant to the Asian Development Bank, Timor-Leste, and adviser to Timor-Leste's Ministry of Public Works, Transport and Communications.

Joanne Wallis is a Senior Lecturer, Strategic and Defence Studies Centre, The Australian National University.

Acknowledgements

This edited book originated in the inaugural Timor-Leste Update held at The Australian National University (ANU) from 28–29 November 2013. Entitled 'Timor-Leste: A New Era? Prospects and Challenges for Timor-Leste', the Update was an occasion for focused analysis and lively debate on a broad spectrum of issues facing the nation over the next 5–10 years. Attended by around 150 policymakers and scholars, and hosted by the State, Society and Governance in Melanesia (SSGM) program at ANU, there was general consensus that the Update should become a biennial event.

In planning the Update, we were generously assisted by a group of dedicated and enthusiastic colleagues who joined us on an organising committee that met regularly during 2013 to refine the topics and program. Our sincere thanks go to committee members Susan Harris-Rimmer, Janet Hunt, Joanne Wallis, Ruth Nuttall and Pyone Myat Thu. We also wish to acknowledge the professional staff who worked with us on the staging of the Update, most importantly Joel Nilon, whose experience and calm manner were critical to ensuring the event ran smoothly, and to Peta Hill, for negotiating complex travel arrangements. We also thank Louana Gaffey for administrative support and Jonathan Barrett, for ensuring the event was recorded and podcast.

We are extremely grateful to the Embassy of the Democratic Republic of Timor-Leste, in particular His Excellency Ambassador H.E. Mr Abel Guterres who collaborated generously with us as the program took shape. To mark Timor-Leste's Proclamation of Independence Day, the Embassy organised a very successful celebration on the evening of the 28 November, to which all Update speakers and participants were invited, and at which the then Australian Minister for Foreign Affairs, the Honourable Julie Bishop, offered commemorative remarks.

The Update would also have been impossible without the sponsorship of the Australian Government's Department of Foreign Affairs and Trade, ANU's Research School of Asia and the Pacific, the State, the Society and Governance in Melanesia Program, and the Asia Foundation Timor-Leste.

Much work has gone into preparing this edited book for publication. We are extremely grateful to Lindy Allen and Geoff Hunt, who provided exceptional copyediting and formatting support. We also thank Emily Tinker at ANU Press for guiding us through the publication process.

Finally, we sincerely thank the conference presenters who took time out of their busy schedules to attend the event. Many travelled from Dili, others from Indonesia, Thailand and Portugal. Particular thanks are due to those who contributed to this volume. In planning the Update and the edited book, we aimed to bring together a group of leading scholars, policy analysts and political leaders, including many from Timor-Leste itself. This volume reflects that mix. It also reflects the thoughtful analysis that each brought to bear on specific aspects of Timor-Leste's development a decade out from its rebirth as a nation, and the challenges for the future. We are grateful to them for devoting the time to this project.

Sue Ingram, Lia Kent and Andrew McWilliam
Canberra, June 2015

Acronyms and Initialisms

Note: The Portuguese or Tetum is given first, followed by the English translation

ADB	Asian Development Bank
AECCOP	*Associação de Empresários de Construção Civil e Obras Públicas*; Association of Entrepreneurs for Construction and Public Works
AMP	*Aliança da Maioria Parlamentar*; Alliance of the Parliamentary Majority
ASEAN	Association of Southeast Asian Nations
CAC	*Comissão Anti-Corrupção*; Anti-Corruption Commission
CAVR	*Comissão de Acolhimento, Verdade e Reconciliação de Timor Leste*; Timor-Leste Commission for Reception, Truth and Reconciliation
CAAC	*Comissão para os Assuntos dos Antigos Combatentes*; Commission for the Issues of Former Combatants
CAVF	*Comissão para os Assuntos dos Veteranos dos FALINTIL*; Commission for the Issues of FALINTIL Veterans
CAQR	*Comissão para os Assuntos dos Quadros da Resistencia*; Commission for the Issues of Cadres of the Resistance
CNRT (1)	*Conselho Nacional da Resistência Timorense*; National Council of Timorese Resistance (in existence from 1998–2001)
CNRT (2)	*Congresso Nacional para a Reconstrução de Timor-Leste*; National Congress for the Reconstruction of Timor-Leste (a political party formed in 2007)
CHART	Clearing House for Archival Records on Timor

CPD-RDTL	*Conselho Popular pela Defesa da República Democrática de Timor-Leste*; Popular Council for the Defence of the Democratic Republic of Timor-Leste
CPLP	*Comunidade dos Países de Língua Portuguesa*; Community of Portuguese Language Countries
FALINTIL	*Forças Armadas da Libertação Nacional de Timor-Leste*; Armed Forces for the National Liberation of East Timor
FRETILIN	*Frente Revolucionária de Timor-Leste Independente*; Revolutionary Front for an Independent East Timor
G20	Group of Twenty (international forum for the governments and central bank governors of 19 major economies plus the European Union)
g7+	Association of 20 countries that are or have been affected by conflict and are now in transition to the next stage of development
GDP	gross domestic product
GFC	Global Financial Crisis
ICG	International Crisis Group
IDPs	internally displaced persons
INTERFET	International Force for East Timor
JICA	Japan International Cooperation Agency
MAE	*Ministério da Administração Estatal*; Ministry of State Administration
MDGs	Millennium Development Goals
MP	Member of Parliament
MSS	*Ministério da Solidariedade Social*; Ministry of Social Solidarity
NGO	Non-government Organisation
NLC	National Liberation Combatant
OECD	Organisation for Economic Co-operation and Development
OPEC	Organization of the Petroleum Exporting Countries
PDID	*Planeamento de Dezenvolvimentu Integradu Distritál*; Integrated District Development Planning
PDL	*Programa Dezenvolvimentu Lokal*; Local Development Program

PNDS	*Programa Nasional Dezenvolvimentu Suku*; National Village Development Program
PNTL	*Polícia Nacional de Timor-Leste*; National Police of Timor-Leste
PSD	*Partido Social Democrata*; Social Democratic Party
RDTL	*República Democrática de Timor-Leste*; Democratic Republic of Timor-Leste
SDP	*Strategic Development Plan*
UDT	*União Democrática Timorense*; Timorese Democratic Union
UN	United Nations
UNDP	United Nations Development Programme
UNHCR	United Nations High Commissioner for Refugees
UNMIT	United Nations Integrated Mission in Timor-Leste
UNTAET	United Nations Transitional Administration in East Timor
WHO	World Health Organization
ZEESM	*Zona Espesial Ekonomia Sosial Merkadu*; Special Economic Zone for Social Market Economy

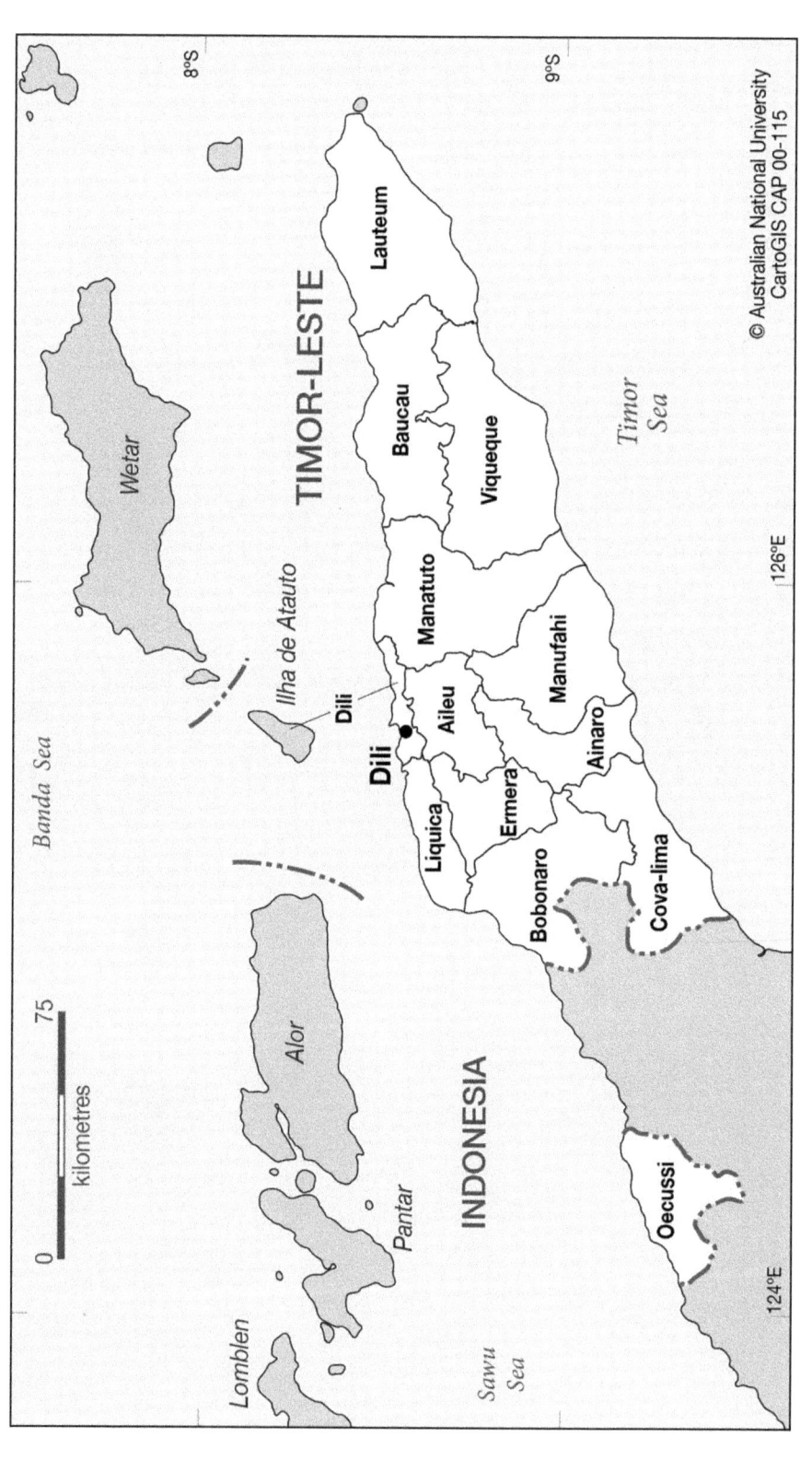

CHAPTER 1

Introduction: Building the Nation: Legacies and Challenges for Timor-Leste

Sue Ingram, Lia Kent and Andrew McWilliam

Background to the update

Timor-Leste has made rapid progress in its first decade as a new state, casting aside the instability that blighted its early years and achieving strong economic growth and institutional development. During 2012, the nation experienced peaceful presidential and parliamentary elections, the winding-up of the Australia-led International Stabilisation Force, and the completion of the United Nations (UN) peacekeeping mission after 13 years of UN presence. But significant challenges remain for the fledgling nation as it struggles to diversify its economy, implement its ambitious social and economic development plans, and preserve stability in the face of projected declines in petroleum revenues.

To mark this transition and reflect on the road ahead for Timor-Leste, the College of Asia and the Pacific at The Australian National University (ANU) convened an inaugural Timor-Leste Update on 28–29 November 2013. The opening day of the conference was set to coincide with Timor-Leste's national Restoration of Independence Day—the date on which the nation unilaterally declared its independence in 1975 and experienced a short-lived independence of 10 days before the Indonesian takeover that lasted 24 years. Full independence was eventually restored on 20 May 2002, following two-and-a-half years of transitional UN administration.

The Timor-Leste Update was designed with a number of complementary objectives in mind. Firstly, it was intended to contribute to Australia's developing knowledge of and engagement with a close regional neighbour by providing a public forum to discuss recent developments and plans. The Update also aimed to sustain and strengthen relationships between government agencies, civil society organisations and research institutions working on Timor-Leste, while helping to build the profile and capacity of East Timorese researchers and policy analysts.

Highlights of the two-day event included an opening address on Timor-Leste's 'path to prosperity' by His Excellency, Agio Pereira, Minister of State and of the Presidency of the Council of Ministers, entitled 'The Challenges of Nation State Building'. His remarks were underscored by a presentation from Mr Fidelis Magalhaes, Presidential Chief of Staff, Presidency of the Republic of Timor-Leste, who spoke on the topic 'Timor-Leste, Past, Present and Future; Why History Matters'. Their considered remarks provided the platform for a series of presentations by Timorese and Australian speakers around three framing topics:

- trends in economic development
- stability
- active citizenship.

The lively discussions that accompanied the presentations, the high level of interest shown in the proceedings, and strong audience attendance from the academy and government, all pointed to both the success of the Update and support for a continued forum of this kind that facilitates shared understandings and critical debates between the two nations. It is hoped that the Timor-Leste Update will become a biennial event.

Key themes

A number of broad themes ran through the presentations at the Update. They reflect Timor-Leste's remarkable politico-historical journey to independence and the subsequent gradual progress in defining values and building the structural, political and institutional foundations of the newly independent nation. We have identified five key themes, each of which is discussed in detail below:

1. achievements and challenges
2. legacies of the past and future prospects
3. theories of the liberal democratic state versus the *realpolitik* of state-building and participatory democracy
4. national and sub-national governance
5. policy intent and policy action: bold visions, modest progress.

1. Achievements and challenges

'Achievements and challenges' was a framing idea for the Update, and was something of a *leitmotif* through the two days of discussions. Timor-Leste has made huge achievements in the 11 years since independence. Stability was quickly restored following the internal divisions and build-up of conflict that came to a destructive head in 2006. Following the 2008 attacks on the president and prime minister, the leadership responded swiftly and effectively within the framework of the constitution, preventing collateral damage to the state and redoubling efforts to strengthen security.

Today, while the country is not conflict-free, episodes of civil discontent are minor in character and do not threaten development or political stability. The last few years have seen effective democratic consolidation, with a maturing of the institutions of the state and an active civil society. The nation is also emerging as a significant player on the international stage: chairing the g7+ forum, which is leading the discourse on the way that the international community engages in conflict-affected states; positioning for membership of the Association of Southeast Asian Nations (ASEAN) in the near future; and chairing the Community of Portuguese Language Countries (CPLP) in 2014.

Nonetheless, serious challenges remain. Timor-Leste is the second or third most petroleum-dependent state in the world, with a downstream risk of petroleum revenue collapse if new fields are not quickly brought on-stream. The state also faces a looming fiscal crisis unless revenue and outlays are brought into line and expenditure from the Petroleum Fund returned to the calculated sustainable level. The prospect of greater fiscal restraint in turn risks a rise in grievances and instability where declining public revenues translate into a paring back of generous social transfers, particularly to veterans, and reductions in public sector employment. The economic and social gulf between urban and rural areas continues to widen, despite a significant increase in social transfers and infrastructure development beyond the capital, Dili. Timor-Leste has experienced rapid population growth since the end of Indonesian occupation, and the population is projected to double in 17 years. However, the burgeoning numbers of school leavers face a weak labour market with little capacity to absorb the growing demand for jobs.

Timor-Leste is also marked by significant gender inequalities, despite constitutional guarantees of equality in all areas of family, social and cultural life and reasonable levels of representation of women in public office. As Laura Abrantes' presentation at the Update noted, women hold 25 out of 65 seats in the national parliament, equating to 38 per cent of seats—the highest percentage in Asia. In the newly constituted Araujo government, 3 of 17 ministers, 2 of 11 vice ministers and 3 of 9 secretaries of state are women, equating to just over

20 per cent. Nonetheless, the influence of women parliamentarians in lawmaking and oversight arguably remains limited—women hold few of the top executive posts, and the sphere of local politics remains overwhelmingly male dominated. Looking beyond their representation in public life, it is apparent that women remain significantly disadvantaged *vis à vis* men in the private sphere: they are poorer and have a lower literacy rate, have a lower rate of participation in the workforce, and are usually in lower level positions than men. Fertility and maternal mortality rates are among the highest globally. Rates of domestic violence continue to soar. All of this suggests that in Timor-Leste, as in many other societies, the process of translating women's formally guaranteed rights into substantive equality remains an ongoing challenge.

2. Legacies of the past and future prospects

Timor-Leste's past—its history of decolonisation and occupation, of political divisions and violence—informs the present. On the one hand, the strength of Timorese national identity lies in its history. On the other hand, the absence of a shared elite history through the 24 years of Indonesian occupation has set up divisions that are still playing out. There is controversy over what constitutes the 'true' history of the past and who controls that history—a feature most evident in continuing public disputes over historical events and the role of particular identities in relation to them. There is also contestation over who has a place in that history and who should be recognised for their contribution: the claims of FALINTIL (*Forças Armadas da Libertação Nacional de Timor-Leste*; Armed Forces for the National Liberation of East Timor) veterans are being treated very differently from those of other groups in society, for instance women, young people and former members of the clandestine front.

A powerful actor in Timor-Leste's political history that continues to shape the present is the Catholic Church. It was a bulwark for the Timorese people during the Indonesian occupation, a defender of their security and cultural integrity, a crucible for youth activism, and an early and influential proponent of a referendum on Timor's political future. It has continued to play a political role after independence where it perceives a threat to its interests, as in the 2005 demonstrations challenging the government's plan to withdraw religious education from the formal primary school curriculum. Two of the presentations touched on the Catholic Church's continuing role both as a pastoral carer and a service provider to the people.

History also shapes Timor-Leste's democratic development path and the policy and the structural choices that it makes. A number of presentations at the Update highlighted how veterans are becoming a privileged group in society due to the size of veterans' pensions. While Timor-Leste seeks to honour the struggles of the past, the spotlight is strongly on the future. The country's *Strategic Development Plan*, launched in 2011, charts an ambitious path for the inclusive development of Timor-Leste through to 2030. Its vision is to create a middle- to high-income country with a diversified economy and strong human capital by the target date. Yet there are real doubts whether the vision is achievable, and whether its major focus on infrastructure development—the aspirational Tasi Mane program and the high modernist master plan of the special economic market zone in Oecussi[1]—are well conceived. The alternative is to shift investment to Timor-Leste's people, investing in education, nutrition, food sovereignty and manufacture for local consumption. One speaker at the Update called for a greater focus on the children of Timor-Leste, who are its future. That the bilateral relationship with Indonesia is also forward-looking, rather than dwelling on the past, is a source of consternation to those still searching for criminal accountability for the crimes committed during the 24-year occupation.

Just days before the Update was held, Timor-Leste's Prime Minister, Xanana Gusmão, announced his intention to resign mid-term in 2014. The prospect of his imminent departure signalled a profound political transition for the young nation. Gusmão is a towering and revered figure who has led the Timorese people in different capacities—as head of the Resistance, as president and as prime minister—for 30 years. Many Timorese were fearful of a return to instability when he relinquished the helm. In the quest for a new leader, there were calls for a generational transfer of political power, but no clear successor was apparent beyond speculation about a possible move by the President, Taur Matan Ruak, to the prime ministership. An important question discussed during the Update was whether the next generation of leaders could command the same authority and the same commitment to constitutionality as the current leadership, whether they would feel the weight of other, non-democratic narratives that are powerful in the region, and the extent to which a growing engagement with Indonesia would influence public policy.

Gusmão delayed his resignation until 5 February 2015—the precise mid-point of his term—and in the weeks leading up to it he worked to secure the succession, eventually anointing the highly regarded Dr Rui de Araújo from the official opposition party, FRETILIN (*Frente Revolucionária de Timor-Leste Independente*; Revolutionary Front for an Independent East Timor). The move was dramatic: it guaranteed the total overhaul of Gusmão's bloated and underperforming

---

1 Tasi Mane refers to the development of three industrial clusters and interlinking infrastructure along the south coast of Timor-Leste to support the planned domestic petroleum industry. The Oecussi special economic zone refers to the development of a trade, commerce and tourist hub in the enclave of Oecussi; the initiative is known as the *Zona Espesial Ekonomia Sosial Merkadu* (ZEESM; Special Economic Zone for Social Market Economy).

government since constitutionally the resignation of a prime minister triggers the departure of the entire government; it marked the transfer of power from the '75 Generation to the *Jerasaun Foun* (New Generation)[2]; and it marked Gusmão's own victory over partisan politics, which, ever since his youth, he has regarded with suspicion.

In persuading his own coalition parties to support Araújo, Gusmão encouraged them to put the interests of the state above the interests of the parties. Prime Minister Araújo, in his inauguration speech, echoed this theme, pledging that the national interest would be paramount and committing the members of his government to putting the interests of the people above partisan interests. The president, in his speech at the inauguration ceremony, captured the essence of the political and policy transition underway, describing the transfer of power 'from the generation which has conquered liberation to that which must conquer development'. This is the huge challenge now confronting the country.

3. Theories of the liberal–democratic state versus the *realpolitik* of state-building and participatory democracy

Institutional choices and the drivers of those choices emerged in various ways through the course of the Update as a domain of contest and competition between international policy orthodoxy and endogenous approaches anchored in local context and realities. A decade after independence, there is evident frustration over homilies on good governance by development partners whose own institutions may be less than exemplary. Equally, there is frustration at the criticism of approaches pursued in Timor-Leste that do not adhere to orthodox models of the structure of the liberal democratic state when patently the home-grown approaches work on the ground. 'Democracy' was described as both an end and a means; there is a form of 'democracy *à la* Timor' that arguably works in context, even if it does not always accord with liberal democratic prescriptions. Those prescriptions may sound noble, but they can work against sustainability. Either way, the question of democracy and development remains a lively and contested arena, both within Timor-Leste itself and as a continuing dialogue among critics and interested observers.

Several examples emerged over the course of the Update illustrating the difficulty of striking the right balance between fiscal or policy ideals and shoring up the stability and security of the state. For example, the design

---

2   '75 Generation refers to the older generation of Timorese leaders who emerged over the period from Portugal's decision to decolonise its territories in April 1974 to the invasion by Indonesian forces in December 1975 and the subsequent armed resistance. *Jerasaun Foun* refers to the younger generation who spearheaded the campaign of civil disobedience of the late 1980s and 1990s that put the question of East Timor back on the international agenda.

and implementation of the 2009 *Pakote Referendum* (Referendum Package) to initiate public works on a massive scale was heavily criticised for bypassing ordinary budgetary approval processes. While there have been allegations that project funds have been manipulated, not implemented, or implemented below standard, others argue that the package was a critical mechanism for stability that necessitated some trade-offs around procurement processes. Similarly, the decision to bring the police and the military together operationally under a joint command following the crisis of 2008 was criticised at the time but has, arguably, proven to be an effective response that is widely endorsed by the population. A third example was the decision to pardon Maternus Bere, the former Laksaur Militia Leader indicted for crimes against humanity for his role in the 1999 Suai Church massacre. Although attracting significant local criticism from human rights groups, this decision can also be understood as a pragmatic response by the Timor-Leste state to larger security interests, and one that signalled the importance of the Indonesia relationship. A fourth example is the collaboration and rapprochement now evident between the government and opposition parliamentary benches. An important point of discussion was where the line should be drawn between liberal democratic templates and *realpolitik*, and how well the benefits of endogenous approaches to nation-state building are understood by the international state-building fraternity. These were flagged as potential areas for research.

A larger, related question that was canvassed as a major political challenge was how Timor-Leste would use its wealth into the future. Two alternative paths were outlined: would the state establish firm rules for all areas of public expenditure with a neutral state apparatus disbursing funds; or would it further entrench a patron–client system that is fundamentally anti-democratic and based around elite interests and political favouritism?

4. National and sub-national governance

Timor-Leste remains two very different worlds: divided between the globalised capital Dili and the isolated and poorly serviced rural hinterland; and between relative wealth and extreme poverty. Troublingly, key indicators suggest that the gap is widening. Several factors were discussed that both informed understanding of and affected developments in these two contrasting worlds. First, gross domestic product (GDP) is a very poor indicator of real per capita incomes as it is dominated by Timor-Leste's oil wealth, much of which is transferred off-shore. Wealth is concentrated in Dili, and distributional inequity across the population is extreme, despite significant levels of social transfer payments since 2008. Distributional inequity mirrors the split between participation in the formal economy and largely subsistence-level rural livelihoods.

That said, there are clear and positive changes occurring across the hinterland, not least with the near completion of the national electricity grid that was rapidly rolled out from 2010. The benefits of lighting and power have extensive multiplier effects, including much more widespread access to communications and the internet, which Timorese, like people everywhere, are embracing with enthusiasm.

The government has also invested extensively in a range of decentralised construction projects, including new health centres, school buildings, road maintenance, and monuments to the nationalist struggle. And despite criticism over tendering processes for these contracts and the quality of construction, most district centres have at least seen a revival of local enterprise and contract services companies.

There remains an ongoing debate about expenditure priorities—in particular, the very large commitments to big-ticket physical infrastructure versus the very modest investments in human services and agriculture—and the beneficiaries of these priorities. The current policy to distribute cheap imported rice at discount retail prices, for example, provides short-term benefits to rural households but inevitably undermines incentives for local rice production to the long-term detriment of East Timorese producers.

Timor-Leste is experiencing a brain and age drain, with young, educated people relocating from the rural areas to the capital seeking further education and job opportunities absent in the regions. Small but significant numbers of young people are travelling overseas for employment, and their remittances are highly visible in upgraded housing stock in rural areas. Social transfers and remittances are also underwriting household expenditures in the districts, but are very unevenly spread, with veterans receiving the lion's share of these publicly funded distributions.

Sub-national governance remains a key systemic question to be resolved, and a critical component of the unfinished agenda of state-building. Earlier enthusiasm and policy discussions around the organisation and implementation of decentralised government have seemingly stalled. The result is that regional government programs and participatory decision-making across the region are constrained and remain heavily dependent on Dili based national level directives.

5. Policy intent and policy action: bold visions, modest progress

A number of presenters commented on the apparent marked disjunction between stated policy intentions of the government and parliament and the decisions actually taken. At the next level down, policies approved are then poorly executed. Institutional capacity and organisation, in its many elements, is the central factor. One aspect highlighted was the insufficient separation of political and technical responsibilities in the implementation of policy. Other organs of state, including parliament and its associated accountability structures, as well as media and civil society, have an active role to play in ensuring that policy translates into effective and responsive service delivery. Recent criticism and controversy over cases of alleged and, in some cases, proven corruption among high officials and ministerial appointments have caused reputational damage to government and politicians among the citizenry. These high-profile cases of apparent conflicts of interest and misappropriation of funds only highlight the need for stronger institutional and public systems of transparency and accountability. Despite its best efforts, the *Comissão Anti-Corrupção* (Anti-Corruption Commission) still struggles for legitimacy and strong political backing.

Contributing papers

We are pleased that the great majority of speakers at the inaugural Timor-Leste Update have been able to prepare written versions of their presentations for this volume. Other than acknowledging the recent change of prime minister, most chapters describe the status quo at the time of the Update. Some authors whose texts were affected by the political transition or the release of more recent data revised their chapters immediately prior to publication. The updated chapters are those by Charles Scheiner, Rui Feijó, Michael Leach, and Saku Akmeemana and Doug Porter, while Cillian Nolan has added a postscript.

The organisation of the book largely mirrors the structure of the conference itself, and while we have sought to encapsulate some of the sentiments and criticism offered by the audience during the Update sessions, we are unable to publish these commentaries within this online book format. For those who are interested, we direct you to the following ANU Timor-Leste website, which provides a number of additional recorded materials and associated discussions: ips.cap.anu.edu.au/ssgm/events/2013-timor-leste-update-follow.

Part One of the volume, Building a Nation-State in the Shadow of History, sets the scene for the remainder of the collection. Each chapter reflects on the achievements and challenges of nation-state building and engages, either explicitly or implicitly, with the legacies of history. Agio Pereira's chapter—a revised version of his keynote address—provides an 'actor's perspective' on the challenges of building peace and securing development since the nation's independence. While acknowledging that many outstanding issues remain, Pereira points to the nation's high levels of economic growth; reduced rates of infant mortality and increased life expectancy; improvements in the provision of water, sanitation, and electricity; positive bilateral relations with Indonesia; and Timor-Leste's leadership roles within international forum such as the g7+, as evidence that Timor-Leste has made great strides since 2002.

Complementing this piece, Fidelis Magalhães's chapter similarly reflects on achievements since independence, while also highlighting a number of significant challenges confronting the nation. Key issues include high youth unemployment, high levels of mal- and under-nourishment, poor-quality education, and the growing dependency of segments of the population on cash transfers. Magalhães is more pessimistic in his assessment of the economy than Pereira, pointing out that the increasing level of state expenditure is a serious issue when the country faces a more than US$1 billion non-oil fiscal deficit each year. More so than Pereira, Fidelis Magalhães engages with the legacies of history, arguing that a number of Timor-Leste's problems—for instance, its lack of human and financial resources—are linked to the underdevelopment of the territory during foreign occupations.

Like Magalhães, Michael Leach tackles the theme of historical legacies. In a reflective piece, Leach discusses the ongoing contested 'ownership' of the national liberation narrative and the 'struggles for recognition' by those who perceive themselves to be excluded. He suggests that not only is there a 'politics of recognition' in Timor-Leste, but there is also a 'political economy of recognition' given that those who can successfully claim veteran status receive significant annual pensions. He notes that the lack of a consensus among political elites about what constitutes the 'true' history of the Resistance also poses difficulties for the writing of a national history curriculum for primary and secondary schools. Leach asks whether the recent rapprochement between factions of the political elite may create more favourable conditions for dealing with controversial issues in the curriculum. He also wonders whether the rise of the post-'75 Generation might transcend the divisions embodied in the leaders of the '75 Generation.

Rui Feijó reflects on key challenges for the consolidation of democracy. Like Leach, Feijó raises the issue of generational turnover, asking what will become of the legacy of Xanana Gusmão and other leaders of the '75 Generation once they reach the end of their active political careers. He identifies other key challenges including that of managing the nation's wealth in line with democratic precepts and building a decentralised state that will make democracy both more representative and more participatory.

Part Two, Trends in Economic Development, reflects on economic developments at both national and sub-national levels. The first chapter, by Charles Scheiner, a researcher with the civil society think tank *La'o Hamutuk*, is entitled Can the Petroleum Fund Exorcise the Resource Curse from Timor-Leste? The answer presented in compelling detail is a pessimistic one, and points to a range of risks and concerns over the sustainability of the Petroleum Fund itself. Drawing largely on data from the government's own statistical compilations, Scheiner argues that Timor-Leste's currently active oil and gas fields may be dry by 2020 and that the Petroleum Fund may be empty within five years after that. While this should underscore the urgency to develop Timor-Leste's non-oil economy, increase revenue and use public money wisely, Scheiner believes that the Petroleum Fund may have created an 'illusion' of financial security that has allowed difficult decisions to be postponed. Scheiner's presentation at the Update resulted in a lively 'Q and A' discussion, and drew attention to the critical importance of the fund and additional fossil fuel development to the future prospects for Timor-Leste.

The following chapter, by Mr Antonio Vitor, Adviser to the Minister for Public Works, provides a measured account of progress made in the area of infrastructure development. Vitor cautions that infrastructure built prior to 1999 is deteriorating, and that ports, airports, major road networks, and telecommunications urgently need upgrading. While some progress has been made—in particular, in the sectors of rural water supply and sanitation, and electricity—key constraints are limited public sector capacities and capabilities to deliver infrastructure and poor co-ordination between relevant ministries.

The subsequent two chapters focus on economic developments at the sub-national level. World Bank governance specialist Saku Akmeemana, and Douglas Porter, consultant adviser at the World Bank, provide an overview of sub-national spending programs and the pragmatic increase of public expenditure directed to the regions in the aftermath of the 2006 crisis. They offer instructive lessons about the need to balance often competing technical, social, and political priorities, and adjust to changing needs over time. Meabh Cryan tackles the issue of continuing tensions over land use. She draws attention to how the lack of legislation for the resolution of land rights claims, and the increasing demand for land from the state for domestic and foreign investment, is contributing to land deals, alienation and forced evictions. She describes the flawed consultation process surrounding the 2009 draft transitional land law (which was later vetoed by President Ramos-Horta), which was the impetus for an alternative, civil society-driven process. The civil society consultations highlighted that land holds multiple meanings for East Timorese communities and challenges the government's view that so-called *rai mamuk* (empty land) can be easily appropriated for development purposes.

Part Three turns to the theme of Stability and Social Cohesion. Cillian Nolan offers a detailed and insightful reflection on the post-Xanana political landscape and the role of different influential segments of society in national politics. His chapter offers an excellent entrée to the two chapters that follow, by Catharina Maria and Damian Grenfell, which move beyond a focus on national-level stability issues to offer 'bottom-up' perspectives on achieving peaceful solutions to conflict. Maria's chapter reflects on her experiences as a peace-building practitioner with the *Laletek* (Bridge) Project—a combined effort of the Catholic Relief Services and the Diocesan Justice and Peace Commission of Dili—that encouraged opposing groups to find common ground and collaborate on issues of mutual interest. Her chapter is a reminder that there are no 'quick fixes' to communal conflict and that peace-builders need to invest time and resources in understanding and responding to each local context. Grenfell's chapter is a more conceptual piece that explores possible applications of customary connections and practice as part of the peace-building process. He argues that politics in Timor-Leste, while frequently represented as essentially 'modern' in form, also encompasses 'customary' and 'traditional' systems of power. He suggests that the concept of 'hybrid political orders' might assist those involved in peace-building to better recognise and engage with different kinds of social practices and meanings that coexist in Timor-Leste, allowing practitioners to locate 'sustainable practices amidst the intense pressure of social change in Timor-Leste'.

Part Four is entitled Citizens, Inequalities and Migration. The five chapters presented in this part focus on the challenges of building a society that encourages the participation of its citizens, recognises their diverse experiences, and addresses enduring inequalities. The first chapter, by Adérito Soares, former anti-corruption commissioner, reflects on how the problem of corruption in Timor-Leste might be addressed. Soares argues that, given the difficulties of law enforcement, comprehensive efforts to combat corruption must include public awareness-raising as a critical component. These efforts are needed especially at the subdistrict and district levels, where more and more projects are being initiated.

Turning to the issue of gender inequalities, Lia Kent and Naomi Kinsella highlight the policy discrimination evident in the veterans' valorisation scheme's lack of recognition of women's roles in the Resistance. They are also critical of the way in which the scheme is elevating the status of former male combatants over that of other citizens through the provision of symbolic recognition and material benefits. This, they argue, is leading to a militarised construction of citizenship in which women's inequality is further perpetuated. Andrew McWilliam explores the continuing disparities and inequalities between the bustling capital of Timor-Leste, Dili, and the majority rural populations. The lure of the city is seeing a continuing rural–urban drift, especially by young people in search of opportunities, and a small but significant number who are pursuing labour migration opportunities and education overseas.

Joanne Wallis's contribution explores the recent and important impacts of cash payments and social transfers to the rural hinterland. She finds that they have been an important mechanism to facilitate and support stability after the 2006 crisis, but have also created a legacy of welfare dependency that will inevitably burden the state with long-term financial commitments. In the final chapter, Pyone Myat Thu examines the complex social politics and legacies of displacement and return that were experienced by many communities in the violence of 1999. Drawing on case studies from Baucau, Thu demonstrates how changing patterns of cross-border communication and kinship networks enable communities to gradually rebuild their lives with minimal government assistance.

Other presentations at the Update

In addition to the papers that appear in this collection as book chapters, the Timor-Leste Update was enriched by the presentations delivered by a number of other invited speakers. James Scambary offered a provocative presentation as part of the panel on economic development trends, casting doubts on the feasibility of the much-vaunted Tasi Mane economic zone development project on the south coast of Timor. Deb Cummins presented a paper on the theme of decentralised development as part of the panel on sub-national development. Drawing on her experience with the Asia Foundation, working with community-driven development initiatives, she reflected on achievements and challenges in this field. Santornino Amaral, also of the Asia Foundation, presented another paper as part of this panel, which reinforced ongoing concerns about inequality of opportunity in the rural areas and highlighted the challenges of effective decentralisation. Ines Martins of *La'o Hamutuk* co-presented a paper with Meabh Cryan examining tensions around land use.

As part of the panel on active citizenship, peace-building specialist Laura Abrantes discussed women's representation in the political arena, and the need for greater opportunities for women to contribute their voices and opinions in public debates and policy development. Parliamentarian Lurdes Bessa discussed the relationship between the national parliament and civil society, arguing that there are many positive signs that show that civil society is helping to shape decision-making on key pieces of legislation and policy. Jose Neves provided a paper reflecting on the work and challenges of the Anti-Corruption Commission in pursuing its important work supporting transparency and accountability in government and public expenditure. As part of the panel on stability, Nelson Belo offered an analysis of the security sector situation and the role of security forces in the stability of the state. Belo noted that, given the central role of the police and military in previous periods of instability, effective management of the security sector is vital. Last but not least, Gordon Peake provided some pertinent concluding remarks. He commented that the papers presented over the course of the two days highlighted Timor-Leste's growing self-confidence as a nation, and the extent to which, after 13 years of UN presence, East Timorese are making their own decisions (including their own mistakes), and firmly charting their own course. This is, of course, how it should be.

Conclusion

Following the turmoil and destruction in the wake of the 1999 popular referendum, the half-island territory of Timor-Leste emerged as the first newly independent sovereign state of the 21st century. Its democratic credentials established, the country has become a poster state for managing internal conflict and demonstrating strong policy leadership both domestically and internationally. Its windfall oil revenues from the Timor Sea have provided much-needed funding for critical infrastructure and important social transfers for pensioners, the disabled and veterans of the independence struggle. At the same time, the still very significant challenges of nation-building, of developing capable statecraft and participatory democracy mean that Timor-Leste remains a work in progress—one where popular expectations are often frustrated by the incremental pace of progress. The chapters that follow do not attempt to present a straightforward or unified narrative of these developments. Rather, they serve to highlight the richness of public debate and the diversity of views that exists on Timor-Leste's achievements, frictions and challenges.

PART ONE
Building a Nation-State in the Shadow of History

CHAPTER 2

The Challenges of Nation-State Building

Agio Pereira

Introduction

Eleven years since Timor-Leste became a nation-state, it is now timely to reflect upon where the country has come from, what has been done to build the state—particularly the institutions of the state—and to lay out the direction that nation-state building has taken and will continue to take into the future. This nation-state account is done by way of a narrative, as it comes from an actor's perspective, an actor who is actively involved in driving the state apparatus, charged with legal-rational responsibility to do so. I do this with honest reflection.

I shall also account for the development, design and delivery of the country's *Strategic Development Plan 2011–2030* (RDTL 2011). This seminal work and the commitment to its steady implementation will see Timor-Leste develop into a society that has a large middle class, a vibrant private sector with a diversification of the resources economy, an educated and healthy population, and, importantly, a society based on the rule of law. For Timor-Leste, it is not a case that development must come first and democratic values will follow, but a case that both should proceed simultaneously. The *Strategic Development Plan* is the culmination of years of painstaking work, replete with consultations, debates and discussions, leading to multipartisan political agreement and acceptance by the people.

The task of nation-state building is not one that comes easy or naturally. One has to learn, and be willing to learn. One has to be courageous enough to fail and to admit failure and to change course. All failures are of course loudly trumpeted, with successes receiving much less attention.

After the jubilation of the 20 May 2002 restoration of independence celebrations, the political leaders had to quickly absorb the mammoth challenge that lay ahead. The dawning day brought with it the reality of government. We now had our own executive, parliament and judiciary—and indeed the nation and the state—and we were responsible for it. We had barely a dollar to bless ourselves with, but we had our freedom, our dignity, and some very capable leaders. The latter cannot be underestimated, as political leadership is one of the key determinants of successful nation-state building, but not much touted and largely absent from the development nomenclature. Technocrats alone do not a nation-state build. The nation requires nurturing; it requires care; it requires leadership. The state requires institutions to be created and given competency with staff and systems.

On 20 May 2002, there was no blueprint handed to our political leaders or to our handful of public servants that said: 'This is a How to Build a Nation-State'. There were no 30-second nation-state building books available. The United Nations (UN) had kick-started the process in 1999, also without a blueprint or guides. The UN had never in its history had to build a state or govern one. There was no red book as there is in Australia to prepare incoming governments. There was no blue book either presented from the UN Transitional Administration in East Timor (UNTAET), when they handed over power. There was no guide.

I recall here what our former Prime Minister Xanana Gusmão said in a speech he gave at the Johns Hopkins University in 2011. The speech captures the challenges that our people and political leaders faced:

> When, on 20 May 2002, we became the masters of our fate, as a State that was finally independent and sovereign, the expectations were that we, Timorese, might decide the future of our Nation. Naturally we believed that this future, in freedom, was promising. But I would like to remind you that there were some factors that seriously threatened this ideal, namely: lack of prepared and qualified human capital; lack of political experience in democratic governance—a system that was completely new to our society; lack of basic infrastructure and other essential equipment; and most importantly, the lack of financial resources of the Country itself (Gusmão 2011).

I have read the critiques of our nascent state, which cause me to take a sober look at how we are building the nation-state. Frequently, though, they draw their critique from a 'developed state' perspective, with little understanding of nation-state building and the heavy impact of donor policies and approaches.

They are mostly post-hoc, detailing where they think we have gone wrong, or have given too much here or too little there; not spending enough resource fund money, or spending too much; doing too little for health and education, and too much for the veterans, with no real impact on living conditions. Critiques are valued but one cannot ignore the fact that nation-state building is a daunting, long-term process.

The birth of the state

The official name of our state is Timor-Leste. This name was agreed to and acquired on 20 May 2002, when Timor-Leste became a sovereign independent state. As the national flag of the Democratic Republic of Timor-Leste was raised at midnight, the world's then newest independent country was born. Given the great jubilation of the people, the ceremony itself was solemn. The secretary-general of the UN, Kofi Annan, Australian Prime Minister John Howard and Indonesian President Megawati Sukarno Putri witnessed the birth of the new nation-state.

Our nation-state's momentous birth became a reality after almost a quarter of a century of conflict imposed by the illegal occupation of the territory by the Republic of Indonesia, with full support from Australia, the United States and the United Kingdom. In the UN, however, international law prevailed, and the question of East Timor remained on the list of the Special Committee on Decolonization until the territory exercised its inalienable right to self-determination and independence. There is much to be said for international law, even if it is sometimes said that it is soft law. Importantly, it carries moral persuasion.

Soon after, in September of the same year, Timor-Leste became a full member of the community of nations—becoming the 191st member of the UN. In his first speech to the UN General Assembly, president Xanana Gusmão reminded the international community that the core reason for Timor-Leste's success in achieving independence was its people. He noted that:

> Our people proved to the world to be worthy of the respect that we all owe and know'. It is the respect that we, one of the world's smallest states, is starting to garner for our solid work to consolidate peace and to take our place as an open democracy in the international community (Gusmão 2002).

It is against this backdrop of history that one can begin to understand the Timor-Leste of today. First, it is a democratic republic subject to the rule of law. Its constitution is recognised as one of the finest examples of liberal constitutions in the world. It is a constitution that the people take pride in. The respect for law and human decency is enshrined in the constitution and the objectives of the state are in accord with the most valued principles of the UN. These are values I know are shared by Australians as well, including the refusal to accept capital punishment.

Security Council Resolution 1272, which authorised the establishment of UNTAET on 25 October 1999, mandated that it would have full responsibility for the administration of East Timor and control of the executive, legislature, and the administration of justice. UNTAET would also maintain law and order, assist in the development of the civil services, facilitate the delivery of humanitarian aid and humanitarian assistance, support capacity-building, and establish an effective administration and conditions for sustainable development. This resolution bestowed upon the transitional administrator, Sergio Vieira de Mello, the powers of a Roman governor. He exercised executive, legislative, and judicial powers. Under UNTAET, transitional governance institutions were established (UNSC 1999). These institutions were developed from the perspective of what was required in a post-conflict, war-torn country that needed time to recover and to identify the best possible ways to move forward.

At the same time, intense consultation with the leadership of Timor-Leste was occurring to ensure that whatever the UN was planning to do not only reflected the best possible expectations of the Timorese people, but would also have sufficient legitimacy to survive the challenges of a post-UN era. For our leadership, that was one of our most pressing challenges; given that the UN had some human resources and some expertise, we had ourselves and our friends from the years of the struggle. We drew heavily on our friends for advice and information, and set about making new friends who had the human resources, the skills and the expertise we needed.

We actively participated in the consultative and governance mechanisms established by UNTAET regulations, but we were not in charge—the UN was. The Timorese political leadership, however, were not passive during this period, undergoing whatever preparedness technical training and professional development for independence we could muster, but there was no corporate governance history or architecture to step into, to inform us and to build on.

From September 1999 until May 2002, East Timor evolved steadily into a nation-state, with its sense of sovereignty enhanced and with a strong sense of pride for finally attaining the goal of independence. The road ahead was filled with uncertainties. Who were our true friends? Who were or could become our enemies? These were legitimate concerns for a nation embracing peace after almost 25 years of living in an environment of conflict against illegal occupation. We asked ourselves which nations were truly receptive to our national interest and our future and which nations may not be. We understood that Timor-Leste would stand the best chance of survival if it had no enemies. We also recognised that in a world dependent upon energy self-sufficiency, and with Timor-Leste being a country rich in oil and gas, we ought to expect the best but be prepared for the worst, hoping that the latter would never materialise.

In the first decade after May 2002, Timor-Leste strove to consolidate peace-building, and, despite a number of serious internal conflicts, there is a general consensus that it succeeded. As we enter the second decade of independence and sovereignty, Timor-Leste has said goodbye to conflict, to welcome development. Development is being carried out within the framework of the *Strategic Development Plan*. This conflict-free phase gives the government the breathing space it needs to focus on development. For development to succeed, any country needs, above all, to be conflict-free. Timor-Leste is no exception. I am not referring to small-scale conflict which every country, big or small, developed or developing, necessarily confronts every now and again, particularly in the political sphere, but conflicts that can derail national development. Timor-Leste has evolved since 1999 as a post-conflict nation.

From the Restoration of Independence Day on 20 May 2002 (which we mark and celebrate every year) until 2006, Timor-Leste experienced its own serious conflicts that arose almost at the rate of one a year. In 2007, this trend was finally broken when our leader, Kay Rala Xanana Gusmão took over the executive of the country and successfully strengthened governance. The period from 2007 to 2012 was the first time a prime minister had managed the country for a full five-year mandate. While the surprise attempt to assassinate President Ramos-Horta on 11 February 2008 and the attack on Prime Minister Xanana Gusmão shook the nation, the Timorese leadership successfully took control and prevented undesired collateral damage against the state. Both these attempts, in fact, were not part of a new development, but were a direct consequence of the unfinished saga of our 2006 crisis.

From a positive point of view, 11 February 2008 set a benchmark for the capacity of the country to act with resilience and to sustain serious conflict without allowing collateral damage to further hinder national peace and stability. The manner in which the pillars of sovereignty handled this crisis was exemplary. The international community recognised the maturity of our leadership at this time. It was a significant benchmark in the process of nation-state building. February 2008 represented a turning point. It demonstrated that the resilience we had exercised during the long and brutal occupation was transferable to nation-state building. We had achieved our own successful skills transfer, and a significant one at that.

Our people acted with shock, yes, but restraint, as did the leadership. As President Ramos-Horta recovered in Darwin Hospital, cared for by the Australian and Timorese community, Prime Minister Gusmão took over the security portfolios, including the armed forces and police. His leadership enabled both forces to build their own capacity while having their most trusted leader at the helm. This demonstrated again the primacy of trusted and effective leadership.

Key themes in the *Strategic Development Plan*

Since 2007, a conflict-free nation-state has been evolving. Ideas are maturing and governance capacity grows. The nation's very first *Strategic Development Plan* became the official long-term plan of the country. It envisages that by 2030 Timor-Leste will have a population that is healthy, well educated and prosperous, with a mature and diversified private sector supported by productive infrastructure, including a national road network, an extensive electricity generation and distribution system, and efficient ports and airports. Our strategic aim is to have a broad and large middle class by 2030. Some question its attainability, but if we do not set these goals, we shall never realise them. The key themes for the government in 2014 were:

- implementation of the *Strategic Development Plan*
- decentralisation of governance
- implementation and socialisation of law.

The latter two themes are key to sustainable development.

Development of Timor-Leste's institutions of law and order, defence, governance, pillars of sovereignty, and civil society are of paramount importance. These are integral to the successful implementation of the *Strategic Development Plan*. The state, as a juridical entity, needs to be equipped with the necessary capacity to safeguard the country's sovereignty—a nation-state's primary duty. Institutional capacity-building becomes, therefore, the central focus of nation-state building.

We were told by the international community that we must decentralise and we agreed, but we first needed to strengthen the centre before we could competently do this. At an international decentralisation conference, sponsored by the Timor-Leste Government and held in Dili in 2013, Prime Minister Xanana Gusmão, during his keynote presentation and reflections during the conference, stated that social, economic and political components vary from country to country and that 'all theories are good; but the only one that is useful, is the one that fits the reality of our country' (Gusmão and Soares 2013).

Australia, Cabo Verde and other nations took part in this conference, sharing their experiences of successes and challenges in the building of local power. Lessons learned were presented along with the benefits and constraints for Timor-Leste if the decentralisation models of other countries were to be adopted without taking into account the importance of specific local realities. We also learned from presentations during the conference that the process of setting up local government and of creating and developing municipalities to make local power work effectively takes considerable time, and, in some cases, has taken more than 100 years.

During this same conference we laid out our decentralisation plans and sought constructive support, yet we were criticised by some of our development partners for not devolving sooner. The question we faced was 'which structures to devolve and to whom?'. We knew that decentralisation was for the benefit of people at local level, to enable them to receive services directly and to have a voice in decision-making. Yet we needed to develop structures and systems to deliver those services. That required some central core to work with and from. Without the machinery of government in place (and we started with none) this would be next to impossible.

So what can be said now by way of an update?

Timor-Leste's leaders recognise that the most important indicators of development are the happiness and well-being of the people. In this context, our challenge effectively becomes implementing inclusionary policies leading towards an equitable sharing of all the nation has to offer. The leaders of Timor-Leste are very conscious of this priority, and this in itself is already a major step forward towards successful nation-state building.

As a good example, CNRT (*Congresso Nacional para a Reconstrução de Timor-Leste*; National Congress for the Reconstruction of Timor-Leste) and FRETILIN (*Frente Revolucionária de Timor-Leste Independente*; Revolutionary Front for an Independent East Timor)—the two major political parties in Timor-Leste—are working in consonance with national priorities. Liberal democracy is adversarial, but institutional solidarity is much needed to forge the mentality that democracy is positive; it can be a uniting force benefiting nation-state building and national sovereignty.

In the Five-Year Program of the Fifth Constitutional Government, social inclusion features as an important strategic policy (RDTL 2012). This entails not only the need to support the elderly and the disabled, but also to support the veterans and the poor, while striving for full gender equality. The youth are also not ignored. The government has a secretary of state solely dedicated to youth and sport. Having a majority young population, Timor-Leste needs to always build in the needs of the youth in national policies.

Like any other country, Timor-Leste places employment generation on the list of top priorities. Timor-Leste also needs to constantly focus on generating employment for the young generation—the future leaders. That is why vocational training programs and employment policies and programs are also given such high priority.

A country can only truly be happy if the most vulnerable of its population are cared for. A fund for human capital development has been established by law, which provides scholarships for Timorese to build their skills to match the needs of the country to achieve inclusive national development.

Development is also about the economy. And the economy is also about industries and international relations. It is also about regional economic co-operation as we strive to become a member of the Association of Southeast Asian Nations (ASEAN). The complex, interconnected nature of development means that Timor-Leste requires sophisticated know-how and this, in turn, means that building adequate human capital is a determining factor for the success of national development. In addition, sustainability requires basic skills to build roads, schools and hospitals, and manage, install and fix electricity, plumbing, cars, computers, and more.

A fund for infrastructure has also been established with the expectation that infrastructure development will enhance inclusiveness and offer opportunities for all, without neglecting the most disadvantaged. As a result, a national electricity grid, together with fibre-optic cables for internet access, is almost completed across the country. The range of benefits deriving from easy access to electricity for a developing country is immeasurable. Health, education, agriculture, business and economic progress draw their vigour and higher productivity from the power of electricity.

Along with roads and bridges, which are a key part of the infrastructure fund's priorities, one can say with a satisfactory level of confidence that Timor-Leste is heading in the right direction, on an inclusive and sustainable development path, guided by its *Strategic Development Plan*.

Another key challenge is foreign investment. Although not a new challenge in developing nations, for Timor-Leste this means a stable legal framework, and a capable and internationally competitive labour force with salary levels and incentives that are competitive with similar countries in our region. Timor-Leste enjoys national stability and peace, which can be a determining factor in attracting foreign investment. This peace and stability is promising and will be long-lasting.

In due course, the development of human capital and infrastructure will reach a higher level and the attractiveness of the country for foreign investment will also be enhanced. There is no reason why Timor-Leste will not succeed in this path. We know we have to succeed. Our leadership, the business community, and civil society are all conscious of and committed to this.

Ultimately, the challenge for any government is to create sufficient employment to respond to current and emerging needs. Foreign investment is also an important factor in providing jobs, as is infrastructure development. Successful diplomacy is yet another important factor. Smart politics, which is often underestimated by governments, has a vital if not overarching role. It is interesting that in the world of aid and development, political development is usually a low priority or does not rate. Yet without it, institutions do not develop.

Those who choose to stay aside will perish. Those who embrace the challenges of competition within the rule of law, including international law, will survive. Those who, in spite of opting to be in the competition ring, choose to adopt dishonest and illegal means to defeat their adversaries will, sooner or later, pay a high price. It is imperative that the global competitive environment is strongly guided by the rule of international law, because this is where countries such as Timor-Leste, existing between two regional giants, identify fairness and legality as their own national interest.

We are getting tired of being lectured about the need for good governance by some of our development partners, when the principles that underpin good governance—a commitment to the rule of law, accountability, and transparency—are sometimes lacking in our bilateral relations.

Setting new boundaries

Timor-Leste strives to work together with other countries to establish new boundaries. In our short history, we have had very positive bilateral relationships with our regional giant neighbours, Indonesia and Australia. In the case of Indonesia, we have demonstrated the importance of defining our relationship by looking forward rather than looking back. We do not and can never forget the past and we have a strong responsibility to care for our people who were traumatised. As a government, we cannot, however, be captive to our past. We now consider Indonesia one of our closest friends. We share more than a land border (which is about to be finally settled following a respectful negotiation process). We share a history of colonisation and oppression and a striving for democracy.

In the case of Australia, our bilateral relationship has also been positive. Australia led the International Force for East Timor military mission in 1999, with Sir Peter Cosgrove at the helm. Australia contributes more direct development assistance than any other development partner. However, there is one aspect of our relationship with Australia that has not been so positive: our efforts to negotiate a permanent maritime boundary in the Timor Sea. In the spirit of looking forward, and not back, this is something I hope can be resolved sooner rather than later. It will also provide certainty for our friends in the oil and gas industry, and an equitable outcome negotiated according to the principles of good governance and international law.

Maritime boundary issues cannot be resolved without both parties entering into a structured engagement negotiations framework. This is very difficult considering that in 2002 Australia withdrew from the jurisdiction of the International Court of Justice regarding the UN Convention on the Law of the Sea and the International Tribunal on the Law of the Sea in matters of the delimitation of maritime boundaries. This leaves no regular umpire to settle such matters, leaving it up to Timor-Leste and Australia to resolve the issues themselves.

New boundaries are important in relationships as well, as there are times in which they should be reset. In our engagement with fragile states, including Timor-Leste's leadership of the g7+, we have succeeded in forging the New Deal.[1] What's 'new' about this deal is that it focuses on promoting peace-building and nation-state building as a foundation for sustainable development among g7+ countries. Timor-Leste was the architect of this New Deal and has been investing in setting the right pace towards transforming mindsets. There is a compelling need to set new boundaries in regards to the way states share information, such as the commitment already stated by the G20 in terms of collaboration beyond borders to counter corporations' tax evasion. Setting new boundaries in terms of the delineation of national borders also needs to occur, with particular consideration to where they should fall, because this will allow for the enhancement of co-operation in trade, investment, regional stability and prosperity for all. It is also vital for a nation-state's sovereignty.

---

1   The New Deal for Engagement in Fragile States (the New Deal) was advocated by the g7+ and developed through the forum of the International Dialogue for Peacebuilding and Statebuilding. It was presented at the fourth High Level Forum on Aid Effectiveness in 2011, where it was widely endorsed.

Timor-Leste is clear about its strategic national interest and is committed to promoting and protecting it. It builds the best possible relations with its neighbours and, within this realm, Australia and Indonesia occupy a very important place. Timor-Leste also sees its accession to ASEAN as part of its national interest. Strong relations with the countries of the Portuguese-speaking community, which includes Brazil, Portugal, Angola, Mozambique, Cabo Verde, São Tomé e Príncipe and Guinéa-Bissau, are also extremely important, due to the historical and cultural attachments between the governments and peoples of these countries that have been forged over many centuries. Such an alliance can also be very useful in the political power posturing that is played out at the UN. It was certainly one of the most important factors in our victory in the struggle against the illegal occupation of East Timor by Indonesia, which occurred with the full connivance of successive Australian governments.

The way forward

Timor-Leste has recently completed the cycle of the budget debates within the parliamentary standing committees. The national parliament has now adopted the law pertaining to the state (national) budget that has become the 2014 Budget. This is a process that sees the prime minister actively involved. He both provides oversight of early bids and reviews final ones from ministers before proceeding to the parliament to promote and defend the budget. In developing our budget, the government placed particular emphasis on the Millennium Development Goals (MDGs). This includes funding the rehabilitation of schools and providing them with the equipment, security and minimum conditions necessary for the students to achieve what their intellectual potential allow them to. The MDGs, and improving the educational environment of the younger generation, will now fall under the direct responsibility of the prime minister.

Our nation has moved from an annual budget of under US$63.4 million in 2002 to a current budget of US$1.6 billion. We have also moved from a situation in which our infrastructure was lacking or destroyed to one in which we now have basic infrastructure such as the national electricity network detailed above. Schools and health clinics are being built or repaired. We are moving at a faster pace to provide water and sanitation, and to grow a mature private sector to play a more effective role as a partner of the government.

We know that our citizens want a reliable power supply, safe roads, good education and employment opportunities, and we are working right now to realise them. These issues are central to the program of government and reflected in our *Strategic Development Plan*.

We have many positive indicators that are consolidating each year. Here are a few:

- Economic growth has been high and non-oil growth averaged 11.9 per cent between 2007 and 2013.
- Agricultural output of major crops is on the up each season.
- The number of tourists in 2013 was 74 per cent higher than in 2012.
- Timor-Leste has reached the 2015 MDGs target in reducing infant and maternal mortality.
- Timor-Leste joined other Southeast Asian nations in being officially certified polio free by the World Health Organization (WHO).
- WHO also declared Timor-Leste to be on target for more than a 75 per cent reduction in the incidence of Malaria cases.
- Timor-Leste is one of the top six countries where life expectancy increased the most between 1990 and 2012 from 50 to 66 years. During that same period, Australia increased from 77 years to 83 years. (WHO 2014).

Australian politicians of all persuasions so often say that 'Australia punches above it weight'. So does Timor-Leste, and our leadership has a unique and keen understanding of the UN and the international community. Timor-Leste has worked with both in ways that very few nations get to do, in order to garner support for our legal and just cause of self-determination, and in partnership to build our nation-state. Timor-Leste takes seriously its role as an international citizen and strives to be a good one, given our singular experience.

On the international stage, our nation has landed a number of global governance roles. These include:

- chairing the United Nations Economic and Social Commission for Asia and the Pacific (ESCAP) with its 62 member countries
- chairing the g7+, which represents 20 conflict-affected countries and which Timor-Leste was instrumental in establishing
- representation on the board of the Extractive Industries Transparency Initiative (Timor-Leste also being the third country in the world to achieve compliance status with it)
- presidency of the *Comunidade dos Países de Língua Portuguesa* (Community of Portuguese Language Countries)
- representation on the United Nations Committee on the Elimination of all Forms of Discrimination Against Women
- joining ASEAN when the preparedness work is finalised to satisfy the criteria.

When we give it proper thought and consideration, we can comfortably state that much has been achieved since 1999. But we must also be frank in acknowledging that much still has to be accomplished before our people can be fully satisfied; before we can say that the sacrifices made during 24 years of conflict have been honoured with the transformation of our nation from being a victim to one where the international community praises our advanced progress in nation-state building in accordance with the rule of law.

References

Gusmão, X. 2002. Speech on the Occasion of the Admission of the Democratic Republic of Timor-Leste to the United Nations at the United Nations General Assembly, 57th Session, New York, 27 September 2002. etan.org/et2002c/september/22-30/27onthe.htm.

Gusmão, X. 28/5/2011. Goodbye Conflict: Welcome Development: The Timor-Leste Experience. *Tempo Semanal* [Weekly Times]. www.temposemanaltimor.blogspot.com.au/2011/02/goodbye-conflict-welcome-development.html.

Gusmão, X. and F. Soares 2013. *The Policy for the Preparation of the Administrative Pre-Decentralisation Structure: The Beginning of the Second Maubere Miracle?* International workshop proceedings, 27 February 2013, Dili.

RDTL (*República Democrática de Timor-Leste*; Democratic Republic of Timor-Leste) 2011. *Timor-Leste Strategic Development Plan 2011–2030*. Dili: RDTL. www.timor-leste.gov.tl/wpcontent/uploads/2011/07/Timor-Leste-Strategic-Plan-2011-20301.pdf.

RDTL 2012. *Program of the Fifth Constitutional Government, 2012–2017 Legislature*. Dili: RDTL. timor-leste.gov.tl/wp-content/uploads/2012/09/Program-of-the-5th-Constitutional-Government.pdf.

UNSC (United Nations Security Council) 1999. Resolution 1272 (1999): Adopted by the United Nations Security Council 4057th Meeting, 25 October 1999. www.un.org/en/peacekeeping/missions/past/etimor/docs/9931277E.htm.

WHO (World Health Organization) 2014. Global Health Observatory (GHO) Statistics 2014. www.who.int/gho/countries/tls/en.

CHAPTER 3

Past, Present and Future: Why the Past Matters

Fidelis Magalhães

Future is past's child, and has the father's face.

This chapter presents my analysis of the current state of Timor-Leste's development process. It is divided into the following sections. First, I discuss the tension between the theory and the *realpolitik* of state-building. Second, I discuss Timor-Leste as a country in the making. Third, I discuss the path to independence, the current Timorese leadership and the present political landscape. Fourth, I touch on the roles and the five-year plan of the president. Finally, I try to paint a picture of the future and identify challenges.

The theory and the *realpolitik* of state-building

I hold the view that most of the contemporary analyses on the socioeconomic development of Timor-Leste suffer from a serious historical deficiency. It is common for expert opinions to make claims about Timor-Leste's current economic performance while seldom referring to the course on which the country has sailed. Like driving a car, one ought to have a rear mirror to look behind. If the mirror is too big the driver will be distracted; but without one, the car cannot be driven safely.

Moreover, expert opinions seldom acknowledge that the development process is largely a political process. Beyond having the right economic theories and formulas, it is only through having strong political commitments and sensitivities that a recently independent, economically underdeveloped country can progress. To succeed, it requires strong political will on the part of the leadership to build democratic governance based on the rule of law, yet at the same time ensure that the state is capable of creating consensus among main political forces that can otherwise be belligerent towards the state. The state needs to be creative in finding ways to ensure mid-term peace and stability so that attention can be given to building institutions and governance systems, and ensuring that services are delivered to its population. There is no development without peace and stability.

In fact, some of the inherent difficulties of state-building in Timor-Leste arises from the prescriptions of liberal democratic theory. It appears that interest groups, peace and stability, and electoral politics are interconnected. The question is how to ensure that the state maintains control over all the interest groups while not being hijacked by them. To only base our analytical approach on rent-seeking theories and to be overtly suspicious of the elites can be misleading. This is true since history has taught us that the elites and, of course, their political will, played an important role in most of the development success stories, *inter alia*, as in the case of South Korea and Singapore.

Timor-Leste: a country in the making

Snapshots of Timor-Leste's history can be divided into the following periods: pre-colonial, Portuguese colonial, Indonesian occupation, and post-independence. Not much can be said about the precolonial period. In fact, more archaeological and historical work is needed in order to establish accounts of that period. The Portuguese established their first trading post in 1562. However, it was not until the 1700s that more efficient commercial exploration of resources began. Primary cash crops such as sugar cane and coffee were introduced *circa* 1815 after the depletion of sandalwood, and an *imposto* (head tax) was introduced in the 19th century for all adult males between 18 and 60 years old. In general, during the period of Portuguese colonialism, Timor-Leste remained a backwater colony. Portuguese colonialism was not conducive to growth and had little impact on technological advancement. There was a serious lack of investment in both infrastructure and human development. The literacy rate at the end of the Portuguese rule in Timor-Leste was at 10 per cent (Saldanha 1994). School enrolment rates were low, despite having increased during the last several years of Portuguese occupation, after the Viqueque Rebellion in 1959. In the 1960s, the number of students enrolled in primary education climbed from less than 5,000 to 27,000 and, in the first half of the 1970s, reached a peak of 57,500 students (Saldanha 1994). Literacy rates in Timor at the end of the Portuguese presence reflect a very limited effort by the Portuguese dictatorial regime of Salazar to provide education to the population of Timor. Salazar was the founder of *Estado Novo* (New State)—the regime established after the 1926 military *coup d'état*—and ruled from 1932 to 1968. Measured by these results, his policies represented a serious neglect of the interests of the Timorese people. The neglect and abandonment of the interests of the population is a typical characteristic of colonial policies.

Comparatively, in Indonesia for example, the impressive progress in literacy rates between 1945 and 1971 was a result of the radical change of state priorities—in contrast with the priorities of the Dutch colonial administration. This change was only possible with independence and with the establishment of a national government. What I am attempting to draw by comparing Timor-Leste's literacy rate and that of Indonesia during the first decades of its independence is that the lack of qualified human resources is due to colonial disinvestment in the sector. As a consequence, postcolonial governments struggle to build their countries with scarce human resources and at the same time invest in the education of the current generation.

To conclude this brief reflection on the past, I will focus on the insufficiencies of the development policies of the governments led by Indonesian dictator Suharto. Suharto was the founder of New Order—the regime established after the 1965 coup, and presided over by the Indonesian government between 1967 and 1998. The development policy of Jakarta for Timor was accelerated from the mid-1980s, in the final 15 years of occupation.

I will not expand further on this, but will instead focus only on education as a measure of development: the policies of Suharto were characterised by a strong investment in equipment and infrastructure. These investments partially benefited the population and partially benefited the military leaders.

In 1985, there was already one primary school in each village, with a total of 497 schools (for 442 villages). By 1996—three years before the UN referendum for the self-determination of Timor-Leste—there were 736 primary schools. In 1996, there were also 112 junior high schools, 37 senior high schools and 16 secondary education vocational schools. There were seven universities, with the first one—Universitas Timor-Timur—having been established in 1986. In 1990, adult literacy had reached 33 per cent (Jones 2003: 41).

Throughout this period, the number of university students in Timor-Leste and Indonesia and the number of university graduates grew exponentially, although starting from a very small baseline. Those youths who were educated in Indonesia became a powerful force of resistance to the Indonesian occupation.

The growth in the number of schools was accompanied by the construction and opening of public facilities, from health to infrastructure and other sectors of public administration. Nevertheless, despite this progress, the country's human resources continued to be undervalued by the foreign administration throughout the entire period of the occupation. The paradox can be explained by the convergence of two factors. In both, consideration for the interests of the Timorese people was absent.

First, *developmentalism* was used by the Suharto regime for propaganda purposes. Consequently, the numbers quickly gained a life of their own, with statistics being more valued than the quality of the results on the ground.

Second, the jobs created in Timor by the investment in public services were often used by Jakarta to reassign Indonesian teachers and other professionals and staff. Once again, the preparedness of East Timorese senior staff to take on positions of increasing responsibility was neglected, as a matter of policy. This translated into another serious negligence.

Therefore, when the Indonesian administration withdrew in 1999, the destruction did not only affect the public and private buildings and equipment. That withdrawal left the country bereft of teachers, engineers, doctors, and other senior officers, who had been primarily Indonesian. The public administration in Timor-Leste was not only left without physical facilities (destroyed by arson), it was bereft of experienced officers and emptied of structures.

The path to independence and the present political landscape

I have discussed how underdeveloped Timor-Leste had been throughout foreign occupations. In fact, it was a planned underdevelopment of the country for centuries. Against this backdrop, many of our current development challenges cannot be solved overnight. Our challenges remain large. We became independent with little qualified human and financial resources, and our institutions were almost non-existent. Our society had never previously been democratic.

What was it that made our path to independence different from other countries that underwent similar experiences? First, we became independent under the auspices of the UN in the new millennium. Upon independence, we were thrust into a new and more demanding reality. We were expected to ascribe to all the existing international norms and conventions and to uphold liberal democracy without the know-how and existing institutions. What's more, this was at a time when the majority of the electorates were illiterate and heavily traumatised by past violations. Our population became more oriented towards the attainment of individual rights and completely ignored their collective duty. This was difficult to manage, especially when mixed with the post-conflict sense of entitlements, or with the narrative of *terus* (suffering). In short, an essential part of nation-state building in the post-conflict context was to manage people's expectations.

We were fortunate, however. We were fortunate because we had individuals with a real sense of purpose at the helm—the running of the state. They tried (though not without episodes of near despair) and succeeded in sticking to democratic ideals while guiding the country through the first decade of self-rule. Even in the darkest periods of the *krize* (crisis) in 2006, and the assassination attempts against both the president and the prime minister, in which the president was seriously wounded, constitutional order prevailed. We opted to follow constitutional arrangements without creating negative precedents. Presidential and parliamentary elections were held in 2007 according to the electoral calendar, and with almost 75 per cent voter turnout.

The leadership has changed over the years since 2002. The elections in 2012 resulted in Taur Matan Ruak becoming president of the Republic. Even though occupying an important role in the Resistance as deputy commander of *Forças Armadas da Libertação Nacional de Timor-Leste* (FALINTIL; Armed Forces for the National Liberation of East Timor), Taur Matan Ruak does not belong to the '75 Generation. He joined FALINTIL when he was 18 years old and ascended through the ranks.

The top leadership roles are now occupied by Taur Matan Ruak, Xanana Gusmão and Mari Alkatiri. José Ramos-Horta, although no longer occupying a formal role, still holds an important political influence. Taur Matan Ruak plays an important role as the bridge between the '75 Generation and the younger generation. Most political parties, including major parties such as the CNRT (*Congresso Nacional de Reconstrução de Timor*; National Congress for the Reconstruction of Timor-Leste) and FRETILIN (*Frente Revolucionária de Timor-Leste Independente*; Revolutionary Front for an Independent East Timor), give more prominence to younger leaders. Most government ministers belong to the *Jerasaun Foun* (New Generation) and the president's team is composed mostly of young people.

In terms of the contemporary political landscape, we are enjoying a very solid relationship among the leaders. This positively contributes to peace and stability. The president holds weekly meetings with the prime minister. Moreover, the relationship between the prime minister and the leader of the opposition has never been so solid. Rather than political posturing, the opposition has opted for constructive engagement in which it supports programs it considers good and continues to challenge those that it considers unsound. This new form of political manoeuvring is not without its critics. There are many who argue that while the current CNRT–FRETILIN relationship is good for national unity, it significantly weakens democracy because it deprives the parliament from having a real opposition. However, this view has to be carefully weighed against many factors. I do think that at this stage of our nation- and state-building process, it is essential to build a broad consensus. During parliamentary debates, the opposition continues to be critical of government programs with which it disagrees, while at the same time offering more measured comments on those policies and plans with which it disagrees. I think we are simply becoming a mature democracy, where consensus building and conflict resolution is an integral part of the democratic exercise. This is in contrast to past practices where the parliament used to be a chamber for personal attacks.

Looking beyond current political culture, it would be a mistake to brand all radical political manoeuvres as anti-democratic. For example, mechanisms such as grand coalitions between major parties are not completely alien to political scientists. While I do not have a personal opinion on the subject, I nevertheless think it is important to keep it within the realm of what is possible and not dismiss it out of hand as anti-democratic.

Roles and the five-year plan of the president of the Democratic Republic of Timor-Leste

Having discussed broadly the changes in relationships among political leaders and institutions, I now would like to discuss in a more in-depth way the roles of the president of the Democratic Republic of Timor-Leste. I will frame this discussion within the context of institutional relations.

The president plays an important role in using his soft power to build political consensus. In Timor-Leste, we informally refer to this type of power in the words of one of our nation's founders, Dr Roque Rodrigues, as *poder da influenciação* (the power of influencing) and *galvanisador* (galvanising force). The fact that the president acquires his legitimacy from the following sources gives additional strength to his authority. First, the president is elected by popular vote. Second, more than holding a symbolic role constitutionally, the president himself is the symbol of national unity, the head of state, and the guarantor of the healthy functioning of state institutions. Third, also in accordance with the constitution, the government reports to both the president and parliament.

In practical terms, we are witnessing a solid co-ordination between all constitutional pillars. In fact, the relationship between the president and the opposition has now evolved into a much stronger one. The president holds regular meetings with the prime minister, government ministers, and parliamentarians. Meetings with the opposition are held periodically. All these initiatives have cemented mutual trust and respect among political leaders.

The following list of goals shows how, with the existing mutual trust and close institutional collaboration, the president has managed to push some of his own priorities ahead. President Taur Matan Ruak's five-year plan, produced at the beginning of his mandate, included the following priorities:

1. generational transition
2. regional integration/strategic partnership
3. economic diversification/reduction of economic dependency
4. nutrition and food security
5. good governance
6. rural development
7. land and property issues.

Many of his plans have received positive responses from the government, parliament and civil society organisations. In fact, many have been translated into government policies. As I have outlined, much of the progress is the result of the president's use of *poder da influenciação*. President Taur Matan Ruak also calls for a strategic partnership with Australia, and our membership in the Commonwealth of Nations.

But of the many achievable goals in the short term, there are those that still require persistent hard work. Although all state institutions are working hard to achieve results, they require both time and improved administrative skills. For example, the public administration must continue to develop its capabilities to respond to national needs. Public services are still concentrated in Dili, whereas 80 per cent of the population live in the districts where the quality and reach of public services are insufficient.

The president of the republic has called for the introduction of rules for performance assessment that would guide career advancement and remuneration for civil servants.

The quality of public tenders and of public works also still needs improvement. In many cases, the state's ability to supervise contracted work is poor or non-existent. Sometimes, money is spent on works that deteriorate almost as quickly as the time it took to build them.

Another challenge that we need to overcome is legal uncertainty. I will not expand on this subject except to mention the land law because of its importance from the point of view of the community and of investors.

Land ownership continues to be a source of conflict and, again, this is a lingering issue. Two land law proposals have been presented in recent years: the first proposal was approved by the national parliament, having been vetoed by the then President José Ramos-Horta; a new, modified proposal is now under review. This is a priority for President Taur Matan Ruak.

Finally, yet another important issue is the integration of our youth in the economy and in the construction of a country that will be theirs to run soon. This topic on its own would require a full seminar. There have been calls recently for the creation of some civic and national service to give the younger generation a sense of duty towards the country and a new sense of purpose. We are currently gathering ideas and we hope to kick-start a nationwide discussion in the near future.

The future

In general, we are optimistic about the future. We hope to become an upper middle-income country by 2030. While monetarily it should not be too difficult to achieve, socially the challenges remain enormous. According to our *Strategic Development Plan*, development is categorised into four pillars: social capital, infrastructure development, economic development, and institutional framework.

Now we face the following real challenges:

1. High youth unemployment. Around 70 per cent of Timor-Leste's population is under 30 and 54 per cent is of productive age. Of those belonging to the productive age category, only around 30 per cent are employed. At the moment, around 27,000 youths enter into the job market every year, while only a handful of job opportunities are being created yearly.
2. High incidence of malnutrition and undernourishment: 45 per cent of children are underweight, with 33 per cent stunting and 19 per cent wasting. (This requires a national consensus. Any government would need to pledge to put an end to malnutrition and undernourishment.)
3. Poor-quality education and poorly trained human resources. Many children who have been through schooling continue to be illiterate and do not possess even elementary maths skills.
4. Veteran issues/cash transfers. In 2012, public transfers were US$233.7 million, or approximately 12.6 per cent of the annual state budget. For 2013, this figure was about US$239 million, or 17.3 per cent of the annual state budget. Of the overall figure for cash transfers, around US$84 million is designated for veterans alone (the rest to support poor families through the *Bolsa da Mae*

(Mother's Purse) program, subsidies to the elderly, and public transfers to civil society organisations). While cash transfers are an important tool to achieve short-term peace dividends, we shall, however, establish a fund that would lead to the reduction of dependency on the state. The president has been calling for veterans to establish a nationwide initiative where they fund health services and scholarships to their children using a portion of their monthly state subsidy. It is hoped that in the future the fund can also invest in various portfolios.

To conclude, the state's expenditure is more likely to continue to grow, especially the recurrent expenditure. This is a serious challenge when we are facing a more than US$1 billion non-oil fiscal deficit every year. The non-oil revenue remains bleak with only US$146 million in revenue for the last year.

Conclusion

Timor-Leste is a country in the making that has many potential and specific challenges. While it is true that many of our problems cannot be solved instantly, a great number of them are the result of our history. We have achieved a great deal since the restoration of independence in 2002, but we are aware that challenges remain. Our development process has been arduous, yet I am confident in saying that we are on the right track. We may have to make concessions, and engage in political manoeuvres and consensus-building along the way. These strategies are, nevertheless, short-term in nature and designed to achieve a specific end goal. Despite all these challenges, the foundations of our society are unshakeable. We continue to see democracy as both a means and an end. We do not believe economic development justifies the suspension of civic rights and participation. This option—the democratic option—may make the road bumpier but the result will certainly be more long-lasting.

References

Jones, G.W. 2003. East Timor: Education and Human Resource Development. In J.J. Fox and D. Babo-Soares (eds), *Out of the Ashes: Destruction and Reconstruction of East Timor*. Canberra. ANU E Press, 41–52.

Saldanha, J.M. 1994. *The Political Economy of East Timor Development*. Jakarta: Pustaka Sinar Harapan.

CHAPTER 4

The Politics of History in Timor-Leste

Michael Leach

National history remains an important concern of East Timorese public life. While surveys demonstrate high levels of popular pride in East Timorese history (Leach 2012), the very centrality of the Resistance to East Timorese nationalism has resulted in considerable political conflict over the symbolic ownership of that history: over who is included, excluded, or recognised in the central narrative of *funu* (struggle; see Ramos-Horta 1987), and, also, how younger people can feel part of the national story. Major episodes of civil unrest since independence (the 2002 riots, the 2005 Catholic Church protests over voluntary religious education, the 2006 political-military crisis, tensions with veterans' groups) have normally contained a strong element of demand for recognition of contributions to the achievement of independence. This has been a prominent theme in post-independence electoral contests as well. As was evident in the 2012 elections, participation in the resistance to the Indonesian occupation remains a powerful source of political legitimacy, and debates over and inclusion or exclusion of certain actors from the narrative of national liberation have been tools in electoral campaigning and public discourse (Powles 2012).

Since independence, formerly suppressed political tensions within the modern nationalist movement have also posed notable difficulties for writing the national history curriculum for schools. Following the replacement of the former Indonesian history curriculum, interim curricula have typically covered history up to 1974 more thoroughly than the critical and difficult years that followed. The legacies of divisions within East Timorese society and political elites from the 1974–75 civil war era, the 1999 referendum, and the political-military crisis of 2006 have posed difficulties for drafting a national history curriculum, with some areas still considered politically difficult or 'too hot to handle' (Leach 2007, 2010).

There are, however, some recent signs of *rapprochement* in these post-independence 'history wars', and a moderation of political conflict since the 2012 elections. This chapter briefly examines some of these divisions since independence, and the way these can be seen in part as symbolic struggles for recognition (Honneth 1995). It examines how history is deployed in national politics, recent developments in the drafting of national history curricula in schools, and the ongoing process of filling in the gaps of resistance history. It then focuses on the way these tensions have been reconfigured in recent years.

The history wars: fault lines and constituencies

As with other postcolonial nations, previously suppressed political divisions within the independence movement emerged in the wake of national liberation. With deep divisions within its small political elite dating to the late colonial era, a range of interconnected 'history wars' have created ongoing challenges for writing a history curriculum since independence, with different internal divisions stemming from events of 1974–75, 1999, and 2006 (Leach 2007, 2009). For some East Timorese, writing the national history is still too controversial a task, with tensions over the divisive civil war period, divisions within the independence movement, and the collaboration of segments of an occupied civilian population still close at hand. As numerous commentators have noted, reconciliation between the parties in the short-lived but bitter civil war in 1975—FRETILIN (*Frente Revolucionária de Timor-Leste Independente*; Revolutionary Front for an Independent East Timor) and UDT (*União Democrática Timorense*; Timorese Democratic Union)—is incomplete, despite the formation of the more inclusive united front *Conselho Nacional da Resistência Maubere* (National Council of the Maubere Resistance) in 1986 (transformed into the CNRT (*Conselho Nacional de Resistência Timorense*; National Council of Timorese Resistance) in 1998) and the efforts of the *Comissão de Acolhimento, Verdade e Reconciliação de Timor Leste* (CAVR; Timor-Leste Commission for Reception, Truth and Reconciliation) to facilitate this process. As one East Timorese teacher noted in 2005:

> Where to start? It will be necessary to be diplomatic with Portugal and Indonesia. When it comes to the civil war in 1975, the parties still exist. And some of the Balibo parties—UDT, Apodeti, Kota, Trabalhista—I don't know why you'd give them an opportunity as they brought East Timor to a terrible time. But this is part of democracy, so fine. It will be a controversial issue, very sensitive. So when you start talking history, you come to a sensitive issue (see Leach 2006: 233).

There is also the long-running process of reconciliation between the majority of independence supporters, and the pro-integration minority, arising from the dramatic and violent separation from Indonesia in 1999. While this generates less public heat, owing to the priority of good relations with Indonesia, there are bitter and unresolved legacies of the 1999 referendum just below the surface of East Timorese society, with a largely unaddressed history of violence—including crimes against humanity committed during the Indonesian occupation. Though these issues enjoy little elite support, they rear up as marginal voices, normally from victims' groups protesting the lack of justice for crimes committed during the occupation (Kent 2012).

Other fault lines appeared after the nation's independence during the period of the first constitutional government from 2002–06. Backgrounded by unmet material expectations, a range of political, cultural and intergenerational tensions emerged, including political divisions between the government and president in the freshly minted semi-presidential system. There were also growing fissures between a largely secular government and the powerful Catholic Church. These wider fault lines were catalysed by tensions between the security forces allied to different elite political factions, and exploded in the political-military crisis of 2006. Though the crisis was triggered by claims inside the military that those from 'eastern' districts had contributed more to the resistance, and from junior 'western' officers claiming discrimination in promotions, a wide range social tensions contributed to the 2006 crisis.

Some of these fault lines were strongly related to the history of the Timorese Resistance. Primary among these issues were intra-elite conflicts between FRETILIN and non-FRETILIN members of the former 'united front' of the CNRT (Leach 2006: 233), and, notably, ongoing tensions between FRETILIN and former CNRT figures over the symbolic 'ownership' of the Resistance, its powerful narrative of national liberation, and the fruits of post-independence political power. In the early years of independence, some Timorese felt that FRETILIN's self-styling as the inheritor of the independence struggle was too narrow and excluded too many. On the other hand, other political actors felt that the importance of FRETILIN resistance in the late 1970s and early 1980s has been neglected in favour of a more unifying and politically palatable emphasis on the subsequent CNRT 'united front' years. Some of these tensions between FRETILIN and the reconstituted political party CNRT (*Congresso Nacional para a Reconstrução de Timor*; National Congress for Timorese Reconstruction) can be traced to internal conflict within FALINTIL (*Forças Armadas da Libertação Nacional de Timor-Leste*; Armed Forces for the National Liberation of East Timor) itself during the late Resistance era (Niner 2009).

Notably, despite the so-called 'east–west' regional conflict that flared violently in 2006 and left 150,000 internally displaced persons (IDPs) in Dili, there were no examples of 'separatist' discourses at any point of the crisis. Even at the peak of these short-lived but intense conflicts, none of the protagonists sought to deny a common historical bond, nor the view that all East Timorese should form a single nation—even if, as Kammen (2003) has observed, the nationalist/traitor trope is frequently employed in a range of social conflicts. As such, the crisis and other precursor conflicts are perhaps best viewed, using Axel Honneth's (1995) term, as 'struggles for recognition': they seek to secure acknowledgement of contributions to the valued common project of East Timorese nationalism; or, at times, to secure recognition of other identities that remain important to these actors, including local and 'traditional' forms of identity.

Broadly speaking, a recognition approach examines the way distorted or inadequate forms of recognition may become important sources of motivation for political mobilisation and resistance (Honneth 1995: 138–39). Perceived 'disrespect' to a group's sense of self, to its traditions and values, or a perceived 'misrecognition' of its contribution to shared and valued social goals, such as national independence, may create the conditions for political conflict (Honneth 1995: 121–43). A 'recognition' dynamic was evident in other political divisions since independence, such as those between 'diaspora' and 'local' independence movement figures, with widely reported popular resentment against exiled political leaders 'taking over' post-independence politics, having been in the diaspora during the Indonesian occupation.

The return of a largely secular leadership also saw tensions with the Catholic Church, which had played a key role in the Resistance. Others noted a growing gap between elite and popular values. For Trindade and Castro (2007: 14), for example, a widely held view across Timor-Leste was that 'the nation-state seems to benefit only the political elites … which in turn come mainly from the eastern region that claimed to have fought more in the resistance and from the returned Timorese diaspora'. In sum, the 2006 crisis highlighted the way the nation-building process had been greatly complicated by 'recognition' style struggles over the relative contributions of various political actors to the achievement of East Timorese independence, or the apparent misrecognition by the new state of key popular values. Some aspects of intergenerational tensions have also assumed the character of 'recognition' struggles. These included the obvious issue of language policy, especially in the early post-2002 years, but also wider conflicts over the political and cultural dominance of older nationalists in post-independence political settlements. These tensions extended to the comparative neglect of the youth-dominated civilian resistance in the national memorial landscape, compared with the greater public valorisation of armed combatants of FALINTIL and senior FRETILIN and CNRT 'national heroes' (Babo-Soares 2003; Leach 2009).

Against the backdrop of these fault lines, a range of constituencies have been making recognition-style claims against the East Timorese state. At various times, these constituencies have included veterans and military petitioners; IDPs during the crisis of 2006–07; the former clandestine resistance; youth; traditionalists favouring a greater role for customary law; the Catholic Church; victims groups; and others.[1] It is worth noting that when taken together, FALINTIL veterans, youth, traditionalists (including *liurai*—traditional rulers), and victims of violence from 1974–99 potentially represent a substantial percentage of the population, which has at times expressed dissent at their perceived exclusion from forms of institutional and symbolic recognition by the state. In addition, key veterans groups such as the Committee for the Popular Defence of the Democratic Republic of Timor-Leste (CPD-RDTL) and Sagrada Familia have explicitly denied recognition of the 2002 constitution, questioning the wider political settlement as a whole.

The politics of demanding recognition of contributions to the Resistance, or acknowledgement of suffering during the occupation, has been the basis of many political claims on the state. Indeed, it might be argued that there is not only a politics of recognition, but also a political economy of recognition. In 2013, there were some 37,000 registered veterans, receiving annual pensions worth US$67 million, along with one-off payments worth US$62 million (*La'o Hamutuk* 2013). Veterans are also frequently recipients of contracts under infrastructure and referendum funds; emergency projects to veterans totalled US$78 million in 2010–12—a figure set to increase by 4 per cent annually (*La'o Hamutuk* 2013). These programs represented a substantial feature of the 2013 budget at 5.8 per cent, exceeding both security sector and health expenditure.[2] While veterans payments enjoy a high level of popular legitimacy, in part because they are considered due recognition, some types of payments to veterans have drawn criticism.[3] It is also true that other groups perceived to be less deserving than veterans have also benefited from large infrastructure contracts. Timor-Leste has witnessed more malicious attempts to mimic recognition claims, from criminal gangs and conflict entrepreneurs leveraging threats of unrest and conflict as a means of rent-seeking (Scambary 2009; ICG 2013).

---

1   See for example, Traube (2007) on the notion of 'unpaid wages', and popular claims for compensation for sacrifices made during the independence struggle.
2   These figures do not include the civilian clandestine list, former military petitioners, and a range of other important new pensions, including payments to the elderly and single mothers.
3   *La'o Hamutuk* (2013) noted that some of the largest payments distributed in June 2012 before the parliamentary elections were directed to 'these warriors, genuine heroes of our independence, (who) deserve attention from the state, but we worry when this rectification is used to pay for party political promises'.

Finally, these patterns of recognition and misrecognition have also been evident in state-sanctioned forms of 'official' history, including the cultural heritage and memorial landscape (Leach 2009). For example, the critical contributions of the youth-dominated clandestine resistance have taken a long time to be recognised in both the history curriculum and the memorial landscape of the independent state. While 12 November is a national public holiday, and there is a system to award medals to veterans of the clandestine resistance, it was only in 2012 that a monument was built to remember the victims of the Santa Cruz massacre—an event widely regarded as a turning point in the campaign for independence. Publicly, the extent of the *juventude*'s (youth) contribution tends to be neglected in post-independence politics, with military veterans' issues and histories strongly dominant. In a parallel feature, as Fernandes (2011: 125) notes, the civilian clandestine resistance has been relatively neglected by historians.[4] As he argues, the history of the clandestine front movements and their 'vital yet often unacknowledged role' in the independence struggle is yet to be fully documented. It is also true that women's contribution to the Resistance remain an area of enquiry to be more fully explored, despite some notable pioneering contributions (Amal 2006; Conway 2010), and the more recent, as yet unreleased, work of the *Secretarido da Comissão de Pesquisa e Elaboração da História da Luta da Mulher Timor* (Secretariat for the Commission for Research and Development of the History of the Timorese Women's Struggle). Women's contribution to the Resistance is also notably absent in official commemoration and memorial landscapes.

Recent developments

Debates over history have taken on a new flavour in recent years. With Xanana Gusmão reviving the name of the former united front for independence (CNRT) as a political party in 2007, leadership credentials in the military wing of the resistance proved a strong theme in both the 2007 and 2012 election campaigns, highlighting the political legitimacy still associated with these attributes. In 2012, Gusmão campaigned again as *Lider Maximo* (top leader) of the Resistance, with a high-profile media campaign, including photos of himself in uniform, which gave full exposure to his role as leader of the resistance era. Likewise, the 2012 presidential election campaign heavily featured references to the past in Taur Matan Ruak's campaign slogan 'Together with you in the past, our blood intertwined towards our independence. Together again with you today, we toil towards a better future' (Powles 2012). The labelling of a

---

4   Exceptions include *Chega!* (CAVR 2006, Chapter 5: Resistance Structure and Strategy); Fernandes (2011); Babo-Soares (2003); and Nicholson (2001).

small pro-CNRT breakaway group from the main opposition party FRETILIN as 'FRETILIN Resistencia' highlighted the way these ideas were deployed as an electoral strategy to delegitimise the major opposition party.

Since 2012, however, there have been clear signs of public *rapprochement* between the two key figures of Prime Minister Gusmão and the opposition FRETILIN leader and former Prime Minister Mari Alkatiri. Following the coalition-building among non-FRETILIN forces from 2007, the profound nature of CNRT's 2012 victory seems to have reduced political conflict between the elites, with a new political settlement or consensus politics emerging. This has reflected Gusmão's successful and long-term strategy of using political victories as a basis for coalition and unity-building, though these developments have also been driven in part by FRETILIN's continuing support among voters from the eastern districts. The influence of President Taur Matan Ruak is also seen to be a factor in the new working truce between the two leaders.

This new style of politics was evident in FRETILIN's unprecedented support for annual budget votes in parliament, and in the appointment of Alkatiri as the head of a major project to develop the exclave of Oecusse as a special economic zone (*Suara Timor Lorosa'e* 2013). It was also reflected in Gusmao's overtures to the 2014 FRETILIN conference, at which he acknowledged its key role in the Resistance. Conversely, Alkatiri publicly acknowledged Gusmão as a former FRETILIN leader himself, and was vocal in encouraging him not to retire early. His party also conspicuously dropped the label '*de facto* government' it had used after the 2007 election, when the CNRT had won fewer seats than FRETILIN. The two leaders were frequently seen travelling together, showing an external unity to the world. In the wake of departing international peacekeeping forces, these developments were critical, and led to wider interpretations within the political elite. Most notably, Minister of State and President of the Council of Ministers, Agio Pereira (2014) wrote of these developments as a 'new politics of national consensus' to overcome failed state syndrome, seeing them as an example to other developing post-conflict countries of 'transforming belligerent democracy into consensus democracy'. On FRETILIN's part, it made references to a new 'pact with the regime' (Lusa News Agency 2014), which it sees as a 'necessary consensus for state-building'.

The remarkable culmination of this trend occurred in early 2015 with the formation of a new government, dominated by CNRT ministers, but led by FRETILIN's Rui Araujo as Prime Minister. With Gusmão stepping down from the prime minister's office to become the Minister for Planning and Development, the new power-sharing executive, involving the two major parties, also represented a major intergenerational shift in the political leadership (Leach 2015). The move toward a semi-formalised government of national unity was important as this generational handover (signalled in 2013, then delayed at the CNRT party congress in 2014) was always likely to be a watch point for political stability. There were clear signs that the 'history wars' were cooling as Gusmão prepared to depart the centre of the political stage, with Alkariti already installed as the head of a new body charged with promoting development in the exclave of Oecusse. These developments answered some of the questions about what to do with the *katuas*—the senior leadership of the 1975 era, including José Ramos-Horta—beyond their departure from formal political life. The rumour mill had entertained various speculations as to how their historic role would be preserved, ranging from proposals of a Lee Kwan Yew–style 'senior ministry', to a more probable, and perhaps inevitable, role as an informal 'council of elders'.

This new moderation of political conflict also saw the state seek to tackle anti-system actors including the CPD-RDTL, with significant developments across 2013 and 2014. Throughout 2013, increased activity and political conflict was evident from disaffected veterans groups, including an extended CPD-RDTL confrontation with police in Manufahi. Late in 2013, calls by a former FALINTIL commander Paulino 'Mauk Morak' Gama, for a 'revolution against poverty and early elections'[5] brought older divisions within the former FALINTIL military resistance to the fore. This raised heated debates in the country, to the extent that a special forum of political leaders had to be convened, with the president himself offering to mediate.[6] This conflict has deeper origins in Gusmão's reformation of the FALINTIL resistance in the 1980s, taking it from the armed wing of the pro-independence party FRETILIN to a non-partisan military force representing all nationalists. This move toward a policy of *apartidismo* (non-partisanship) ultimately led to the creation of the CNRT—a broad nationalist front representing all East Timorese nationalists, with no ideological goals other than national liberation, and with FALINTIL as its military.[7] At the time of the initial split in 1984, Mauk Moruk was among a small group of disaffected FALINTIL officers who rejected the strategy and attempted an internal coup against Gusmão's leadership.

This episode amply demonstrated the ongoing power of history in East Timorese political life. Moruk is now associated with Sagrada Familia—a former clandestine group during the occupation—who, like CPD-RDTL, remains outside the mainstream of post-independence politics. Many in Dili expressed relief that all major parties, including FRETILIN, supported Prime Minister Gusmão in the special forum, which Moruk did not attend. Moruk and his veteran-dominated group, the *Konseilu Revolusionariu Maubere* (KRM; Maubere

---

5   *Timor Post* 21/10/2013.
6   *Suara Timor Lorosa'e* 11/11/2013.
7   See Niner (2009: 105–06) for historical background to these events.

Revolutionary Council), later called for protests on 28 November 2013—the 38th anniversary of Timor-Leste's unilateral declaration of independence in 1975, but these actions ultimately did not proceed.

In March 2014, the parliament moved to proscribe CPD-RDTL and KRM, after members wearing uniforms had conducted military exercises in the Baucau district. Following a reported shoot-out between KRM and police, Moruk and CPD-RDTL leader Aitahan Matak were detained in Dili, and Moruk's brother and Sagrada Familia leader Cornelio 'L7' Gama were placed under house arrest. Moruk surrendered to police but warned that 'all of Dili would burn' at his command. This threat was followed by Moruk visiting the attorney-general with a military escort, and reported attempts to register as a legal organisation. Local security NGO Fundasaun Mahein (2014) subsequently expressed concerns that despite the government's new resolve, veterans groups operating outside the law may bring the government to the bargaining table over registration. While new forms of elite unity were evident in the face of ongoing sources of historical division, as other commentators have noted, beneath the new confidence of a more united elite lie ongoing tensions, with parallels to those that lay behind the 2006 crisis (Powles and Sousa Santos 2013):

> The standoff between Gusmao and Mauk Moruk reflects a potentially dangerous schism between two groups: on the one hand, Gusmao, the former clandestine groups allied to him and the national police; and on the other hand, the Gama brothers, Sagrada Familia, and the national military whose Chief, General Lere Anan, publicly stated his support and membership of Sagrada Familia during the resistance struggle.

While Moruk's challenge was met with a firm and unified response from the elite, to the relief of many in the country, there were also fears that popular disaffection with the slow progress of development may yet assist these groups' message, and in mobilising potential supporters. As Mattheos Messakh (cited in Gonçalves 2014) argues, the wider question is whether disaffected veterans groups are capable of becoming a lightning rod for those who feel left out of progress and economic patronage:

> It is likely that Mauk Moruk's strategy is to captivate young people who feel increasingly marginalized and who can be easily taken advantage of ... to fill a void left by the prohibition of martial arts groups created during the clandestine resistance and involved in the violence of 2006.

By mid-2014, tensions surrounding disaffected veterans groups appeared to calm considerably, only to flare up again in January 2015 in a standoff between the PNTL (*Policia Nacional de Timor-Leste*; National Police of Timor-Leste) and the KRM in Laga. Though the government's resolve remained firm, and the KRM's popular support base was uncertain, these developments also showed that so long as participation in the military resistance remains a keystone of political legitimacy, historical divisions and associated claims for recognition would continue to prompt powerful reactions. While the present government can win these symbolic battles on the same ground of veteran credentials, future governments will need to establish alternative criteria for legitimacy.

Thinking about post-conflict history

It should first be noted that difficulties in writing the national history in Timor-Leste are common to post-conflict societies. As in Bosnia and Kosovo, Timor-Leste is not alone in having to replace the history component of otherwise retained textbooks, following national independence (Höpken 2001: 3). Similarly, several post-conflict societies have delayed history education in favour of a less controversial and general focus on human rights education and civics curricula (Cole and Barsalou 2006: 12). This pattern, evident in Rwanda and Bosnia, has been apparent in Timor-Leste, with civic education curricula development far in advance of history curriculum development through the early years of independence (see Leach 2007, 2010). Some post-conflict countries have gone further, and chosen to ignore the recent past of violent conflict in newly developed national history textbooks (including Mozambique and Cambodia), or have openly postponed inclusion (Rwanda) (see Höpken 2001: 2).

A key issue in post-conflict societies is how the role of the history curriculum is conceived. As Höpken (2001: 12) notes, peace-building and reconciliation will not necessarily be promoted by curricula primarily designed to promote officially sanctioned versions of national identity and foster loyalty to the state. Equally, teaching students core historical methods of critical inquiry, such as the capacity to evaluate the merits of competing historical claims, may not be compatible with the goals of official histories that seek to inculcate 'national values' and loyalty. This is a critical issue for Timor-Leste, particularly as it seeks to move on from the authoritarian epistemology of the New Order (Indonesian regime 1967–98) approach to national history as a single, authorised, pan-archipelagic narrative. Indeed, understanding historical knowledge as a process of evaluating competing historical claims, and teaching students the processes of gathering evidence to test them, are essential skills of democratic citizenship. As Cole and Barsalou (2006: 1) note teaching these skills of critical inquiry may be a more effective focus in resource-poor environments than developing new history textbooks. Yet this focus can also attract opposition from new ruling elites and policymakers, as 'few post-conflict societies are ready to accept an approach that promotes critical thinking, since it is often perceived as flying in the face of traditions that respect expertise, seniority, and authority and promote group honour as more important than any forensic truth' (Cole and Barsalou 2006: 10).

In Timor-Leste, the link between history curriculum development and transitional justice is also a critical one. Certainly, the failure to implement the recommendations of the CAVR report strongly parallels the challenges in writing the national history. Thorny and highly politicised debates over justice and reconciliation, along with questions of how to deal with legacies of internal division, and the relationship with Indonesia, are common to both challenges. Both point to a present lack of political will and a working consensus to deal with the complex and divisive issues of historical justice. While the CAVR has produced an essential range of educational materials, as the *Secretariado Tecnico Pos-CAVR* (Post-CAVR Technical Secretariat) itself notes (CAVR 2008: 39), *Chega!* was not written directly for the classroom and still needs to be 're-presented … appropriately for different levels and subject areas'. This is an important caveat, as the 'socialisation' of CAVR findings can only truly take place at a national level through their reproduction as curricula. At present, CAVR materials are left to the discretion of individual teachers to incorporate into classroom practice. This is regrettable, as representative personal stories—of the sort employed by the CAVR report—are considered to be very helpful methodologies for dealing with complex issues of historical justice in school curricula (Cole and Barsalou 2006: 10).

The role of a history curriculum development in nation-building is also a critical one. Compulsory schooling is, of course, a key site of integration around national values and identities. Gellner even goes so far as to argue that 'the monopoly of legitimate education: is more important than the classic Weberian monopoly of legitimate violence' (Gellner 1983; Tawil and Harley 2004: 9–10). A key issue is how to promote a social cohesion that is respectful of diversity (Tawil and Harley 2004: 4) without exacerbating social tensions. As was abundantly clear in the 2006 crisis, Timor-Leste's past can easily be recruited to the purposes of creating discord; highlighting the urgent need to promote social cohesion.

Finally, compulsory education is also a key site for promoting a postcolonial cultural identity in the wake of colonialism and civil conflict. As Tawil and Harley argue (2004: 20), Mozambique is a good example of a society seeking to assert a post-independence national identity that also accommodates a diverse multilingual, multicultural society. However, as Rønning notes (cited in Tawil and Harley 2004: 20), accommodating multiple languages and local identities may be seen by some nationalists as a form of tribalism that questions the project of national unity. In Timor-Leste, the 'Mother Tongue' Multilingual Education Program has certainly faced criticisms of this type, despite the strong evidence base suggesting its effectiveness in promoting literacy. Key questions in the process of promoting an inclusive national identity via compulsory education include who is consulted about these issues, how non-elite voices are heard, and the ways conflict is dealt with (Tawil and Harley 2004: 19). Where there are ongoing divisive issues, there may be a clear role for outsiders in the process of curriculum development; indeed, this was the 'circuit-breaker' in reforming the national curriculum after the conflict in Rwanda (Cole and Barsalou 2006: 7).

History in progress

Major developments have occurred in the national history curriculum in recent years. The most significant of these is the redevelopment of the year 1–9 primary curricula, with a major effort to 'indigenise' a range of curricula for primary schools. This includes a stand-alone history curriculum at primary level for the first time, replacing the previous syllabus (Leach 2007), which saw primary school history covered under the general subject of *'Estudo do Meio'* or 'Environment'. Units will have a strong early focus on pre-colonial history, to encourage an understanding of Timorese cultures and identity as the products of societies pre-dating the colonial era, before examining the impacts of colonialism (*Reforma Curricula de Ensino Básico*—Curriculum Reform for Ensino Basico project team; interview with author 2014).[8] East Timorese curriculum developers are the primary writers for the first time, supported by international consultant teams, with the additional involvement of teachers and the teacher training college. Importantly, the *Ministério da Educação* (Ministry of Education) curriculum development team is also working with teachers to develop lesson plans—something that was previously relegated to the school or teacher level (see Leach 2007)—and a mentoring scheme for new teachers. In terms of pedagogical approach, lesson plans include a strong focus on asking questions—a seemingly straightforward approach, but one that challenges previous schooling cultures in a profound way, and may take considerable time to implement. Importantly, the curriculum seeks to encourage the development of critical reasoning skills and basic research techniques, including oral history projects at 4th and 5th grades; encountering the idea of stereotypes; understanding different perspectives on historical issues; and introducing students to different types of historical evidence at 5th and 6th grades. Taken together, these approaches represent a significant departure from the former curriculum. The influence of a very active vice-minister for primary education is widely acknowledged as a key factor in these changes. At the secondary level of years 10–12 the approach is more standard, with curriculum development

---

8   Interview with Curriculum Reform for Ensino Basico project team, Dili, 18 August 2014. At this point, the reformed curriculum covers the first and second cycle only (years 1–6).

teams from Portuguese universities working on the upper history curriculum. The strong base in national culture at primary level, and a more generic 'national and world history' approach at secondary school may prove complementary, although it remains to be seen how more controversial episodes and periods of conflict in East Timorese history will be dealt with in the upper years of schooling.

Other neglected elements of East Timorese history are also starting to receive due attention. The women's history project *Secretarido da Comissão de Pesquisa e Elaboração da História da Luta da Mulher Timor* (Secretariat for the Commission for Research and Development of the History of the Timorese Women's Struggle) is researching the role of East Timorese women in the Resistance. This work is well in progress and the project expects to launch their report in 2015. The history of the clandestine movements is also expanding slowly, though there is considerable work to do in this area. As noted above, in recent years the relative lack of recognition of the clandestine resistance is starting to be addressed by both historians and formal state memorialisation. There is, however, also some controversy attached to the new Santa Cruz monument at Motael, which was installed without consultation with the 12 November committee led by Gregorio Saldanha (da Silva 2012); and there is still no progress on a memorial at Santa Cruz itself, despite a government-announced design competition co-sponsored by the 12 November committee in 2010 (RDTL 2010). Slow but steady progress on the history of the clandestine resistance is also evident in some newer publications, most substantially in Fernandes's *The Independence of East Timor: Multi-Dimensional Perspectives* (2011). It is to be hoped that a new generation of East Timorese historians will build on—and perhaps revise—early attempts made by external historians, and the relatively few East Timorese accounts made following independence (de Araujo 2003; Babo-Soares 2003; Pereira 2009). In terms of documentation, the national archive still requires support to fully catalogue and digitise its materials, and a formal legislative framework to define its responsibilities. The *Arquivo & Museu da Resistência* (Archives & Museum of East Timorese Resistance) in Dili is strongly supported by government, and also performs some of these archival functions. Outside the country, CHART (Clearing House for Archival Records on Timor) is being funded by the East Timorese Government and other donors to preserve and digitise the archives of the Timorese diaspora in Australia[9].

---

9   See timorarchives.wordpress.com/chart/.

Conclusion

International experience suggests that certain pre-conditions must be met before compulsory history education can be seen as a resource to foster reconciliation and peace-building. These pre-conditions include a favourable post-conflict environment where violence has ended, a strong commitment to peace-building from political elites, a sense of common national values, and a general social consensus for reconciliation (see Höpken 2001: 5–8). Until recently in Timor-Leste, many of these basic issues were still unsettled, with a highly fractious political elite, divisive legacies of the 2006 crisis, and a small but influential cohort of anti-system groups that routinely questioned the state's monopoly on legitimate force. The 2006 military-political crisis was a clear setback to the peace-building process, as are the still divisive debates over reconciliation, forgiveness and justice.

However, recent developments in political stability raise grounds for greater optimism. In the wake of the *rapprochement* between fractions of the political elite, are conditions favourable for dealing with more controversial issues in the national history in upper levels of schooling? While there are grounds for positive assessments, including a strong political commitment from relevant ministers to producing culturally relevant education, some caveats are clear. First, there is little political will to deal with internationally sensitive issues arising from the Indonesian occupation, the violence of 1999, and the unresolved grievances of victims groups. While much of the tension from 2006 has been worked through, and post-independence relations between the political elite are at a high point, events associated with the 2006 crisis are still sensitive, and attempts at writing their history may prove challenging. Another caveat concerns the extent to which these welcome developments should be understood as transformations within the political elite alone, or whether they are subject to more popular consensus. Behind the elite political *rapprochement*, victims groups still feel marginalised, and an uncomfortable level of popular support can be sensed around some of the disaffected veterans groups' criticisms, particularly when they speak of those who have missed out on the fruits of development or economic patronage.

Equally, with the departure of Xanana Gusmão from the prime minister's office in early 2015, other questions attend the new moderation in political conflict. Will the new consensus continue in a post-Gusmão electoral environment after the 2017 elections? How will the emergence of the post-'75 Generation alter these inter-party dynamics? Can a new generation address divisive social issues with the same sort of historical legitimacy as the *katuas*? Or, indeed, will a new generation more easily transcend these divisions associated with the leaders of the '75 Generation? More broadly, questions remain about the role of the military. Will the army stay out of politics once senior civilian leaders are no longer former FALINTIL commanders, whose political control ensures the close ear of government (see Feijo in this collection). If recognition-style claims from former veterans groups continue to catalyse some popular economic discontent, the combination of high unemployment and a growing youth population could again reveal a latent potential for significant social unrest. It remains to be seen if claims from victims groups can be addressed with cash transfers and pensions, in the absence of meeting more difficult demands for justice. Time will tell if the 'history wars' are cooling, or simply in abeyance in formal elite politics.

References

Amal, T. 2006. *Sete Mulheres de Timor – Feto Timor Nain Hitu* [Seven Women of Timor]. Granja do Ulmeiro: Acção para a Justiça e Paz [Action for Justice and Peace].

Babo-Soares, D. 2003. Branching from the Trunk: East Timorese Perceptions of Nationalism in Transition. PhD thesis, The Australian National University.

Babo-Soares, D. 2003. Political developments leading to the referendum. In J.J. Fox and D. Babo-Soares (eds), *Out of the Ashes: Destruction and Reconstruction of East Timor*. Canberra: ANU E Press, 53–73.

CAVR 2006. *Chega!: The Report of the Commission for Reception, Truth and Reconciliation, Timor-Leste*. Dili: CAVR.

CAVR 2008. *The Chega! Resource Kit*. Dili: Post-CAVR Technical Secretariat.

Cole, E.A. and J. Barsalou 2006. Unite or Divide? The Challenges of Teaching History in Societies Emerging from Violent Conflict. *United States Institute of Peace Special Report* 163. Washington DC: USIP. www.usip.org/files/resources/sr163.pdf.

Conway, J. 2010. *Step by Step: Women of East Timor, Stories of Resistance and Survival*. Darwin: Charles Darwin University Press.

da Silva, M. 2012. Harii Monumentu 12 Novembru St. Cruz Sai Fali Estatua [Statue built to commemorate 12th November]. *Jornal Independente* [English translation]. 14 November.

de Araujo, F. 2003. The CNRT Campaign for Independence. In J.J. Fox and D. Babo-Soares (eds), *Out of the Ashes: Destruction and Reconstruction of East Timor*. Canberra: ANU E Press, 99–116.

East Timor Law and Justice Bulletin 2013. Violations of the Law by Both the State and CPD-RDTL Dissidents in Manufahi. 20 February. www.easttimorlawandjusticebulletin.com/2013/02/violations-of-law-by-both-state-and-cpd.html#sthash.WHzAlz8N.dpuf.

Feijó, R.G. 2014. Timor-Leste: Challenges to the Consolidation of Democracy. SSGM *In Brief* 2014/5. Canberra: State, Society and Governance in Melanesia Program, ANU. ips.cap.anu.edu.au/sites/default/files/SSGM%20IB%202014_5.pdf.

Fernandes, C. 2011. *The Independence of East Timor: Multi-Dimensional Perspectives—Occupation, Resistance and International Political Activism.* Brighton: Sussex.

Fundasaun M. 2014. Rule of Law or Rule of the Deal in Timor-Leste? *East Timor Law and Justice Bulletin* 9 March. www.easttimorlawandjusticebulletin.com/2014/03/fundasaun-mahein-fm-rule-of-law-or-rule.html#sthash.ZUs92sIy.dpuf.

Gellner, E. 1983. *Nations and Nationalism.* Ithaca: Cornell University Press.

Gonçalves, M. 1/4/2014. Ex-Guerrillas Threaten Political Stability in East Timor. *Global Voices.* globalvoicesonline.org/2014/04/01/ex-guerrillas-threaten-political-stability-in-east-timor/.

Honneth, A. 1995. *The Struggle for Recognition: The Moral Grammar of Social Conflicts.* Cambridge: Polity.

Höpken, W. 2001. History-Textbooks and Reconciliation—Preconditions and Experiences in a Comparative Perspective: Draft. World Bank meeting, 11 November, Washington DC. siteresources.worldbank.org/INTCEERD/Resources/EDUCwolfganghopken.pdf.

ICG (International Crisis Group) 2013. Timor-Leste: Stability at What Cost? Media release 8 May. www.crisisgroup.org/en/publication-type/media-releases/2013/asia/timor-leste-stability-at-what-cost.aspx.

Kammen, D. 2003. Master-Slave, Traitor-Nationalist, Opportunist-Oppressed: Political Metaphors in East Timor. *Indonesia* 76:69–85.

Kent, L. 2012. *The Dynamics of Transitional Justice: International Models and Local Realities in East Timor.* Abingdon: Routledge.

La'o Hamutuk 2013, The National Impact of Benefits for Former Combatants. BELUN Seminar on the Social Impact of Administration Processes for Veterans Payments, Dili, 5 March. www.laohamutuk.org/econ/pension/VetPension6Mar2013en.pps.

Leach, M. 2006. East Timorese History after Independence. *History Workshop Journal* 61(1):222–37.

Leach, M. 2007. History Teaching in East Timor: Challenges and Alternatives. In D. Kingsbury and M. Leach (eds), *East Timor: Beyond Independence*. Clayton: Monash Asia Institute Press, 193–207.

Leach, M. 2009. Difficult Memories: The Independence Struggle as Cultural Heritage in East Timor. In W. Logan and K. Reeves (eds), *Places of Pain and Shame: Dealing with 'Difficult Heritage'*. Abingdon: Routledge, 144–61.

Leach, M. 2010. Writing History in Post-Conflict Timor-Leste. In Leach, M., N. Canas Mendes, A. da Silva, A. Ximenes and B. Boughton (eds). *Understanding Timor-Leste: Proceedings of the Timor-Leste Studies Association Conference*. Dili, 2–3 July 2009. Hawthorn: Swinburne Press, 124–30.

Leach, M. 2012. Longitudinal Change in East Timorese Tertiary Student Attitudes to National Identity and Nation Building, 2002–2010. *Journal of the Humanities and Social Sciences of Southeast Asia and Oceania (Bijdragen tot de Taal-, Land- en Volkenkunde)* 168(2–3):219–52.

Leach, M. 18/2/2015. Generational Change in Timor-Leste. *Inside Story*. insidestory.org.au/generational-change-in-timor-leste.

Lusa News Agency 6/4/2014. FRETILIN Explains 'Regime Pact' with Xanana Gusmao to Cadres.

Nicholson, D. 2001. The Lorikeet Warriors: East Timorese new generation nationalist resistance, 1989–99. Bachelor of Arts (Honours) thesis, Department of History, University of Melbourne.

Niner, S. 2009. *Xanana: Leader of the Struggle for Independent Timor-Leste*. North Melbourne: Australian Scholarly Publishing.

Pereira, A. 26/1/2014. Timor-Leste Transforming Belligerent Democracy into Consensus Democracy. *Tempo Semanal*. www.temposemanal.com/opiniaun/item/474-timor-leste-transforming-belligerent-democracy-into-consensus-democracy.

Pereira, N. 2009. *Catatan Seorang Peompat Pagar* [Memories of a Fence Jumper], Dili: RENETIL (*Resistencia Nacional dos Estudantes de Timor Leste*; National Resistance of East Timorese Students).

Powles, A. 27/4/2012. Nationalism and Nostalgia Win in Timor Leste. *Asia Times*. www.atimes.com/atimes/Southeast_Asia/ND27Ae03.html.

Powles, A. and J. Sousa Santos. 5/12/2013. Xanana Gusmao-Mauk Moruk: Timor Struggles With its Past and Future. *Lowy Interpreter*. www.lowyinterpreter.org/post/2013/12/05/Gusmao-Mauk-Moruk-Timor-struggles-with-its-past-and-future.aspx.

Ramos-Horta, J. 1987. *Funu: The Unfinished Saga of East Timor*. Trenton: Red Sea Press.

RDTL 25/10/2010. Open Competition for the Best Drawing of the Monument Dedicated to the 12th of November 1991 Massacre. News release. timor-leste.gov.tl/?p=4153&lang=en&n=1.

Scambary, J. 2009. Anatomy of a Conflict: The 2006–07 Communal Conflict in East Timor. *Conflict, Security and Development Journal* 9(2):265–88.

Suara Timor Lorosa'e 9/4/2013. Xanana Gusmão Appoints Alkitiri to Improve Oe-cusse's Economy.

Suara Timor Lorosa'e 11/11/2013. Xanana Wants to Tell True History.

Tawil, S. and A. Harley (eds) 2004. *Education, Conflict and Social Cohesion*. Geneva: International Bureau of Education. www.ibe.unesco.org/conflict/ConflictSCohesion.htm.

Timor Post 21/10/2013. Mauk Moruk Calls for Revolution.

Traube, E.G. 2007. Unpaid Wages: Local Narratives and the Imagination of the Nation. *Asia Pacific Journal of Anthropology* 8(1):9–25.

Trindade, J. and B. Castro 2007. *Technical Assistance to the National Dialogue in Timor-Leste: Rethinking Timorese Identity as a Peacebuilding Strategy: The Lorosa'e–Loromonu Conflict from a Traditional Perspective*. Dili: The European Union's Rapid Reaction Mechanism Programme.

CHAPTER 5

Challenges to the Consolidation of Democracy

Rui Graça Feijó

Introduction

On 1 January 2013, Timor-Leste initiated a march on its own feet. The United Nations Integrated Mission in Timor-Leste (UNMIT)—the last of the special missions that started back in 1999—as well as the International Stabilisation Force convened in the wake of the 2006 crisis, departed then, heralding a new phase in this new nation's political life. So far, the country has responded positively to this change and maintains a stable political situation. The fact that in 2012 Timor-Leste organised presidential and legislative elections considered free and fair complying with international standards, reinforced the country's legitimacy to fully dispose of political autonomy, which it is now enjoying.

Both the majority of authors writing on Timor-Leste (for example, Kingsbury 2009; Molnar 2011; Leach and Kingsbury 2012) and international organisations who elaborate indices of democratic performance (for example, Freedom House, Polity IV, The Economist Intelligence Unit) agree that Timor-Leste has achieved the status of a democratic polity. Freedom House has long considered Timor-Leste an 'electoral democracy' and a 'partly free' country, rating it 3.5 points on a scale in which those who have less than 3 points are free and those scoring above 5 are not free. The overall figure combines a score of 3 for political rights and 4 for civil liberties. Among the factors that prevent a more positive evaluation, this organisation ranks problems with freedom of the press, which is deemed to exercise self-censorship in the context of the existing defamation laws; limits to the freedom of association; weak rule of law and a culture of impunity associated with episodes of violence perpetrated by the police forces; the status of refugees; and gender discrimination sustained by customary law.[1] Polity IV uses a classification ranging from −10 to +10, in which countries scored 6 to 9 are considered as democracies (and those scoring 10 are full democracies). Timor-Leste has been consistently classified in recent years with 7 points, that is, as a clearly democratic country. All three sub-criteria receive the same classification.[2] Finally, The Economist Intelligence Unit's Democracy Index ranks Timor-Leste as the 43rd country in the world in terms of its democratic performance. The country is regarded as a 'flawed democracy' (a category that comprises countries with marks between 6 and 7.99, and encompasses most of the European Union members) and is rated at 7.16. This overall figure is the result of five independent indices, and there Timor-Leste receives high marks for its political process and pluralism (8.67, in line with a 'full democracy') and civil liberties (7.94), and lower for political participation (only 5.56). Both the functioning of government (6.79) and political culture (6.88) are in line with the overall classification.[3]

These three examples reveal that a consensus exists as to the classification of Timor-Leste as a functioning and apparently stable democracy. As Damien Kingsbury has noted, meaningful elections capable of producing alterations in the orientation of the country (peaceful replacement of two presidents, change of parliamentary majority, and substantial alteration in the composition of the government basis of support) seem to have been incorporated in the popular culture and became equated with *lulik* (sacred) rituals (Kingsbury 2014). A clear symbol of this evolution can be grasped in the vivid images of citizens emerging from the polling booths and proudly exhibiting their ink-marked fingers as proof of their participation in the electoral process, discharging a community service. However, the apparent stability of the country in the recent past cannot be equated with the consolidation of democracy or the absence of serious challenges to the way the political regime responds to popular demands and delivers tangible outcomes. As Robert Elgie and Sophia Moestrup put it, Timor-Leste enjoys a stable but not yet consolidated democratic regime (Elgie and Moestrup 2011).

In this brief essay, I will consider, among the myriad pertinent challenges to democratic consolidation and the improvement of its performance, three aspects that I regard as critical: the generational turnover, the relationship between prosperity and democracy, and the mandatory constitutional reform supposed to produce a decentralised state administration.

---

1   See www.freedomhouse.org/report/freedom-world/2013/east-timor-0#.U5x9DCjJ4UU.
2   See www.systemicpeace.org/polity/polity4.htm.
3   See portoncv.gov.cv/dhub/porton.por_global.open_file?p_doc_id=1034.

Generational turnover

The presidential elections in 2012 offered a glimpse into the ongoing generational turnover. The incumbent president, a leading member of the '75 Generation, was eliminated in the first round, leaving the second round to be contested by two candidates who were in their teens or just beyond in 1975. This highlights the onset of a process of generational turnover, as the most relevant political positions have consistently remained in the hands of the elder generation. The recent decision of Gusmão to step down from his prime ministership and pave the way for a new incumbent from the *Gerasaun Foun* (New Generation) further stresses the importance of this process.

Timor-Leste is a complex and paradoxical case. The typical case of generational turnover associated with transitions from authoritarianism considers that when the generation who negotiated the political change gives way to a new one, the latter emerges fully socialised in democratic politics and formatted to operate within the system—not to challenge or discuss its merits once again. This generally means that democracy has been consolidated and in most cases has become 'the only game in town'. In Timor-Leste, a country in which different notions of political legitimacy (in the classical sense of Max Weber's 1947 work) concur to create a complex landscape, a critical element in the rooting of democracy, was the espousal of democratic principles by a strong charismatic leader. Charismatic and legal-rational legitimacy merged to produce a democratic polity. Now that the charismatic leader has stepped aside, what will become of his legacy? The question is further amplified by the fact that the members of the generation of which Gusmão is a leading and persuasive member, and which broadly accommodated his vision, are rapidly coming to the end of their politically active lives: Ramos-Horta has been performing international duties for the UN; Mário Carrascalão no longer leads his PSD (*Partido Social Democrata*; Social Democratic Party); and the replacement of Alkatiri as leader of FRETILIN (*Frente Revolucionária de Timor-Leste Independente*; Revolutionary Front for an Independent East Timor) is expected to take place in the next congress before the general elections.

In parallel with those who espouse the current democratic system, worrying signs are discernible in Dili. First, several 'siren songs' can be heard—some along the path of 'Asian values'; others putting specific emphasis on 'Timorese values'— that are supposed to diverge from the standard democratic ethos. The defeat of Ramos-Horta in the first round of the 2012 presidential election has been read as a signal of the Timorese fatigue with an internationally driven agenda, and the two candidates that made it to the final round converged in praising the Timorese own values and the need to bring them to a more prominent place in the political arena. The fact that both of them had long experience in the home fronts of the Resistance suggests that this factor remains a major element in the recruitment of new political leaders—some of which are already in very high positions, epitomised by Fernando Lasama de Araújo, another offspring of the *Gerasaun Foun* that emerged during the Resistance period—and offers a basis for some form of continuity. But the emphasis on genuine national values can be read to imply a critique of the 'imported' institutions associated with international co-operation. The odds are that democratic institutions prove to be sufficiently plastic to accommodate emerging trends, although they may need to be reconfigured. In this light, the possibility of revising the constitution—a possibility contemplated in its provisions—may be contemplated, if not during the current legislature, most likely after the next round of elections, in which competing actors may formally present some ideas that have been floating around for some time.

Second, the role of the military in political life is open to question. It should be recalled here that the military claims a strong line of continuity from the clandestine guerrilla struggle—which was critical in keeping the flame of the Resistance alive and creating the conditions that eventually led to the proclamation of independence—to the military (and political) foundations of the new nation. In a sense, the military is vested with 'revolutionary legitimacy' derived from its important role in the liberation struggle, in which it kept a united front that combined with the emergence of different (and rival) political forces. The overwhelming value of national unity, which the military claim to interpret better than anyone else, is a critical element in this scenario. For this reason, the discourse of national unity that often goes hand in hand with the recrimination of politicians for artificially dividing the people and pursuing particular interests can easily be amplified when a towering figure the size of Gusmão steps aside.

So far, the will of the military to intervene in the political arena has been confined within the limits of the constitutional order, as the 2012 election of Brigadier General Taur Matan Ruak as president shows. But some signs suggest that among the military there are aspirations to a more prominent role. On the one hand, with the rise in prosperity derived from the exploration of natural resources, the military has been eager to claim a larger share of the budget, including a substantial increase that would result from the introduction of general military conscription for all youth, as advocated by President Taur Matan Ruak. On the other hand, it has been rapid to respond to what is perceived as a lack of capacity of the civilian authorities to deal with security issues. For instance, in the wake of street disturbances that marked the aftermath of the legislative elections in 2012, the military commander did not hesitate to appear on national television and set the terms for the restoration of peace—threatening the intervention of the armed forces. This move was widely regarded as a high-profile intervention on the brink of conflict with the government.

Will the military's appetite for an increased role in the political arena be circumscribed by the constitutional provisions? Or will it lay claim to a new role that has marred some other developing countries, as we have witnessed in Africa or in Latin America in the 1970s and 1980s?

Prosperity and democracy

Timor-Leste, while remaining the poorest country in Southeast Asia (according to the World Bank), is endowed with natural resources that have been translated in the very rapid growth of its Petroleum Fund. However, the rise of nominal gross domestic product (GDP) per capita is not a panacea, and the relationships between prosperity and democracy are far from universally positive. Literature on economic development is rich on the issue of what has been labelled the 'resources curse', which is an expression of the paradox of plenty—countries and regions with an abundance of natural resources, especially non-renewables, tend to have worse development outcomes than countries with more balanced resource structures.[4] It is often the case that an internal conflict grows, in which different groups compete for their share of revenues, increasing social pressure on governments to function effectively, as well as generating new opportunities for the level of corruption to grow and a tendency for a capture of the state administration by private interests to surface. The relationship of this problem to the adoption of a democratic regime is evident from available indices. If some assumptions of the modernisation theory imply that an increase in the level of economic development generally translates to the establishment of democratic polities, examples abound of less positive paths. In their listings of the wealthiest countries of the world measured by their GDP per capita (in purchasing power parities), both the World Bank and the International Monetary Fund have in the top places countries that are long-established democracies (Luxemburg, Norway, USA), alongside countries that derive a great deal of their wealth from non-renewable natural resources and have authoritarian regimes, such as Qatar or Brunei. A glimpse at the political regimes of the OPEC (Organization of the Petroleum Exporting Countries) countries also reveals that oil-producing nations tend to have worse ratings in the Freedom House index than Timor-Leste.

---

4   See Scheiner in this collection.

A major challenge for the new nation is thus to manage its wealth in line with democratic precepts. Two key aspects of this endeavour are the fight against poverty with the construction of a welfare state—which has been pursued by the generous funding of the ministries of education and health, as well as by the creation of the ministry for solidarity and the expansion of pension schemes— and the development of an 'economic civil society'. Both processes will impact the regime's capacity to strengthen its own basis and solidify democracy.

In order to implement this program, two polar conceptions may be adopted. Timor-Leste may choose clearly defined procedures, institutionally framed, and validated through the rule of law. This would promote equity and equal opportunities, and the state would be regarded as a moral figure. An opposite choice could be made to rely on ad hoc policies, and individual negotiation between the state and private agents, privileging personal ties over institutional norms. Such an approach would create confusion as to the role of the state, generate dependency on social and economic actors *vis à vis* those in power, and foster clientele more than satisfy social needs. Neopatrimonialism and corruption would be the inevitable conclusion of this path.

One example that comes to mind is that of the veterans and the generous pension scheme that the government has implemented. In the state budget for 2013, no less than US$96 million was allocated to this purpose, the fastest growing item in public spending, outperforming both health and education—two areas in which the country needs to make serious investments if it is to overcome the dire needs revealed by the United Nations Development Programme (UNDP) Human Development Index—and, therefore, having a major impact on the relationship between the state and its citizens, since it touches tens of thousands of families (*La'o Hamutuk* 2013). A few problems are raised by this scheme, one of which is the transparency in the determination of those entitled to benefit from its provisions. The actual process of ascertaining those who participated in the 25-year struggle, and acknowledging the degree of their involvement— which is the basis for their entitlement—is rumoured to be prone to abuses and manipulations. This is easy to understand when political rivalries are vividly present and pertain to the very history of the Resistance movement, lacking the existence of a clearly defined set of upheld legal procedures.

Another example of generous use of financial resources is the ambitious program of decentralised investments, which has been implemented in recent years. One of those schemes was the 2009 *Pakote Referendum* (Referendum Package), which absorbed US$70 million destined to provide investment in infrastructures mostly in the country's rural districts; it has been replicated in subsequent years in much the same vein. Instead of basing contracts on a widely publicised public tender scheme, the government opted for an ad hoc management of those contracts, arguing with the need to address the needs of national companies that might face difficulties in an open competition, with the result considered 'a glaring example of wasteful, uncontrolled, impetus spending' (*La'o Hamutuk* 2009). Political patronage seems to have been the main force behind the distribution of contracts. Similar schemes are said to have been in operation in the case of the construction of the Garden of Heroes in Metinaro, and in the district-based smaller-scale replicas of this national cemetery destined to honour those who fell for their country.

At present, Timor-Leste seems to be at the crossroads. In a greatly unfavourable regional and historical context, the perception of corruption is not improving. The Transparency International Corruption Perceptions Index for 2014 rates Timor-Leste at 28 points (in this index, 0 represents the most corrupt, 100 the least so)—down from 33 in 2012 and 30 in 2013; in line with Indonesia, rated at 32 points.[5] If it is undeniable that the Anti-Corruption Commission is operating and the judicial system passes condemnations, the frequency of cases brought by the public suggests an unacceptably high level of endemic corruption. The casuistic dependency of society in relation to those who happen to be in power, rather that the deployment of sound rules, is venom for a healthy civil society that democracy requires to thrive. The recent upgrade of the Court of Auditors, with the ensuing increased capacity to uphold clearly defined and institutionalised procedures, is a step in the right direction. However, it still must compete with a political culture that is permeable to ways of performing public duties that conflict with the rule of law. It is not uncommon to hear voices saying 'We have won the elections and this is the time for us to do things our way, and to pay our supporters. When others win the general elections, it will be their time.'[6] Comments such as these suggest a candid justification of patronage as the basic language in the relations between government and civil society.

Grassroots democracy: building a decentralised state

The third challenge to the consolidation of democracy in Timor-Leste is the process of building a decentralised state. The relevance of this endeavour has recently been recognised by Xanana Gusmão, who spoke of it as 'the second Maubere miracle'—one that will be spread over a long period of time and may go beyond one generation (Pereira 2014).

---

5   See www.transparency.org/research/cpi/overview.
6   Interview with a businessman supporter of the current majority, May 2013.

Two independent reasons concur to render the decentralisation reform critical to the fate of Timorese democracy. On the one hand, there is a clear constitutional mandate to build a decentralised administration including institutions of local power. These state organs that need to be established all over the territory are bound by a constitutional provision stipulating that state organs 'in their reciprocal relationships and exercise of their functions shall observe the principle of separation and interdependence of powers'.[7] As such, the constitutional architecture is conceived as being formed by several pillars entertaining 'interdependent' relations in such a way that the overall stability of the institutions rests upon the converging contribution of each one of them— including the organs of local power. In other words, the full scope of horizontal accountability will only be completed when the organs of local power are fully established and operational.

The constitutional mandate, embodied in a number of its sections (directly in sections 5, 63, 71, 72; indirectly in sections 2, 69 and 137, see Amaral 2013) entails a vision that goes beyond a mere administrative construction, and conveys the need to establish and develop a social contract between society at large and the institutions of governance. Without this, one might end up building a hollow or phantom state whose governing institutions might be endowed with material resources but lack the necessary social legitimation (Lemay-Hebert 2012).

On the other hand, ever since the First Constitutional Government of Mari Alkatiri produced the first official documents stating the goals of this reform, three goals have emerged in prominent position: to promote the institutions of a strong, legitimate and stable state across the territory; to promote opportunities for local democratic participation by citizens; and to promote more effective, efficient and equitable public service delivery (RDTL 2002). This makes it clear that a close relationship exists between the proposed administrative reform and the consolidation of democracy, both by enlarging the scope of political institutions that are governed by democratic principles and by offering increased opportunities for citizens to participate in the decision-making process, namely in matters pertaining to their local communities. In brief, this reform is supposed to contribute to make democracy both more representative and more participatory.

Decentralisation reform has been on the Timorese political agenda since independence, but so far only the most timid of steps have been taken. Back in 2003, a major study was presented, entitled the *Local Government Options Study* (RDTL 2003), by a team under the auspices of the Ministry for State Administration and Territorial Management. It contains a thorough analysis of

---

7   Constitution of the Democratic Republic of Timor-Leste, section 69.

six alternative paths, which remain to this day the fundamental options on the table for the 'optimal sub-national configuration'. They include the delineation of the levels of the administrative hierarchy from central government down to the community level that will 'facilitate cost effective and efficient service delivery and enhance community initiative and participation' (RDTL 2003).

Two points of clarification should be inserted at this stage. First, decentralisation reforms have been defended on different grounds, namely on the basis of an alleged greater effectiveness of public administration, and on account of the increased political legitimacy that it is supposed to generate. In this brief essay, only the latter sort of reasons will be considered. Second, the concept of decentralisation covers a vast array of practical situations that can be summarised in the following three models:

- Deconcentration—occurring when the central government disperses responsibilities for certain services to its regional branches without involving any transfer of authority to the lower levels.
- Delegation—taking place when the central authority transfers responsibilities for decision-making and the administration of public functions to local governments or semi-autonomous organisations that are not wholly controlled by the transferring authority, but which remain ultimately accountable to it.
- Devolution—referring to those situations in which the central authorities transfer authority to lower level units that normally dispose of clear geographical boundaries over which they exercise authority and within which they perform public functions, and whose members are accountable to their citizens. Devolution is theoretically justified by the principle of 'subsidiarity' developed by the Catholic theologian Oswald van Nell-Breuning and embodied in the papal encyclical *Quadragesimo Anno* (1931), which posits that matters of societal organisation and administration be conceived in a bottom-up manner, and ought to be handled at the lowest possible level of authority that is capable of solving the problem in an efficient manner. In terms of the impact of a decentralisation process upon democratic performance, devolution is by far the most heavily charged of all those variants, thus it is the one we might expect to see emerging in Timor-Leste.

The seminal *Local Government Options Study* presented six fundamental options. Looking at the current situation in the country, inherited directly from the UN administration but with deeper historical thickness dating back to earlier periods, it considered three main layers of governance: districts, subdistricts, and *sukus* (villages). In all six options, the 'perennial *sukus*'—'the only institution that has remained more or less intact during the history of the territory' (RDTL 2003: 76)—were contemplated as an unavoidable territorial unit with profound resonance in the Timorese populations. Only the sixth option, however, would treat the *sukus* as a formal state organ; all others acknowledging their role as forms of local self-organisation that would not bind the state. As for districts and subdistricts, several hypotheses were discussed, with all of them implying that it would be relatively easy to redefine their status and their boundaries. In fact, no substantial anchorage of these units in the autochthonous system of political legitimacy or self-organisation was observed, thus facilitating the rational bureaucratic manipulation required to install a novel administration.

In the course of the years since independence, different solutions have been adopted regarding *sukus* and the other sub-national units. From 2004, elections have been staged for what has been labelled *lideranças comunitárias* (community leadership) (2004–05, 2009). Rules have been designed and revised to frame the electoral process, and a substantial step in the direction of allocating village chiefs and *konsellus suku* community council] has been taken by the 2009 Bill. However, the most salient feature of village politics is that these institutions remain outside the reach of the state, being merely recognised as organs of self-rule destined to accomplish customary functions. In this light, it is not surprising that no allocation of state funds has been made on a regular basis, only grants decided at higher levels being at the disposal of local leaders for small investments.

As for the mid-level institutions, from 2003 Alkatiri's government opted for a model that would transform subdistricts into the main units, under the aegis of a few 'provinces'. The number of municipalities would be reduced from the current 65 subdistricts to between 30 and 35—implying a substantial alteration of the composition of the new units. The Fourth Constitutional Government of Xanana Gusmão revised this option and became inclined to transform the existing 13 districts into the novel municipalities, eliminating the subdistrict level. Curiously, the district level is the one that fewer Timorese regard as a significant unit of identification, and has little more than administrative significance devoid of any articulation with autochthonous systems of legitimacy (that to a certain extent are still visible in the subdistricts, which are the heirs of historical *reinos* (kingdoms) (Leach et al. 2013)). This option was coupled with the idea of holding elections in 2009, later moved to 2010, before being postponed for sometime after the legislative polls of 2012. The program of the Fifth Constitutional Government promised that a pilot experience be developed in three to five municipalities before the end of the legislature in 2017.

Of more importance seems to be the intention to proceed with what has been called the 'pre-deconcentration' program. The formulation of this program is recent, and was thoroughly exposed by Gusmão early in 2014. The main suggestion arising out of this new approach is that the decentralisation reform that has been in the making for so long will be conceived in conservative terms emphasising deconcentration over any other meaning—namely devolution—and that the time frame for its deployment has increased 'up to one hundred years' (Pereira 2014). A critical new figure is the 'district manager', who represents central government at district level, is empowered with substantial competences, is recruited as a public servant in view of his CV, and forfeits any relation to locally held notions of political legitimacy. If this vision becomes the blueprint for the reform, a very modest process of decentralisation will surface. Little or no devolution will be implied in the process, and its impact on democratic performance cannot be expected to be high. In the meantime, as a district administrator put it in an interview with Tanja Hohe (2004), 'the national government has a roof, but no roots'. The next few chapters in the politics of Timor-Leste will revolve around these issues.

Conclusion

Challenges to democratic consolidation and the improvement of its performance in Timor-Leste come from many different sources, including the ongoing process of state-building (decentralisation), which requires commitment of the ruling elite to a major reform, and the need to adopt an adequate choice of policies in a context where democratic norms suffer the competition of alternative narratives that may subvert the main tenets of the constitutional ethos. Stability, which has marked Timor-Leste's development in recent years, cannot, therefore, be totally equated with the consolidation of democracy. The performance of the regime also needs to improve in order to secure a firm rooting of democratic governance in the political landscape at all levels. Particular attention should be devoted to the plasticity of democratic institutions, and their capacity to adapt to the emerging social forces in the country. If democracy is equated with empowering citizens to take the fundamental decisions regarding the development of their communities and to possess the ultimate control over those who momentarily hold power, it must combine in balanced proportions to the adherence to international standards and recognised procedures with greater responsiveness to local values and forms of political legitimation.

References

Amaral, S. 2013. *Decentralization Policy Issues and Challenges in Timor-Leste: A Grassroots Perspective*. Paper presented at the Timor-Leste Update, The Australian National University, Canberra, 28–29 November 2013.

Elgie, R. and S. Moestrup 2011. *Semi-Presidentialism Outside Europe*. Abingdon: Routledge.

Hohe, T. 2004. Clash of Paradigms in East Timor. *Contemporary Southeast Asia* 4(3):569–89.

Kingsbury, D. 2009. *East Timor: The Price of Liberty*. Basingstoke: Palgrave Macmillan.

Kingsbury, D. 2014. Democratic Consolidation in Timor-Leste: Achievements, Problems and Prospects. *Asian Journal of Political Science* 22(2):569–89.

La'o Hamutuk 2010. Submission to Committee C of RDTL National Parliament Regarding the Proposed General State Budget for 2010. www.laohamutuk.org/econ/OGE10/sub09LHSubOJE10En.htm.

La'o Hamutuk 2013. The National Impact of Benefits for Former Combatants. www.laohamutuk.org/.../VetPension6Mar2013en.pps.

Leach, M. and D. Kingsbury (eds) 2012. *The Politics of Timor-Leste*. Ithaca: Cornell Southeast Asia Programme.

Lemay-Hébert, N. 2012. Coerced Transitions in Timor-Leste and Kosovo: Managing Competing Objectives of Institutional Building and Local Empowerment. *Democratization* 19(3):465–85.

Molnar, A.K. 2011. *Timor-Leste: Politics, History and Culture*. Abingdon: Routledge.

Pereira, A. 2014. *A Politica Para a Preparação da Estrutura Administrativa de Pre-descentralização: O Inicio do 'Segundo Milagre Maubere'*? [A Policy for the Preparation of the Administrative Structure for Pre-Decentralisation: The Start of the 'Second Maubere Miracle'?]. *Tempo Semanal* 13/4/2014. www.temposemanal.com/opiniaun/item/561.

RDTL (*República Democrática de Timor-Leste*; Democratic Republic of Timor-Leste) 2002. *Project Document: Decentralization and Local Governance Options in Timor-Leste*. www.portphilip.vic.gov.au/default/GovernanceDocument/Decentralization_and_local_governance_options_in_Timor-Leste.

RDTL 2003. *Local Government Options Study: Final Report*. www.estatal.gov.tl/Documents/DNDLOT/Option%20Study%202006/LGOS%20Report.pdf.

Weber, M. 1947. *Theory of Social and Economic Organization*. New York: Free Press.

PART TWO
Trends in Economic Development

CHAPTER 6

Can the Petroleum Fund Exorcise the Resource Curse from Timor-Leste?[1]

Charles Scheiner

Introduction

Oil and gas comprised 76.4 per cent of Timor-Leste's gross domestic product (GDP) in 2013 (RDTL GDS 2015) and provided more than 93 per cent of state revenues in 2014.[2] Most of the money from selling off non-renewable petroleum wealth has been saved in the Petroleum Fund—a sovereign wealth fund containing US$17 billion. People expect the Fund to finance state activities after the oil and gas fields are exhausted, which could happen within five years, but the Fund may be empty by 2025. Timor-Leste has about a decade to use its finite oil resources to underpin long-term prosperity and development.

This chapter gives an overview of the consequences of Timor-Leste's reliance on its limited oil and gas reserves, focusing on its impacts on economics and decision-making. It explores how effectively Timor-Leste's Petroleum Fund, established in 2005 with extensive guidance from international agencies, can prevent or ameliorate some of the most serious consequences of the resource curse—the negative impacts of non-renewable resource wealth on citizens of most countries that depend on exporting petroleum and mineral wealth.

---

1   An abridged version of this chapter was published as *SSGM In Brief* 2014/29.
2   During 2014, Timor-Leste received US$1.817 billion from oil and gas revenues and US$502 million from investing the Petroleum Fund, including unrealised stock price changes (CBTL 2015). Non-oil state income totalled US$184 million, of which a significant portion was paid by the state to itself (RDTL MoF 2014; 2015a). Oil revenues dropped 49 per cent from 2012 to 2014, and therefore comprise a smaller percentage of the shrinking total of state revenues (*La'o Hamutuk* 2015c).

I draw on research and analysis by the Timor-Leste Institute for Development Monitoring and Analysis, also known as *La'o Hamutuk*. *La'o Hamutuk* is an independent Timorese civil society organisation founded in 2000 to support the country's political and economic sovereignty, from the perspective of social and economic justice. It analyses reports and proposals from government, international agencies and other sources, compares them with observations and other data, and uses its findings to enhance public and leaders' understanding of the context and likely consequences of policy options. In addition to using published documents, *La'o Hamutuk* consults with officials, experts, practitioners and researchers. It also advocates for policies and programs that will equitably benefit Timor-Leste citizens both now and in the future.

Published statistics and international comparisons involving Timor-Leste are often inaccurate or inconsistent, frequently confusing total GDP with non-oil GDP, even though it is four times larger *(La'o Hamutuk* 2014b; cf. RDTL GDS 2013, 2014a and 2015d). This makes it challenging to understand whether contradictions and retroactive revisions come from improved data or methodology, political motivation, or agencies' reluctance to differ with the government.[3]

Oil swamps the economy

Timor-Leste relies on its petroleum exports more than every nation except South Sudan, Libya, and, perhaps, Equatorial Guinea. However, this dependency is not due to vast oil and gas reserves or high production rates, but because the non-petroleum economy, which scarcely existed when independence was restored in 2002, is still very small.

Although 23.6 per cent of Timor-Leste's US$5.6 billion GDP has been categorised as 'non-oil', about half of this is generated by state spending for public administration, procurement, and infrastructure construction. Since oil money provides the lion's share of state revenues, this will evaporate when the wells dry up. The private sector and consumer-driven portions of the economy—agriculture, manufacturing, and local commerce for businesses and individuals—average less than US$2 per citizen per day, although most citizens make do with far less than the average.

---

3   For example, in December 2013 the IMF estimated that Timor-Leste's total GDP increased by 5.7 per cent between 2011 and 2012 (IMF 2013). Eight months later, however, Timor-Leste Government statistics stated that it had *declined* by 10.4 per cent (RDTL GDS 2014a), and in June 2015, the Government reported that the 2012 GDP increased by 5.5 per cent over 2011 (RDTL GDS 2015d). During 2014, UNDP and the World Bank also published misleading or incorrect data on Timor-Leste (UNDP 2014, 2014a), and the government prevented the IMF from publishing its annual Article IV report on the country because of disagreement over the report's content.

6. Can the Petroleum Fund Exorcise the Resource Curse from Timor-Leste?

Table 6.1 Gross Domestic Product in 2013.[4]

	(million USD)	
Total GDP	$5,596	
GDP from Petroleum Sector	$4,276	76 per cent
Non-oil GDP	$1,319	24 per cent
Of which: Productive GDP (agriculture and manufacturing)	$265	5 per cent

Source: RDTL GDS 2015d.

Government officials have been proud that the non-oil GDP is growing at 'double-digit rates' (RDTL Prime Minister 1/4/2014: 3; *La'o Hamutuk* 2014b; Global Insight 2014: 6), but virtually all of this growth represented rising state spending. When state spending slowed in 2013, non-oil GDP growth virtually stopped. The productive parts of the economy—agriculture and manufacturing—are only 4.7 per cent of total GDP. After adjusting for global inflation and population, these sectors shrank by 13 per cent from 2007 to 2013 (RDTL GDS 2015d). By comparison, public administration and construction (largely paid for with public money) increased 90 per cent and 347 per cent during the same six years (RDTL GDS 2015d).

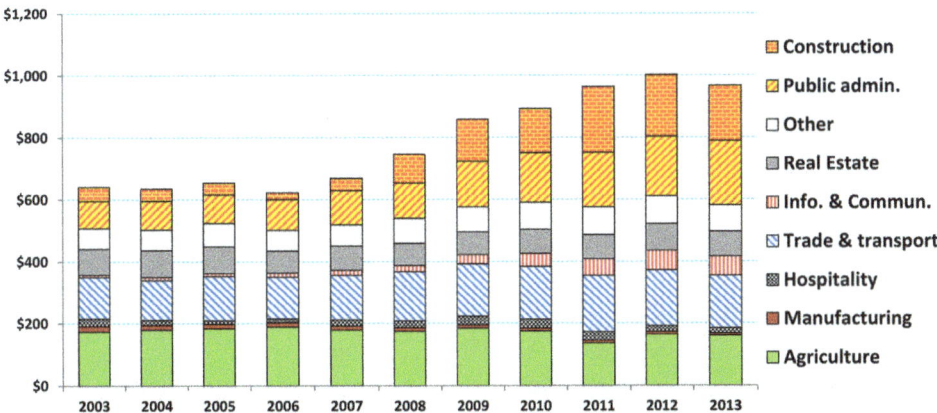

Figure 6.1 Sectoral contributions to Timor-Leste's 'non-oil' GDP per capita in 2013.
Source: RDTL GDS 2015d.

---

4   Total GDP per capita declined 16.7 per cent in 2013 (RDTL GDS 2015d) because oil production and revenues began to drop. As non-oil GDP was essentially unchanged in 2013, the percentage of total GDP from petroleum is declining.

Nevertheless, state agencies and the small middle and upper classes have money to spend, and the absence of convenient local products leads them to purchase goods and services from overseas, as shown in Table 6.2.

Table 6.2 Balance of external trade, 2013.

	(million USD)	
Goods (excluding petroleum sector)	–$497	
Imports	$519	96 per cent
Exports	$22	4 per cent
Services	–$1,458	
Imports	$1,536	95 per cent
Exports	$78	5 per cent
Total trade deficit	$1,955	

Source: RDTL GDS 2015d.

Unfortunately, trade is less diverse and more import-heavy than the numbers show. Most of the exported non-oil goods are coffee, whose value fluctuates with the weather and the global market. More than half of exported services are 'travel'—tickets on foreign airlines sold in Timor-Leste.

Prioritising short-term purchases over sustainable national development results in extreme import dependency. About half of state spending immediately goes abroad, and individuals make little effort to spend in the local economy. Chickens are imported from Brazil, rice from Vietnam, eggs and beer from Singapore, fruit juice from Cyprus, onions from Holland, garlic from China, milk from Australia, and so on. In 2014, more than US$116 million went to Indonesian suppliers for a variety of goods including water, candles, cigarettes, instant noodles, sugary drinks, and canned fish. Although a few agencies advocate 'local content', almost nobody weighs economic sovereignty when deciding what to buy. Current and pending free-trade policies make it even harder to cultivate local production. As oil and gas revenues tail off, there will be little cash to pay to foreign suppliers, and imports will become unaffordable. Without local food production, people will starve.

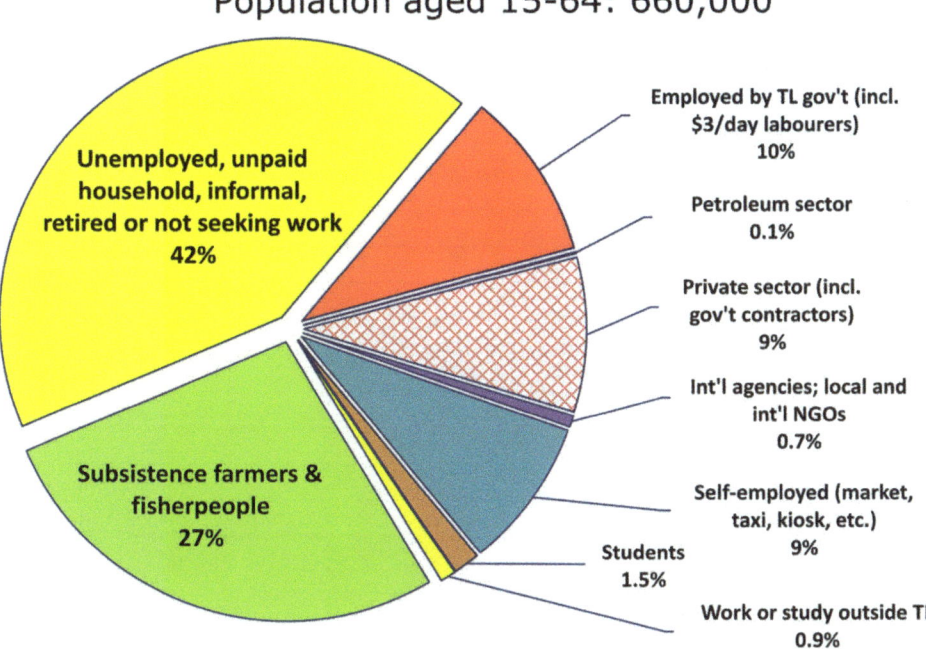

Figure 6.2 What do Timorese people do for work?
Sources: RDTL MF 2015a; RDTL GDS 2013b; 2015b; 2015c; *La'o Hamutuk* research and estimates.

Counting people rather than dollars tells a different story. Timor-Leste is an agricultural country, and most households live mainly by subsistence farming.

The formal economy, both public and private, employs less than a third of the working-age population. Only 9 per cent of the working-age population works for companies, and less than one-fiftieth of those jobs are in the petroleum industry. As the International Monetary Fund (IMF) explains, 'The oil and gas sector is the mainstay of the economy … However … the sector directly accounts for virtually no on-shore employment. Its economic impact is entirely via government spending' (IMF 2013).[5] During 2013, total private sector employment declined because of reduced government spending on infrastructure, although the number of working-age people increased by about 18,000 (RDTL GDS 2015b; 2015c).

---

5   In February 2015, the *Business Activities Survey of 2013* (GDS 2015b) reported that the number of private sector jobs had dropped 4.1 per cent since the previous year, which was confirmed by the Labour Force Survey (GDS 2015c). Female workers disproportionately lost their jobs.

Oil fuels the state machinery

As Table 6.3 shows, more than 90 per cent of Timor-Leste's government revenues are from oil.

Table 6.3: Sources of income in the 2015 General State Budget.

	(million USD)	
Projected revenues (including those deposited into the Petroleum Fund)	$2,461	
Revenue from oil and gas exports[a]	$1,374	56 per cent
Return on Petroleum Fund investments	$916	37 per cent
Non-petroleum (domestic) revenue sources	$170	7 per cent
Budgeted sources for financing state expenditures	$1,570	
Withdrawn from the Petroleum Fund during 2015	$1,327	85 per cent
New loans (to be repaid mostly with petroleum money, if it still exists)	$70	4 per cent
Non-petroleum (domestic) revenues	$170	11 per cent

[a.] This projection is too high. World prices for Brent crude oil fell by more than 50 per cent between mid-2014 (when the 2015 Budget was prepared) and the beginning of 2015. *La'o Hamutuk* (2015, 2015b) suggested that this should be incorporated in the revision of the 2015 Budget but the Ministry decided not to. Nevertheless, the 2016 budget will incorporate these developments (RDTL MoF 2015b).
Source: RDTL MoF 2015.

About US$25 million of the US$170 million in 'domestic revenues' will come from taxes paid by the state to itself (such as import taxes paid by companies working on state-financed projects). Another US$19 million will be the gross receipts of the highly subsidised public electricity system, which recovers only 20 per cent of its operational costs from users and uses oil income to cover its operating deficit and capital outlays.

Policies neglect other domestic revenues: a 2008 'tax reform' slashed import, wage, and business taxes in hopes that this would encourage foreign investment and reduce prices to consumers. As a result, Timor-Leste has the third-lowest total tax rate in the world—one-quarter of the global average (World Bank/PWC 2014).

The sovereign wealth fund saves petroleum revenues

Almost all of Timor-Leste's oil and gas income is deposited into the Petroleum Fund, which serves as a buffer between this income and annual expenditure. This allows the state Budget to respond to public needs, rather than oil price and production fluctuations. Forty per cent of the Fund is invested in the global stock market, with the balance in bonds, mostly from the US Government. Returns from these investments are redeposited into the Petroleum Fund.

When the Fund was being created in 2004–05, designers intended that these earnings would replace oil revenues after the fields run dry (CBTL 2015; *La'o Hamutuk* 2013).

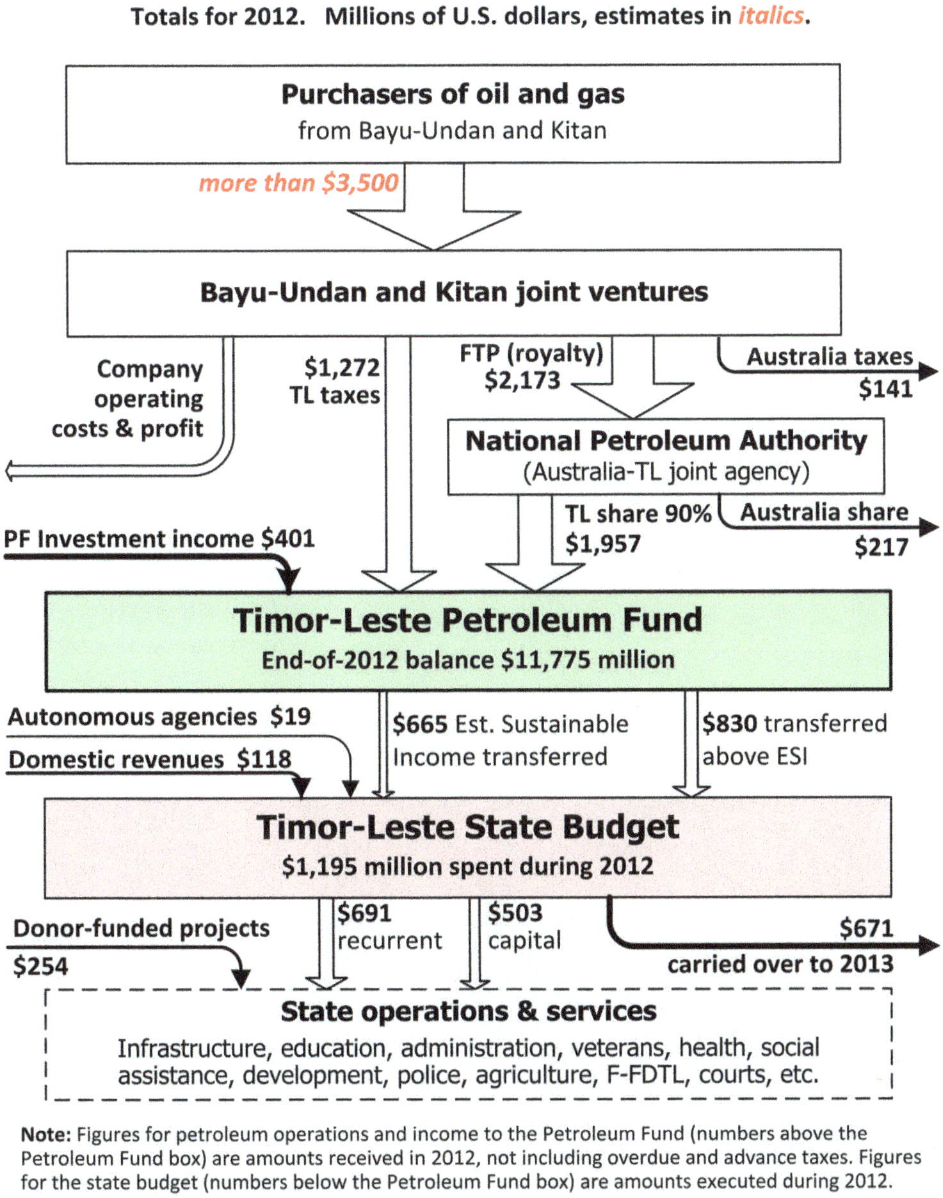

Totals for 2012. Millions of U.S. dollars, estimates in *italics*.

```
┌─────────────────────────────────────────────┐
│         Purchasers of oil and gas           │
│          from Bayu-Undan and Kitan          │
└─────────────────────────────────────────────┘
              more than $3,500
                     ↓
┌─────────────────────────────────────────────┐
│       Bayu-Undan and Kitan joint ventures   │
└─────────────────────────────────────────────┘
   Company      $1,272       FTP (royalty)    Australia taxes
  operating    TL taxes        $2,173            $141
 costs & profit
                          ┌──────────────────────────┐
                          │ National Petroleum Authority │
                          │   (Australia-TL joint agency)│
                          └──────────────────────────┘
                             TL share 90%  Australia share
  PF Investment income $401    $1,957         $217

┌─────────────────────────────────────────────┐
│        Timor-Leste Petroleum Fund           │
│      End-of-2012 balance $11,775 million    │
└─────────────────────────────────────────────┘
 Autonomous agencies $19   $665 Est. Sustainable   $830 transferred
 Domestic revenues  $118   Income transferred      above ESI

┌─────────────────────────────────────────────┐
│        Timor-Leste State Budget             │
│       $1,195 million spent during 2012      │
└─────────────────────────────────────────────┘
 Donor-funded projects  $691       $503                $671
      $254             recurrent   capital    carried over to 2013

┌─────────────────────────────────────────────┐
│          State operations & services         │
│ Infrastructure, education, administration, veterans, health, social │
│   assistance, development, police, agriculture, F-FDTL, courts, etc.│
└─────────────────────────────────────────────┘
```

Note: Figures for petroleum operations and income to the Petroleum Fund (numbers above the Petroleum Fund box) are amounts received in 2012, not including overdue and advance taxes. Figures for the state budget (numbers below the Petroleum Fund box) are amounts executed during 2012.

Figure 6.3 Timor-Leste's petroleum revenue streams.
Sources: CBTL 2015; RDTL MoF 2013; 2014; Santos 2014; ANP 2015.

A New Era? Timor-Leste After the UN

Every year, the Ministry of Finance calculates an estimated sustainable income (ESI) benchmark, equal to 3 per cent of the current Petroleum Fund balance added to the net present value of expected future revenues from oil and gas fields with approved development plans.[6] The ESI informs the decision of how much to withdraw from the Petroleum Fund each year to finance the state Budget, although it was exceeded every year from 2008 to 2012, and again from 2014 onwards (RDTL MoF 2014b).

The ESI does not reflect population growth. It was designed to spend more per person now than later, investing in Timor-Leste's future and being supplemented by other revenues over time. If future oil revenues and investment returns follow ESI's prudent projections, the ESI would be the same amount every year, regardless of population, local inflation (which has exceeded global rates), improved state services, or growing expectations. Unfortunately, overspending ESI has lowered the balance in the Petroleum Fund, reducing its future investment earnings. In fact, the Fund's goal of using return from investments to finance state activities for decades after the oil and gas are gone is unlikely to be achieved, due to transfers above ESI, rapid budget escalation, revision of the Petroleum Fund Law, less prudent price projections, and lower oil production and income.

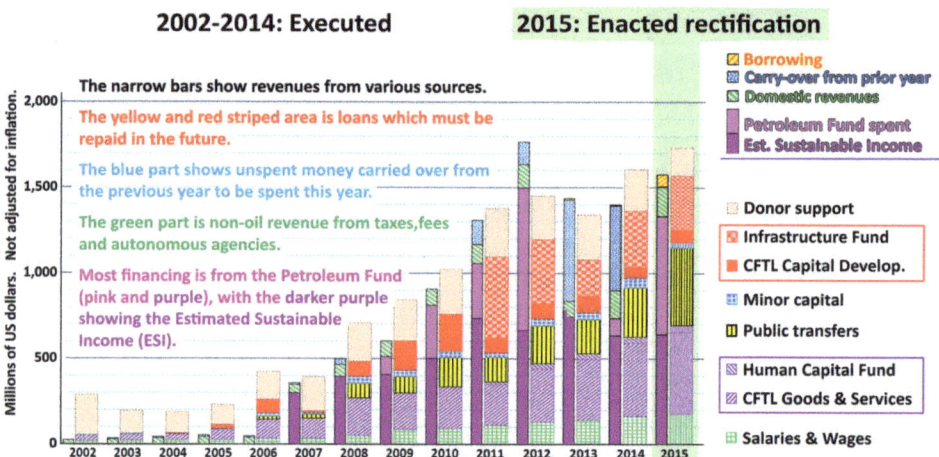

Figure 6.4 State revenues and expenditures.
Sources: RDTL MoF 2013b; 2014a; 2015a; and state budget books for prior years.

Figure 6.4 shows how much money Timor-Leste's state Budget has received and spent since the restoration of independence in 2002. The narrow bars show actual revenues through 2014 and budgeted revenues during 2015. The lowest

---

6   At present, these are the Bayu-Undan and Kitan fields in the Joint Petroleum Development Area, from which Australia takes 10 per cent of the revenue. The Greater Sunrise project has no approved development plan, so it is not part of the ESI.

two segments (solid pink and purple) represent withdrawals from the Petroleum Fund, while the upper segment (stippled blue) is the balance carried over from excess withdrawals from the Fund in prior years. However, the blue (carryover) and yellow/red (borrowing, which started in 2014) segments also mainly come from the Fund in the past and the future.

Large oil revenues began in 2006; they have been declining since 2012. They pay for virtually all state expenditures, which grew more than 25 per cent per year from 2008 to 2012—faster than every nation except Zimbabwe.

The principal source of income is the Bayu-Undan oil and gas field, operated by US oil giant ConocoPhillips. In 2013, the company downgraded its estimate of future revenues to Timor-Leste by 49 per cent, with production to end four years earlier than previously estimated (RDTL MoF 2014a). The Government responded by withdrawing less than the parliamentary limit (which had been set at ESI) from the Petroleum Fund for the first time ever, and financed its operations with the cash balance transferred from the Fund in prior years.[7] During 2014, oil revenues to Timor-Leste dropped 42 per cent, primarily because production fell 24 per cent as the fields near the end of their profitable lives.

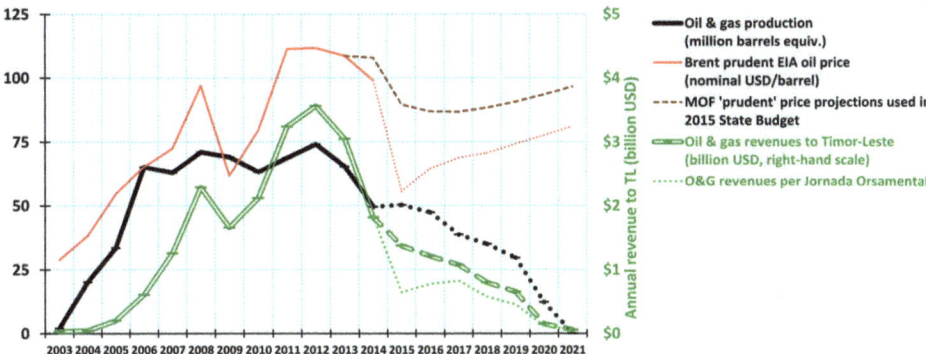

Figure 6.5 Oil and gas income peaked in 2012 and continues to fall.
Sources: US EIA 2015; RDTL MoF 2015; 2015a; 2015b; ANP 2015; La'o Hamutuk 2015c.

Figure 6.5 shows how oil and gas revenues to Timor-Leste (double green line) reflect global prices (red thin line) and local production (thick black line). After 2014, the graph shows price projections used by the Ministry of Finance for the 2015 budget (dashed brown line), and more recent US government

---

7   The 2013 budget authorised US$787 million to be withdrawn from the Petroleum Fund, equal to the Estimated Sustainable Income, but the Timor-Leste Government withdrew only US$730 million because much more had been withdrawn during 2012 than the government could spend (*La'o Hamutuk* 2013a). Nevertheless, 2013 ended with US$634 million in the Treasury account—more than triple the cushion the government says it needs. During 2014, the Treasury again paid for increased spending. However, the balance had been drawn down to US$181 million by year end, leaving little to be rolled over into 2015.

projections (dotted red line). As a result of the price drop, future revenues may be less than the dotted green line, as it does not incorporate likely decreases in production.

The 2014 budget allowed withdrawal of up to US$903 million from the Petroleum Fund—well above the US$632 million ESI, which *La'o Hamutuk* and parliament's Committee on Public Finances had agreed was unnecessary (*La'o Hamutuk* 2013b; RDTL National Parliament 2013). By the end of the year, US$732 million had been withdrawn—US$100 million more than ESI. The 2015 budget limits Petroleum Fund withdrawals to US$1.327 billion, and it is likely to be used because the carried-over balance that had supplemented lower transfers during 2013–14 no longer exists. The government transferred US$140 million from the Petroleum Fund in January and February 2015—the first time a transfer has ever been done during the first two months of a fiscal year.

Spending grows quickly, but not always wisely

State expenditures are shown as the wider bars in Figure 6.4, with the tan upper segment representing donor contributions, which are not included in the state Budget. The next two (red) segments represent physical infrastructure. Infrastructure construction absorbed half of state expenditures while the electricity system was being built in 2011, and it still absorbs more than a third of the Budget. Although spending on large projects has slowed due to delays, it will resurge if projects on the drawing board—including Dili airport, Tibar Port, the Oecusse Special Economic Zone, and the Tasi Mane petroleum infrastructure project —are built.

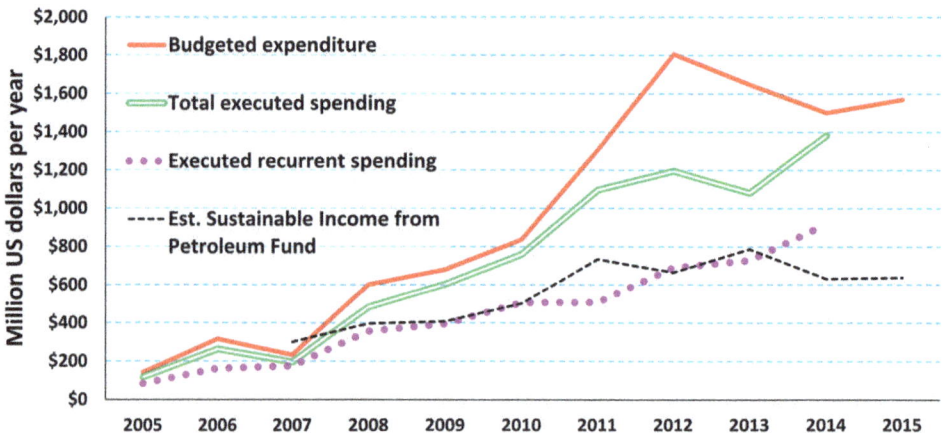

Figure 6.6 Budgeted, executed and recurrent spending year by year.
Sources: RDTL MoF 2014; 2015a.

Spending on recurrent costs (salaries, goods, services, public grants) continues to increase about 20 per cent per year, even though total appropriations went down after 2012.

Timor-Leste continues to under-invest in health and education, spending merely 14 per cent of its budget on these human resources, compared with more than 30 per cent in well-managed developing countries (UNDP 2011). Most children born during the post-1999 'baby boom' are not getting adequate nutrition or education, which will have severe, long-term consequences for the nation's future.

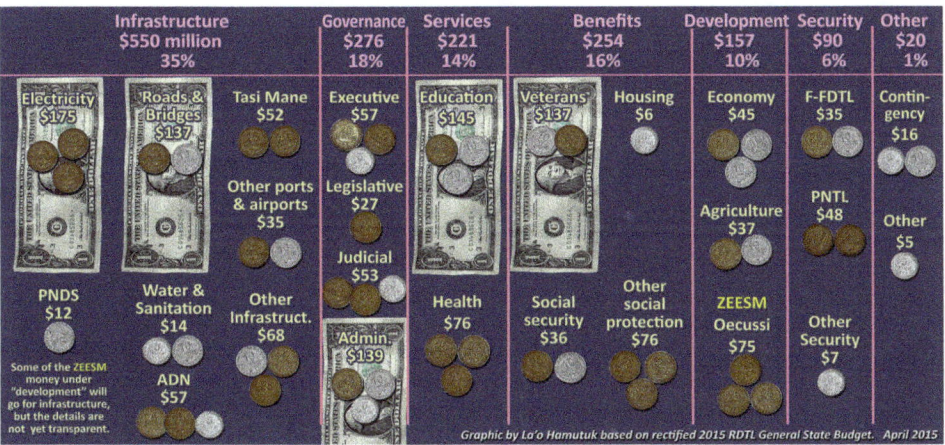

Figure 6.7 Allocation of the revised 2015 State Budget (US$1.570 billion).
Source: RDTL MoF 2015a.

Agriculture, which sustains most Timorese households, receives only 2 per cent of 2015 state spending (*La'o Hamutuk* 2014).

The resource curse has many faces

Timor-Leste's economy and politics are typical of the resource curse (Neves 2013)—a set of conditions, choices and consequences that almost always makes citizens of extractive export-dependent countries worse off than people in countries with little oil or mineral wealth. In general, the resource curse results from easy access to non-renewable wealth, which is seen as a windfall that can be freely spent on short-term desires rather than strategic longer term development. Since there are few taxpayers demanding that their money be used wisely, corruption, conflict and opacity often occur, although Timor-Leste has taken some steps to avert them. At the end of the day, when all the mineral wealth has been converted to cash and spent, the opportunity to develop a sustainable, self-sufficient economy may also have been squandered.

Available wealth attracts shady characters

A cash-rich government with limited experience and safeguards is a tempting target for scammers, tax-evaders, thieves and opportunists from all over the world, as shown by these examples (*La'o Hamutuk* 2012b).

In 2009, Malaysian Datuk Edward Ong promised to build the Pelican Paradise luxury resort just west of Dili. Ong then asked the Minister of Finance to deposit US$1.2 billion from Timor-Leste's Petroleum Fund in a blocked bank account controlled by Asian Champ Investment, Ltd, promising to pay 7.5 per cent interest and to return the money in one year. His proposal was taken seriously, and the Minister travelled to London with the President of Timor-Leste's Petroleum Fund Investment Advisory Board (PFIAB) for further discussions. In the end, prudence prevailed, and Timor-Leste declined to give the apparently fictional company $1 billion. The PFIAB noted that 'worldwide there have been a number of reported cases where institutional investors have fallen prey to fraudulent schemes under arrangements involving apparently secure deposits in "blocked accounts" at reputable banks, higher than market interest rates, a rapid decision-making process, and little if any documentation concerning the parties making the offer' (RDTL PFIAB 2009; *La'o Hamutuk* 2010). Although Ong and Pelican Paradise were invisible after the attempted scam was exposed, they resurfaced in 2015.

On 19 June 2014, US Federal agents arrested Nigerian-born US lawyer Bobby Boye, who worked in Timor-Leste from 2010–13, advising the Ministry of Finance on petroleum tax collection (*La'o Hamutuk* 2014f). US prosecutors charged Boye with wire fraud, alleging that he created a fake company, Opus & Best, and used his influence to have the Timor-Leste government pay O&B US$3.5 million. In April 2015, Boye pled guilty and could be sentenced to four to 20 years in prison. However, many suspect that others were involved in his crimes, either through conspiracy or negligence. It is clear that both the Norwegian aid program, which initially hired him, and the Ministry of Finance, which extended his employment and awarded contracts to O&B, failed to exercise due diligence (*La'o Hamutuk* 2014e), as Boye has a long record of criminal and financial malfeasance (Aftenposten 2014; *La'o Hamutuk* 2014j).

Timor-Leste's state-owned petroleum company, TimorGAP, has spent tens of millions of dollars and signed contracts for billions during its three years of operation, but it has not generated any income. In August 2014, *La'o Hamutuk* suggested that the Court of Appeals audit their finances, as Parliament and the public know very little about the obligations they have incurred on behalf of the state (*La'o Hamutuk* 2014h).

The resource curse is not magic or metaphysical. It occurs in almost every impoverished nation whose economy is dominated by exporting non-renewable resources, including Nigeria, Ecuador, the USSR, Libya, Gabon, Iraq, Congo, Equatorial Guinea, Papua New Guinea, and Nauru. Oil and gas exporters are the most vulnerable, due to the volatility of the international market, avarice of the petroleum industry, and the industrialised world's addiction to petroleum. With most wealth deriving from extractives and state spending, rent-seeking—working to get a piece of this money, rather than to produce something—becomes dominant. Although one form of this is corruption, most resource curse–driven behaviour is legal and accepted, albeit more fundamental and widespread.

Timor-Leste protected itself against one consequence of the resource curse by using an international currency—the US dollar safeguards against runaway inflation and 'Dutch disease'.[8] However, inflation in Timor-Leste has been higher than in its trading partners, due to the lack of local productive capacity and the supply of money exceeding the supply of imports.

Furthermore, the international oil market is priced in US dollars, so when a rising dollar makes oil and commodity prices fall, state revenues also drop. During 2014, the US dollar rose and oil prices fell, lowering inflation but sharply reducing state revenues and the value of Petroleum Fund investments in other currencies (*La'o Hamutuk* 2015, 2015b).

Some structural elements of the resource curse are nearly impossible to control, such as the ruthlessness and amorality of huge international oil companies, global and local environmental damage, invasions and civil wars, and the capital-intensive, high-skill nature of the petroleum industry. Others, however, can be overcome, although it is rare to find political leaders in any country with the far-sightedness, wisdom and courage to make the best decisions for their people's future.

Timor-Leste's history and geography make the resource curse more severe than it would be from petroleum dependency alone, including these factors:

- **Extreme poverty and underdevelopment:** Portugal did little to develop economic production or human resources, while Indonesia destroyed infrastructure and discouraged individual initiative or self-reliance. Only a small fraction of Timor-Leste's 1.2 million people have had access to good education, entrepreneurial skills or managerial experience.

---

8   'Dutch disease' results when mineral rents cause a large inflow of foreign currency, distorting foreign exchange rates and making exports less competitive. By not printing its own money, Timor-Leste has reduced this damaging impact.

- **Emergence from foreign rule:** Until 2002, leaders and citizens never lived under democratic self-government by rule of law. Administrative and legal structures must be built from scratch, overcoming the bad habits civil servants learned while working in and/or resisting inefficient, illegal and corrupt Indonesian and Portuguese administrations. Citizens and leaders alike are learning how to effectively participate in a peaceful, transparent, accountable, stable, democratic society, where government with citizen consent and participation serves the public interest (*La'o Hamutuk* 2015a).

- **Recovery from prolonged war:** Many people are traumatised. Repeated unpredictable, uncontrollable interruptions to people's lives has taught them not to plan for or invest in the future. Leaders who excelled at struggling against foreign occupation lack the skills for peacetime democratic, consultative governance. Around the world, struggles over oil and minerals often lead to war and conflict, but Timor-Leste hopes that that phase of its history is over.

- **Self-interested neighbours:** Although both Australia and Indonesia claim to support the new nation, their thirst for oil and insistence on impunity belie their good will. Australia continues to occupy about 40 per cent of the oil and gas reserves that should belong to Timor-Leste under current international law (*La'o Hamutuk* 2014a).

This toxic combination makes it almost impossible to develop a sustainable, equitable economy. PowerPoint presentations substitute for plans; the *Strategic Development Plan 2011–2030* (RDTL 2011) is an enticing, impossible dream. In search of showy, quick solutions, planning neglects the unglamorous but essential tasks of alleviating poverty, replacing imports, and working toward food sovereignty.

The cash-flush government has hardly any taxpayer-voters demanding financial accountability. The elite and some constituencies believe that they are entitled to a disproportionate share of public resources—a pattern set by rewarding heroes of the liberation struggle and 'buying peace' to neutralise potentially troublesome groups or political opponents. Instead of the give-and-take that constrains state spending in 'normal' countries, the whims of politicians and promises of salesmen are using up Timor-Leste's finite oil wealth. The appointment of Dr Rui Maria Araujo as Prime Minister in February 2015 has prompted optimism that these patterns may change, but former Prime Minister Xanana Gusmão continues in a major role, with responsibility for planning, investment, infrastructure, procurement and other key sectors.

Multi-billion dollar, multi-year infrastructure projects such as the Tasi Mane south coast petroleum infrastructure project and the Special Economic and Social Market Zone in Oecusse are initiated without realistic estimates of their total cost, competitive advantage or economic viability (*La'o Hamutuk* 2013d, 2014g, 2015b, 2015e). Adding to the risk, loans from foreign institutions (sometimes disguised as Public–Private Partnerships) incur hundreds of millions of dollars in debt, which will have to be repaid after the oil and gas are gone (*La'o Hamutuk* 2013c, 2014d).

When a decision-maker has access to money, it seems like the solution to every problem. It's easier to buy a scholarship than to build a quality university—the budget for overseas scholarships is far higher than the appropriation for the National University of Timor-Leste, which educates four times as many students as will receive the scholarships (RDTL MoF 2014a, 2015). Similarly, the state pays for a few well-connected people to fly to overseas hospitals, but most citizens cannot access decent health care. Roads and bridges in the capital used by VIP visitors are repaved frequently, with street vendors and neighbourhood markets moved out of sight, while rural communities struggle with impassable tracks and rivers. Airport and highway construction could consume a billion dollars, yet very few Timorese people will ever fly or own a car. Hundreds of millions more may pay to construct a container port that can handle an eight-fold increase in imports, but without oil money, how will Timor-Leste pay for the imports or guarantee the investor's expected return?

More ominous, petroleum dominates planning, diverting attention from sustainable, equitable, realisable development paths. Because oil is where the action is today, the most persuasive, creative and ambitious people choose to work in petroleum regulatory agencies, oil corporations and TimorGAP (the state-owned oil company). They persuade budgeters to award millions of dollars for concept studies, preliminary designs and promotional presentations. When the resulting proposals are compared with those for agriculture, tourism, or import-substituting manufacturing, the playing field is tilted.

Similarly, the best and brightest university students major in petroleum engineering, similar to the rent-seeking that led many in the West to become stockbrokers and lawyers during the bubble before the 2007 financial crisis (Stiglitz 2014: ch. 2), but few jobs exist for inexperienced graduates in the capital-intensive petroleum industry (*Rigzone* 2015). As a result, less glamorous but more necessary fields like civil engineering, education, business development, management, water supply, sanitation, nutrition, and health care are deprived of both financial and human resources (Neves 2014).

This petro-state doesn't have much petrol

If Timor-Leste's oil reserves were as large as Brunei's or Saudi Arabia's, these problems could be drowned in dollars. Unfortunately, geology has not been that generous to this new nation. Even if the Greater Sunrise field is developed with an LNG plant in Timor-Leste and Australia takes only half of the upstream revenues, total expected oil and gas revenues are not even enough to support one (current) dollar per person per day of public spending over the next four decades. This would be less than one-third of the 2015 state budget, which pays for a level of services that nobody would consider adequate over the long term. If the balance in the Petroleum Fund goes up and the stock market booms, additional revenue from investments could help a little, but recent patterns make this improbable (Scheiner 2014; *La'o Hamutuk* 2015d).

Oil revenues peaked in 2012, and Timor-Leste has already received more than three-fourths of the expected income from its only two producing oil and gas fields. Kitan production will end in 2016 and Bayu-Undan by 2020 (RDTL MoF 2015; *La'o Hamutuk* 2014c, 2015c). By comparison, Australia is richer in petroleum than Timor-Leste, with larger future potential. Indonesian reserves are smaller for its population, but they are being pumped more slowly than Timor-Leste's.

Table 6.4 Oil and gas reserves in nearby countries.

	Timor-Leste		Australia		Indonesia	Brunei
	50 per cent Sunrise	no Sunrise	50 per cent Sunrise	no Sunrise		
Known oil and gas reserves per person	605 barrels	170 barrels	1,170 barrels	1,150 barrels	83 barrels	6,440 barrels
Likelihood of additional discoveries	Low (small area, explored for decades)		High (further offshore)		Moderate (large area)	Moderate (deeper water)
How long reserves will last at 2014 production rates	16 years	4.3 years	51 years	50 years	27 years	23 years

Sources: *La'o Hamutuk* estimates and ANP 2014 for Timor-Leste; BP 2015 for other countries.

Timor-Leste's petroleum officials have faith that Timor-Leste has large undiscovered oil and gas deposits, and that the companies' projections are too pessimistic (*Timor Post* 2014).[9] During the discussion of a preliminary version of this chapter in November 2013, Autoridade Nacional do Petróleo's (ANP) (National Petroleum Authority) President Gualdino da Silva said:

---

9   In 2007, Timor-Leste tried to continue oil production from the Elang-Kakatua field after ConocoPhillips decided it was no longer worth operating. They were unable to attract another company.

> [Timor-Leste] is a proven petroliferous zone. It is also a new frontier; we need more production, we need more discoveries. How could one believe in a conclusion based only on the two production fields? The country is still in an early stage, in its infancy, of researching and discovering more oil and gas. It is too early to reach that conclusion (ANU 2013).

After oil prices crashed in 2014, ANP's director of exploration continued to promote a new bidding round:

> We have 85 percent open acreage offshore in [Timor-Leste's undisputed area] and we still [have] more than 65 percent open acreage in the Joint Petroleum Development Area. We haven't any onshore blocks [that have been offered for exploration] ... This is [a] very new frontier (*Rigzone* 2015).

The director's comment ignores industry-wide retrenchment and the fact that oil companies already explored or declined all open offshore acreage during more profitable times.

Although anything is possible, the country's small and constrained land and sea area, geological structures, and 120-year history of oil exploration make significant additional reserves unlikely. The first Sunrise test well was drilled in 1974, Kitan is the only commercial field discovered since the flurry of exploration after the 1991 Timor Gap Treaty, and more than a dozen test wells have been drilled since the Indonesian occupation ended in 1999, with Kitan the only commercially viable discovery. During Timor-Leste's most recent offshore licensing rounds in 2006, no company that had previously explored the area submitted a bid. Since then, about 90 per cent of the contract areas awarded in 2006 turned out be commercially unviable, and the contract holders have relinquished them (*La'o Hamutuk* 2014i). The next bidding round, which could take place in 2015, has been repeatedly delayed since 2010.

There isn't much time

Timor-Leste does not have enough oil and gas to sustain the country for very long. If the non-oil economy hasn't developed when the last well runs dry in five years, many more people will join the growing majority struggling to live under the poverty line. When state revenues can no longer cover expenses, Timor-Leste will fall into austerity, with drastic implications for the state and its citizens.

Combined with good planning, Timor-Leste's Petroleum Fund could help support sustainability. Although documents and officials often refer to intergenerational equity, suggestions for more serious efforts to develop alternatives to petroleum (UNDP 2011; Scheiner 2011; *La'o Hamutuk* 2012; *Petroleum Economist* 2013) were rebuffed (RDTL Spokesperson 10/5/2011, 21/3/2013) until recently (RDTL MoF 2011, 2013c, 2014b). Nevertheless, Timor-Leste's government continues to boast about its strong, growing, inclusive economy (Global Insight 2014; *Straits Times* 2014), although it is unclear whether policymakers believe their own advertising. After ANU published a two-page summary of this chapter (Scheiner 2014a), the Ministry of Finance responded with an eight-page Briefing Note (RDTL MoF 2014c), narrowly redefining the resource curse and ignoring the main points in the chapter.

However, others are beginning to understand the urgency. After years of echoing the government's petroleum-dominated priorities, the World Bank highlighted the need for non-petroleum economic development in its 2013–17 Country Partnership Strategy (World Bank 2013). When President Taur Matan Ruak promulgated the 2014 state budget, he wrote to parliament:

> Once again, I am concerned about the excessive dependency of government revenue on the Petroleum Fund. I am absolutely convinced that it is urgent to correct this situation ... I believe that it is necessary to adopt active policies to diversify economic development ... (RDTL President 3/2/2014).

Minutes after being sworn into office in February 2015, Prime Minister Dr Rui Araújo hedged his bets:

> [W]e know that these petroleum reserves are not renewable and, in the worst case scenario, may even run out in the years to come. While on the one hand we are fortunate to still have untapped resources, on the other hand we are one of the countries with the greatest petroleum dependency in the world. As such, we must invest in a responsible and sustainable manner (RDTL Prime Minister 16/2/2015).

La'o Hamutuk and others in civil society have encouraged a sustainable course for more than a decade (*La'o Hamutuk* 2002, 2005a, 2015; Scheiner 2011, 2013; FONGTIL 2013, 2014). In 2012, we began to estimate Timor-Leste's future state revenues and expenditures based on current trends, external factors and anticipated policy choices (*La'o Hamutuk* 2012, 2012a). The spreadsheet model is online as part of an ongoing effort to encourage evidence-based decision-making (Scheiner 2014; *La'o Hamutuk* 2015d, 2015f).

The model uses an engineering approach, based on causality and Timor-Leste's history, rather than correlations with other countries. It does not try to simulate the macro economy and therefore does not estimate GDP, inflation, poverty or trade. Rather, it projects how much the state will receive and spend, based on oil and gas receipts, investment returns, domestic revenues, and policy decisions about recurrent spending, megaprojects, borrowing, Sunrise development, and other factors.

6. Can the Petroleum Fund Exorcise the Resource Curse from Timor-Leste?

The model uses data and estimates from a variety of sources, including state budgets and executed expenditures (RDTL MoF 2013, 2013a, 2013b, 2014, 2014a, 2015a), population projections (RDTL GDS 2013b), oil price projections (US EIA 2015), and *La'o Hamutuk's* calculations of oil and gas production and debt repayments based on information from oil companies and lenders.[10] Detailed descriptions of the model's outputs and suggestions of what should be cut after Timor-Leste runs out of money are beyond the scope of this chapter.

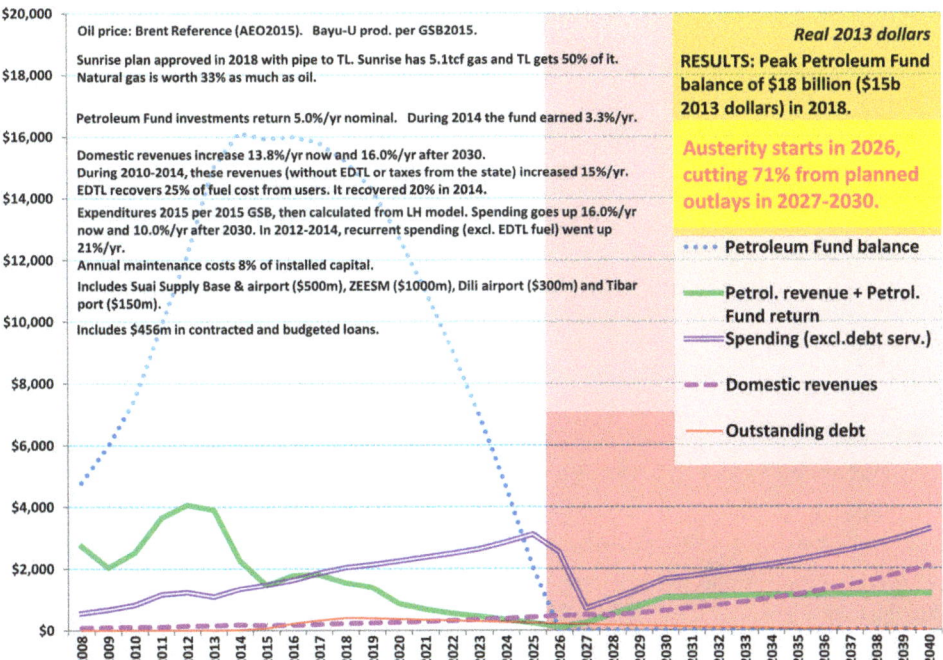

Figure 6.8 Base case scenario from sustainability model.
Source: *La'o Hamutuk* 2015f.

Figure 6.8 shows the model's baseline scenario, which is based on 'best-guess', mid-2015 assumptions of what is likely to happen, and is too optimistic for prudent planning. It uses higher oil prices than the Ministry of Finance uses to calculate the ESI and assumes a better return on Petroleum Fund investments than they earned in 2012–14. It also assumes that much less will be spent to build the Oecusse Special Zone and the Tasi Mane Project than is currently being discussed (*La'o Hamutuk* 2015).

---

10   At the time of writing in June 2015, long-term oil price predictions are tentative, and Timor-Leste's future plans and budgets are being reviewed. Updates will be posted at www.laohamutuk.org/econ/model/13PFSustainability.htm.

With these rosy assumptions, spending exceeds oil and interest income in 2017, and the Petroleum Fund begins to shrink. By 2026, before today's infants finish secondary school, the Fund will be used up, and state spending will have to be slashed by more than two-thirds from desired levels, as shown by the red shaded background.

This scenario assumes that the Greater Sunrise project goes ahead soon with an LNG plant in Beaçu, so that austerity cuts are 'only' 71 per cent. If the companies prevail and they build a floating LNG plant, austerity will be 75 per cent—a little harsher.

In February 2015, Sunrise operator Woodside Petroleum announced that it will 'shelve' the Sunrise project. CEO Peter Coleman told reporters,

> We have exhausted all activities … it's very difficult [for us] to spend any material amount of money [on Sunrise]. We don't know what the regulatory regime is, [and] we don't know what the fiscal regime is (*West Australian* 2015).

If the Sunrise project remains stalled, the model shows that Timor-Leste will have to cut expenditures 87 per cent after 2025, closing even more schools, clinics, offices and police stations.

Changes in other assumptions can bring on bankruptcy and austerity up to three years earlier or seven years later. However, without a dramatic redirection of policy approaches, Timor-Leste's petroleum reserves and petroleum wealth will not be able to finance the state for longer than 15 years, even if the country's wishes for Sunrise development, investment returns and global oil market prices are granted.

Although reducing expenditure and increasing non-oil revenue could delay austerity for a few years, it is inevitable that escalating budgets, increasing population and greater expectations will exhaust the country's finite petroleum wealth in less than a generation. This can only be ameliorated with a rapid, radical shift of direction toward increasing food production, reducing imports, cutting wasteful spending and cancelling unprofitable megaprojects.

Timor-Leste must fortify its strongest resource—its people—by investing in education, nutrition, health care, and rural water and sanitation. It must develop agriculture, the sector that employs most of its workers, to meet basic necessities and reduce the need for imports. Timorese people of all economic classes, genders, regions and generations will have to work together to defeat the resource curse by creating an equitable, sustainable economy.

The Timorese people proved their unity and persistence through their difficult, long struggle to achieve political sovereignty over the Indonesian occupation. Achieving economic sovereignty by overcoming the petroleum occupation may be even more difficult. It will require diverse approaches, building on Timor-Leste's strengths and prioritising medium- and long-term sustainability.

Timor-Leste has about 10 years before the only ship that can take the nation away from poverty—its remaining petroleum wealth—will have sailed. If the nation has not built a solid foundation for its non-petroleum economy, the Petroleum Fund safeguards will have failed to avert the resource curse. Sadly, the Petroleum Fund may have been only a delusion of economic security that enabled Timor-Leste's officials, advisors and donors to delay difficult decisions and avoid challenging tasks.

References

Many documents are referenced on both *La'o Hamutuk* and RDTL Government websites, as the government sites don't always work. All were accessed between December 2013 and June 2015.

Aftenposten [*Evening Post*] 23/8/2014. 'Finansdepartementet sendte svindler for å hjelpe Øst-Timor' [Finance department sends swindler to aid Timor-Leste]. www.aftenposten.no/okonomi/Finansdepartementet-sendte-svindler-for-a-hjelpe-Ost-Timor-7677639.html; English version at www.aftenposten.no/okonomi/Convicted-embezzler-money-launderer-hired-by-Norways-government-7679817.html.

ANP (*Autoridade Nacional do Petróleo*; National Petroleum Authority) 2015. JPDA production data. www.anp-tl.org/webs/anptlweb.nsf/pgLafaekReport.

ANU (The Australian National University) 2013. 'Trends in Economic Development'. Podcast from Timor-Leste Update conference, 28/11/2013, Canberra. ips.cap.anu.edu.au/news-events/podcasts/series/2013-timor-leste-update-podcast-series.

Barma, N.H. 2014. *The Rentier State at Work: Comparative Experiences of the Resource Curse in East Asia and the Pacific*. Asia & the Pacific Policy Studies 1:257–272. Canberra: Wiley Publishing. onlinelibrary.wiley.com/enhanced/doi/10.1002/app5.26.

BP 2015. Statistical Review of World Energy 2015. www.bp.com/en/global/corporate/about-bp/energy-economics/statistical-review-of-world-energy.html.

CBTL (Central Bank of Timor-Leste) 2014. Balance of Payments 2006–2013. Dili: CBTL. bancocentral.tl/Download/Publications/BoP/Excel/BOP%20 2006-2013.xlsx.

CBTL 2015. Petroleum Fund quarterly and monthly reports. Dili: CBTL. www.bancocentral.tl/PF/Reports.asp.

FONGTIL (Forum ONG Timor-Leste) 2013. Civil Society Statement on the Economic Sector to Timor-Leste and Development Partners Meeting, 19 June, Dili. www.laohamutuk.org/econ/13TLDPM/FongtilTLDPMEcon19Jun2013en.pdf.

FONGTIL 2014. Civil Society Statement on the Economic Sector to Timor-Leste and Development Partners Meeting, 25 July. www.laohamutuk.org/econ/14TLDPM/14TLDPMEconEn.htm.

Global Insight 2014. Timor-Leste advertising insert in *Japan Times*, 2 May. info.japantimes.co.jp/international-reports/pdf/20140502-GI-TIMOR-LESTE.pdf or www.laohamutuk.org/misc/promotion/TLPromoJapanTimes2May2014.pdf.

IMF (International Monetary Fund) 2013. Democratic Republic of Timor-Leste: Staff Report for the 2013 Article IV Consultation. Washington DC: IMF. www.imf.org/external/pubs/cat/longres.aspx?sk=41079.0 or www.laohamutuk.org/econ/IMF/IMFArtIVTL2013ReportDec2013.pdf.

IMF 22/10/2014. IMF Executive Board Concludes 2014 Article IV Consultation with Timor-Leste. Press release. www.imf.org/external/np/sec/pr/2014/pr14478.htm or www.laohamutuk.org/econ/IMF/IMFPR14478ExecBdArt4TL22Oct2014.htm.

La'o Hamutuk 2002. With Money, Oil Also Brings Problems. *La'o Hamutuk Bulletin* 3(5) July. www.laohamutuk.org/Bulletin/2002/Jul/lhv3n5en.pdf.

La'o Hamutuk 2005. Public Consultation and Enactment of Timor-Leste Petroleum Fund Act. www.laohamutuk.org/Oil/PetFund/Act/05FundActConsult.htm.

La'o Hamutuk 2005a. Timor-Leste Will Be One of the Most Oil-Dependent Countries in the World. *La'o Hamutuk Bulletin* 6(4) November. www.laohamutuk.org/Bulletin/2005/Nov/LHBv6n4en.pdf.

La'o Hamutuk 2010. Trying to Scam a Billion from the Petroleum Fund. www.laohamutuk.org/Oil/PetFund/ACI/10AsianChampInvestment.htm.

La'o Hamutuk 2012. Timor-Leste is going for broke. laohamutuk.blogspot.com/2012/03/timor-leste-is-going-for-broke.html.

La'o Hamutuk 2012a. How Timor-Leste Got Ten Billion Dollars … and How Quickly We Will Spend It All. laohamutuk.blogspot.com/2012/05/how-timor-leste-got-ten-billion-dollars.html.

La'o Hamutuk 2012b. Ten Billion Dollars is a Tempting Target. laohamutuk.blogspot.com/2012/07/ten-billion-dollars-is-tempting-target.html.

La'o Hamutuk 2013h. [Operation of] Timor-Leste Petroleum Fund. www.laohamutuk.org/Oil/PetFund/05PFIndex.htm.

La'o Hamutuk 2013a. 2013 General State Budget. www.laohamutuk.org/econ/OGE13/12OGE13.htm.

La'o Hamutuk 2013b. Letter to Parliament on the 2014 General State Budget, 8 November 2013, 3. www.laohamutuk.org/econ/OGE14/LHKartaOGE14PN8Nov2013en.pdf.

La'o Hamutuk 2013c. Timor-Leste is Going into Debt. www.laohamutuk.org/econ/debt/12Borrowing.htm.

La'o Hamutuk 2013d. South Coast Petroleum Infrastructure Project. www.laohamutuk.org/Oil/TasiMane/11TasiMane.htm.

La'o Hamutuk 2014. 2014 General State Budget. www.laohamutuk.org/econ/OGE14/13OGE14.htm.

La'o Hamutuk 2014a. Information about the Treaty between Australia and Timor-Leste on Certain Maritime Arrangements in the Timor Sea. www.laohamutuk.org/Oil/Boundary/CMATSindex.htm.

La'o Hamutuk 2014b. The Double Digit Disappears. laohamutuk.blogspot.com/2014/04/the-double-digit-disappears.html.

La'o Hamutuk 2014c. Oil Production Inevitably Declines. laohamutuk.blogspot.com/2014/03/oil-production-inevitably-declines.html.

La'o Hamutuk 2014d. Public-Private Partnerships to Build Grandiose Infrastructure Projects. www.laohamutuk.org/econ/PPP/PPPIndex.htm.

La'o Hamutuk 2014e. Timor-Leste Has Been Robbed! laohamutuk.blogspot.com/2014/06/timor-leste-has-been-robbed.html.

La'o Hamutuk 2014f. Making the Oil Companies Pay What They Owe. www.laohamutuk.org/Oil/tax/10BackTaxes.htm.

La'o Hamutuk 2014g. Special Economic Zone in Oecusse. www.laohamutuk.org/econ/Oecussi/ZEESMIndex.htm.

La'o Hamutuk 2014h. La'o Hamutuk Asks the RDTL Court of Appeals Please audit TimorGAP [Open letter to the Court of Appeals]. www.laohamutuk.org/Oil/TimorGAP/14LHTRTimorGAPaudit5Aug14.htm.

La'o Hamutuk 2014i. Petroleum Production Sharing Contracts. www.laohamutuk.org/Oil/PSCs/10PSCs.htm.

La'o Hamutuk 2014j. Bobby Boye: Convict, Advisor and Fraud. www.laohamutuk.org/econ/corruption/Boye/14BoyeCase.htm.

La'o Hamutuk 2015. PM Araujo, Recognize Falling State Revenues When Revising the 2015 Budget. laohamutuk.blogspot.com/2015/02/pm-araujo-recognize-falling-state.html.

La'o Hamutuk 2015a. It Takes More Than Money to Achieve Development. laohamutuk.blogspot.com/2015/02/it-takes-more-than-money-to-achieve.html.

La'o Hamutuk 2015b. Submission to Committee C, National Parliament, regarding the Proposed Rectification of 2015 State Budget. www.laohamutuk.org/econ/OGE15/OR/LHSubOR15-31Mar2015en.pdf.

La'o Hamutuk 2015c. Timor-Leste's Oil and Gas are Going Fast. www.laohamutuk.org/Oil/curse/2015/OilGoingFast15Apr2015en.pdf.

La'o Hamutuk 2015d. Update: How Long Will Timor-Leste's Petroleum Fund Last? www.laohamutuk.org/econ/model/OilSustain2June2015.pdf.

La'o Hamutuk 2015e. Civil Society Comment to the 2015 Timor-Leste Development Partners Meeting on the Economic Sector. laohamutuk.blogspot.com/2015/06/civil-society-to-development-partners.html.

La'o Hamutuk 2015f. How Long Will the Petroleum Fund Carry Timor-Leste? www.laohamutuk.org/econ/model/13PFSustainability.htm.

Neves, G. 2013. Rentier State, Statism, and Socio-Political and Socio-Economic Dynamic. Paper presented to Timor-Leste Studies Association, July, Dili. www.laohamutuk.org/econ/model/NevesPoliticalRentierTLSA2013.pdf and www.tlstudies.org/pdfs/TLSA%20Conf%202013/Volume%202%20individual%20papers/vol2_paper3.pdf.

Neves, G. 2014. Is Timor-Leste a Failed State? Life at Aitarak Laran (blog of the office of the Presidency of Timor-Leste), September. aitaraklaranlive.wordpress.com/2014/09/15/is-timor-leste-a-failed-state/.

Petroleum Economist 2013. Going for Broke. Editorial, March, 2. www.petroleum-economist.com/Article/3159297/News-and-Analysis-Archive/Going-for-broke.html or www.laohamutuk.org/Oil/TasiMane/2013/PetroEconLeaderMarch2013.pdf.

RDTL (*República Democrática de Timor Leste*; Democratic Republic of Timor-Leste) 2011. *Timor-Leste Strategic Development Plan 2011–2030*. Dili: RDTL. timor-leste.gov.tl/wp-content/uploads/2012/02/Strategic-Development-Plan_EN.pdf or www.laohamutuk.org/econ/SDP/2011/Timor-Leste-Strategic-Plan-2011-20301.pdf.

RDTL GDS (General Directorate of Statistics) 2013. *Timor-Leste National Accounts 2000–2011*. Table 1.1. Dili: RDTL. www.statistics.gov.tl/wp-content/uploads/2013/12/TL-NA_2011_Final_Publishable.pdf or www.laohamutuk.org/DVD/DGS/NatlAccts2011May2013en.pdf.

RDTL GDS 2013a. *External Trade Statistics, Annual Reports 2012*. Dili: RDTL. www.statistics.gov.tl/wp-content/uploads/2013/12/External_Trade_2012.pdf or www.laohamutuk.org/DVD/DGS/DGETrade2012.pdf.

RDTL GDS 2013b. *Timor-Leste Census 2010 Volume 8: Population Projection*. Dili: RDTL. www.statistics.gov.tl/wp-content/uploads/2013/12/PPJ_Monograph.pdf or www.laohamutuk.org/DVD/DGS/Cens10/8Projections.pdf.

RDTL GDS 2014a. *Timor-Leste National Accounts 2000-2012*. Tables 1.1 and 3.1. Dili: RDTL. www.statistics.gov.tl/wp-content/uploads/2014/07/National-Account-2012.pdf or www.laohamutuk.org/DVD/DGS/NatlAccts2012July2014en.pdf.

RDTL GDS 2014b. *Business Activity Survey of Timor-Leste 2012*. Dili: RDTL. www.statistics.gov.tl/wp-content/uploads/2014/07/BUSINESS-ACTIVITY-SURVEY-OF-TIMOR-LESTE-2012.pdf or www.laohamutuk.org/DVD/DGS/BAS2012Jul2014en.pdf.

RDTL GDS 2015. External Trade Statistics, Monthly Reports. www.statistics.gov.tl/category/survey-indicators/external-trade-statistics/monthly-reports/.

RDTL GDS 2015a, Consumer Price Index Reports. www.statistics.gov.tl/category/survey-indicators/consumer-price-index/-lang=en.

RDTL GDS 2015b. *Business Activity Survey of Timor-Leste 2013*. Dili: RDTL. www.statistics.gov.tl/wp-content/uploads/2015/02/Business-Activity-Survey-2013-_English.pdf or www.laohamutuk.org/DVD/DGS/BAS2013en.pdf.

RDTL GDS 2015c. Timor-Leste Labour Force Survey 2013: April 2015. www.statistics.gov.tl/wp-content/uploads/2015/04/LFS_2013_ENGLISH_VERSION.pdf or www.laohamutuk.org/DVD/DGS/LFS2013en.pdf.

RDTL GDS 2015d. *Timor-Leste National Accounts 2000-2013*. Dili: RDTL. www.statistics.gov.tl/wp-content/uploads/2015/06/A4-NA-2014-OK.pdf or www.laohamutuk.org/DVD/DGS/NatlAccts2013Jun2015en.pdf.

RDTL MoF (Ministry of Finance) 2011. Analysis of Fiscal Sustainability in Timor-Leste. www.mof.gov.tl/analysis-of-fiscal-sustainability-in-timor-leste.

RDTL MoF 2013. Petroleum Fund 2012 Annual Report. Dili: RDTL. www.laohamutuk.org/Oil/PetFund/Reports/PFAR12En.pdf or www.mof.gov.tl/petroleum-fund-annual-report-2012.

RDTL MoF 2013a. Fundo Consolidado de Timor-Leste, Declarações Consolidadas Anuais Ano Fiscal de 2012 [Consolidated Fund of Timor-Leste, Annual Financial Statements for Fiscal Year 2012]. www.laohamutuk.org/econ/OR12/CFET_Financial_Statement_2012.pdf.

RDTL MoF 2013b. State Budget 2013: Budget Overview (Book 1), tables 2.5.3.1.1 and 2.5.3.1.2. Dili: RDTL. www.laohamutuk.org/econ/OGE13/BksApr2013/OGE13Bk1en.pdf.

RDTL MoF 2013c. Yellow Road workshop 9–10 May, Dili. Presentations available from La'o Hamutuk at www.laohamutuk.org/econ/OGE14/13OGE14.htm#yrw or www.mof.gov.tl/2013-yellow-road-workshop/?lang=en.

RDTL MoF 2014. Budget Transparency Portal. www.budgettransparency.gov.tl/public/index?&lang=en. Also www.transparency.gov.tl/english.html.

RDTL MoF 2014a. General State Budget 2014. All six budget volumes are available at www.laohamutuk.org/econ/OGE14/13OGE14.htm#docs.

RDTL MoF 2014b. Yellow Road Workshop 29-30 May, Dili. Presentations. www.mof.gov.tl/wp-content/uploads/2014/08/Yellow_Road_Workshop_2014.pdf.

RDTL MoF 2014c. Briefing Note to Respond to 'The Resource Curse in Timor-Leste' Article Authored by Charles Scheiner (La'o Hamutuk). www.mof.gov.tl/briefing-note-to-respond-to-the-resources-curse-in-timor-leste-article-authored-by-charles-scheiner-lao-hamutuk/?lang=en or www.laohamutuk.org/econ/exor/MoFResourceCurse2Sep14.pdf.

RDTL MoF 2015. 2015 General State Budget documents. www.laohamutuk.org/econ/OGE15/14OGE15.htm#docs.

RDTL MoF 2015a. 2015 Rectification budget papers and related documents. www.laohamutuk.org/econ/OGE15/14OGE15.htm#docs.

RDTL MoF 2015b, Jornada Orsamental workshop 14 May 2015, Dili. Presentations. www.mof.gov.tl/wp-content/uploads/2015/05/Jornada_Orcamental.pdf or www.laohamutuk.org/econ/OGE16/yrw/JornadaOrsamental14May2015.pdf.

RDTL National Parliament 2013, Comissão de Finanças Públicas. Relatório e Parecer Sobre a Apreciação Inicial da Proposta de Lei N.º 10/III(2ª)—Orçamento do Estado para 2014 [Report and Opinion on the Initial Proposed Law No. 10/III(2), State Budget for 2014]. Dili: RDTL, 19. www.laohamutuk.org/econ/OGE14/CommCReport3Dec2013pt.pdf; unofficial English translation at www.laohamutuk.org/econ/OGE14/ComCRecomOGE14LHEditen.pdf.

RDTL PFIAB (Petroleum Fund Investment Advisory Board) 2009. Letter to Minister of Finance responding to 'Request for an advice on depositing part of the Petroleum Fund in cash', 18 September. Included in Annex X to the 2009 Petroleum Fund Annual Report, available at www.mof.gov.tl\wp-content\uploads\2011\09\Petroleum_Fund_Annual_Report_2009_English.zip, Part 4, page 23 or www.laohamutuk.org/Oil/PetFund/ACI/IABAsianChamp18Sep09En.pdf.

RDTL President 3/2/2014. *Mensagem ao Parlamento Nacional na Promulgação do Orçamento Geral do Estado para 2014* [Message to the National Parliament on Promulgation of the General State Budget for 2014]. www.laohamutuk.org/econ/OGE14/PR-OGE3Feb2014en.pdf or Portuguese original at www.laohamutuk.org/econ/OGE14/PR-OGE3Feb2014pt.pdf.

RDTL Prime Minister 1/4/2014. Address by His Excellency the Prime Minister of the Democratic Republic Of Timor-Leste Kay Rala Xanana Gusmão at the Forum on Trade and Investment Opportunities in Timor-Leste, Kuala Lumpur, Malaysia. timor-leste.gov.tl/wp-content/uploads/2014/04/Forum-on-Trade-and-Investment-KL-1.4.14.pdf or www.laohamutuk.org/DVD/2014/XG-KL1Apr14en.pdf.

RDTL Prime Minister 16/2/2015. Speech by His Excellency the Prime Minister Dr Rui Maria De Araújo on the Occasion of the Swearing-In of the Sixth Constitutional Government. timor-leste.gov.tl/wp-content/uploads/2015/02/Swearing-in-of-the-Sixth-Constitutional-Government-16.2.20151.pdf.

RDTL Spokesperson 10/5/2011. Transparency and the UNDP Timor-Leste Human Development Report 2011. Press release. timor-leste.gov.tl/?p=5018&lang=en or www.laohamutuk.org/econ/HDI10/SSComNHDR10May2011En.pdf.

RDTL Spokesperson 21/3/2013. Correction of Inconsistencies in International Media Regarding Oil and Gas. Press release. timor-leste.gov.tl/?p=7901&lang=en.

Rigzone 5/2/2015. Timor-Leste Reviews Investment Rules, Plans New Bid Round. www.rigzone.com/news/oil_gas/a/137061 or www.laohamutuk.org/oil/curse/2015/RigzoneBid5Feb2015.pdf.

Santos 2014. Annual Reports for 2012–2014. www.santos.com/share-price-performance/company-reporting/annual-reports.aspx.

Scheiner, C. 3/5/2011. Timor-Leste Must Win Independence from Petroleum. Presentation at launch of UNDP 2011 Human Development Report. www.laohamutuk.org/econ/HDI10/11NHDREn.htm.

Scheiner, C. 18/4/2013. Comments at the launch of the 2013 Economic and Social Survey of Asia and the Pacific. www.laohamutuk.org/econ/ESCAP/ESCAPScheiner18Apr2013en.pdf.

Scheiner, C. 2014. How Long Will the Petroleum Fund Carry Timor-Leste? In *Understanding Timor-Leste: Proceedings of the 2013 Timor-Leste Studies Association conference.* tlstudies.org/tlsa_confpro2013.html or www.laohamutuk.org/econ/model/ScheinerPetrolFund17Feb2014en.pdf with additional information at www.laohamutuk.org/econ/model/13PFSustainability.htm.

Scheiner, C. 2014a. The Resource Curse in Timor-Leste. SSGM In Brief 2014/29. Canberra: ANU. ips.cap.anu.edu.au/publications/%E2%80%98resource-curse%E2%80%99-timor-leste-0.

Stiglitz, J.E. 2014. *The Price of Inequality: How Today's Divided Society Endangers Our Future* New York: W.W. Norton.

Straits Times 31/8/2014. 15th Anniversary Timor-Leste Independence Referendum advertising supplement. Singapore. www.laohamutuk.org/misc/promotion/TLAdSingapore31Aug14.pdf or znx.cc/st/2014/08/31.pdf.

Timor Post 21/5/2014. Timor Gap Preparadu Explorasa Bayu Undang, 11.

UNDP (United Nations Development Programme) 2011. Managing Natural Resources for Human Development: Timor-Leste National Human Development Report. New York: UNDP. www.laohamutuk.org/econ/HDI10/TLHDR2011En.pdf.

UNDP 2014. Human Development Report: Sustaining Human Progress: Reducing Vulnerabilities and Building Resilience. hdr.undp.org/en/2014-report/download.

UNDP 2014a. Timor-Leste Country Explanatory Note for Human Development Report. hdr.undp.org/sites/all/themes/hdr_theme/country-notes/TLS.pdf.

US EIA (Energy Information Administration) 2015. Annual Energy Outlook 2015: With Projections to 2040. Also see associated statistical tables. www.eia.gov/forecasts/aeo/.

West Australian. 18/2/2015. Woodside to Cut Jobs, Shelve Sunrise. www.laohamutuk.org/Oil/Sunrise/2015/WAWoodsideSunrise18Feb2015.pdf.

World Bank 2013. Timor-Leste Country Partnership Strategy for the Period FY2013–2017. Washington DC: World Bank. documents.worldbank.org/curated/en/2013/02/17493182/timor-leste-country-partnership-strategy-period-fy2013-2017.

World Bank/PwC (PricewaterhouseCoopers) 2014. Paying Taxes 2015. Washington/London: PricewaterhouseCoopers. www.pwc.com/gx/en/paying-taxes/pdf/pwc-paying-taxes-2015-high-resolution.pdf.

CHAPTER 7

Progress and Challenges of Infrastructure Spending in Timor-Leste

Antonio Vitor[1]

Background

Most basic infrastructure such as power, water, transport, telecommunications, office and school buildings built by Portuguese and Indonesian administrations in Timor-Leste were destroyed when the country was liberated in 1999.

> Almost everything needed to be rebuilt and the country faced a massive task in planning and executing a wholesale infrastructure investment program valued at more than US$10 billion. Eleven years later, while notable progress had been made in some sectors, Timor-Leste remains far behind its original investment targets. While the country possesses significant oil & gas resources to support infrastructure financing, its capacity for investment planning and implementation remain constrained (Darcy 2012: 1).

Prior to 2006, most public expenditure was funded by the international development community. However, with the creation of a dedicated Infrastructure Fund, Timor-Leste's own resources are now funding around 80 per cent of public expenditure. Operating within the framework provided by the *Strategic Development Plan 2011–2030* (SDP), and the infrastructure

---

[1] The views expressed in this chapter are those of the author's and do not necessarily reflect the views and policies of ADB or its Board of Governors, the governments they represent, or the Government of Timor-Leste.

program of the Fifth Constitutional Government 2012–2017, the government hopes to better direct and measure Timor-Leste's development performance in the infrastructure sector.

Owing to the inflow of funds from petroleum sales over the past few years, Timor-Leste's government has dramatically expanded the level of resources invested in infrastructure development. Since 2007, the budget of the Ministry of Infrastructure (including projects funded under the Infrastructure Fund) has increased by more than an order of magnitude to almost US$200 million a year. In 2013, the country planned to spend about 15 per cent of its gross domestic product (GDP) on infrastructure development. This is an enormous figure by international standards, where developing countries spending 6 per cent of their GDP on infrastructure are generally considered to be making a more than adequate contribution to their infrastructure development needs. Capital expenditure requirements are higher in post-conflict environments, where challenges are often greater in terms of the availability of skilled labour and expertise. Even taking this into account, Timor-Leste's infrastructure expenditure targets are very ambitious.

However, the high and increasing budgetary allocations for infrastructure have added to the burden of implementing agencies, and while disbursement ratios have improved over recent years, the Ministry of Public Works (MPW) is still only able to disburse about two thirds of its budget. Large budgets, combined with the limited implementation capacity of the infrastructure ministries, lead to pressures to divert resources to pay for ad hoc 'emergency projects'. Examples of these projects include the well-known *Pakote Referendum* (Referendum Package), which totalled US$70 million, for which funding was diverted from the National Electrification Project, and an emergency drainage project for which funding was diverted from a multi-year project for drainage.

The current extent and state of Timor-Leste's infrastructure requires substantial investment to meet the growing needs of the country. Therefore, proper prioritisation, effective and efficient implementation of selective infrastructure projects is crucial. Timor-Leste requires extensive and diverse infrastructure development, but in this chapter I limit discussion to issues of roads, electricity, water and sanitation, ports, and airport development.

Targets in the *Strategic Development Plan 2011–2030*

Timor-Leste's SDP sets an ambitious goal to achieve middle-income country status by 2030. This is a reachable goal if Timor-Leste can manage its resources properly and prudently to create a modern and productive economy.

The status of infrastructure remains inadequate and inefficient with increasing development demands. Infrastructure spending should, therefore, be directed towards building and maintaining the core and productive infrastructure needed to support the growth of the nation, increase productivity, create jobs, and support the development of national private sector. In doing so, the scale and cost implications are large and ongoing (RDTL 2011: 70–72).

The relationship between infrastructure and economic development has been widely recognised. Empirical evidence demonstrates that shortfalls in infrastructure lead to declining productivity (Aschauer 1989a, 1989b, 1991). This relationship implies that public capital is an important input in the production function. Many targets set for infrastructure in the SDP should be seen in this context. Building Timor-Leste's infrastructure is not an easy task, particularly where demand for infrastructure is pressing while the cost of supply is enormously high. There are no simple answers, but the targets set for key infrastructure, while ambitious, are tough choices the country has to make to overcome the constraints in socioeconomic development. The design and planning for infrastructure investment are, therefore, key preconditions for social and economic development.

Does the SDP make the right choices for infrastructure spending to establish preconditions for state social services and to support economic growth? This question is hotly debated, but, in my view, the choice to invest in transport infrastructure such as ports, airports, roads and bridges is compelling. As Brooks has commented,

> Asia benefits from market-driven integration, where large trade and FDI [foreign direct investment] flows respond to infrastructure development … and efficient infrastructure services lower transaction costs, raise value-added and increase potential profitability for producers while increasing and expanding linkages to global supply chains and distribution networks (2009: 1).

Conversely, inadequate infrastructure can cost an economy significant unrealised gain from trade, and lead to an 'inability to transport goods and people efficiently, [while] an inadequate power supply to operate machines leads to microeconomic as well as macroeconomics bottlenecks … infrastructure can also yield positive externalities' (Brooks 2008: 1).

The plan for road network development is to deliver a comprehensive road maintenance program, to rehabilitate all existing roads, to construct new bridges, and to provide all-weather access on major routes within five years (RDTL 2011: 75). In Timor-Leste, roads are categorised into national, district, rural, and urban. All national and district roads will be fully rehabilitated to an international standard by 2020. All rural roads are expected to be fully rehabilitated by 2015. A bridge construction program to construct and rehabilitate bridges that are in need of replacement or repair will also be undertaken. There are around 3,200 linear metres of bridges throughout the nation. District roads have been the highest priority for repair. A national highway of two lanes in each direction capable of taking a full-length container at an average speed of 60 km per hour is planned to be built on the south coast, linking Suai in the western part and Beaco in the eastern part of the country. A ring road around the country has also been envisaged (RDTL 2011: 72–76). The SDP's comprehensive, 10-year road-building program will give certainty and ongoing opportunities to international and national road construction companies to encourage such business to invest and grow in Timor-Leste. This will improve Timor-Leste's private-sector development and create jobs throughout the nation (RDTL 2011: 72).

The plan for water and sanitation is to overcome the many challenges involved in providing improved access to clean water and sanitation across Timor-Leste. This includes the construction of a major sewerage collection system in Dili, providing a safe, 24-hour, piped water supply to households in 12 district centres, and installing water systems and community latrines in rural areas. The SDP sets a target that by 2030 all citizens of Timor-Leste will have access to clean water and improved sanitation. The target for urban districts is to provide 60 per cent access to appropriate, improved sanitation facilities by 2015. Alongside sanitation facilities, the SDP also sets out to rehabilitate existing sewers, and separate sewage from stormwater drainage by building intercepting sewers, installing pilot toilet facilities in households and facilitating local treatment of sewerage. These initiatives include building appropriate treatment facilities in a staged way—connecting commercial properties first, then residential septic tank effluent, followed by all houses that have flush toilets. Other options include building a trunk sewer along the waterfront to take effluent from the intercepting sewers. The expectation is that by 2020 there will be appropriate, well-operated and maintained, sustainable infrastructure for the collection, treatment and disposal of sewage in Dili (RDTL 2011: 77–81). While this is an achievable goal, the works must be outsourced, and a proper, operational and detailed infrastructure plan put in place.

'Electricity is seen as a basic right and the foundation for our economic future.' According to the SDP, by 2015 everyone in Timor-Leste will have access to reliable electricity for 24 hours a day. To achieve this, the government has commenced investment in new power plants, substations and transmission lines, as well as distribution systems. An expansion of renewable energy systems is also envisaged in the SDP. The establishment of two power plants for electricity generation, and the roll-out of most transmission and distribution systems have been accomplished. Apart from the national electricity grid, the government has also rolled out a rural electrification program aimed at improving the living conditions of the majority of the population, including more remote communities. The SDP states that by 2020 at least half of Timor-Leste energy needs will be met from renewable energy sources (RDTL 2011: 85–92).

The international airport in Dili will be extended and a new terminal will be built. Rehabilitation of building airstrips for at least Suai, Oecusse/Ambeno, Lospalos, Maliana, Viqueque, Atauro and Same are being considered. While the plan for Baucau airport is for it to be an alternative airport to Dili, it will be also used as aero-military base (RDTL 2011: 97–98).

Two new seaports—one at Tibar near Dili and another in Suai—are envisaged. Construction of these two ports is expected to support the growing economy and meet future industry and freight demands (RDTL 2011: 94). The plan for Tibar port includes the construction of a wharf and onshore facilities, a new road from Dili to Tibar, dredging, and possible construction of a breakwater. These facilities will be built in phases in accordance with growing demand and funding availability. The Tibar Port Project has already commenced, and by 2020 Timor-Leste is expected to have a new, fully operational and efficient major port. A logistics supply base for the petroleum sector will be established in Suai. This is expected to provide capacity for the south coast to develop a domestic petroleum sector along with related and supporting industries and businesses. The expectation is that when this port facility is in place it will attract investment and promote growth, and provide an international access point to Timor-Leste. Alongside these two major ports, regional ports construction will be undertaken over the next 10 years. Port facilities will be built, repaired or substantially expanded (RDTL 2011: 93–96).

What is the progress to date?

> Timor-Leste has an extensive system of national, district and rural roads that provide access to the rural parts of our nation where the majority of the population lives. The network is generally constructed to the Indonesian pavement standard of 4.5 metres width with lined masonry drains and two lane steel truss bridges. The Timor-Leste road network comprises national roads that link districts to each other, district roads that link district centres with sub-districts and rural roads that provide access to villages and the more remote areas. There are around 1,426 km of national roads, 869 km of district roads and 3,025 km of rural roads (RDTL 2011: 70).

The roads network development program is currently undergoing a significant expansion. Remarkable progress is being made on the national roads upgrade. According to the SDP, all national and district roads are to be fully rehabilitated to an international standard by 2020. All national roads will be upgraded to a width of 6 metres plus a 1-metre shoulder on both sides, and will include drainage and slope protection works. From 2011, the Government of Timor-Leste and development partners—namely the Asian Development Bank (ADB), the Japan International Cooperation Agency (JICA), and the World Bank—are co-financing this national roads network development program. The agreement is to upgrade about 600 kilometres out of approximately 1,426 kilometres of the existing national roads by 2017. Percentage-wise, the government's program is securing about 40 per cent of the total length of Timor-Leste's national roads to be upgraded by 2017. Recently, the government and the ADB co-financed the upgrading of about 14 kilometres of Liquiça–Maubara section. This section is part of the main road link between the Nusa Tenggara Timur Province of Indonesia and Dili was due to be completed by December 2013. The civil work contracts for the upgrading of Dili–Liquiça and Tibar–Gleno road sections were awarded earlier in 2014 and works have recently commenced. Heavy maintenance for the section from Batugade to Maliana has been ongoing since 2012.

In 2012, the government and JICA signed a loan agreement to upgrade the Dili–Manatuto–Baucau road link. The following year the design was completed and put out to tender, and the construction of the Dili to Manatuto road was scheduled to commence in 2014, with the remaining section from Manatuto to Baucau to be completed by 2017. Subsequently, the government and the World Bank signed a loan agreement to upgrade the Dili–Ainaro road link. Works were scheduled to commence in 2014 with a completion schedule by 2017. The government has also signed with ADB a new loan to finance the construction of the Manatuto–Natarbora road link, including the design for the upgrading of the Baucau–Lospalos road, the Lautem–Com road link and the Baucau–Viqueque road. This project was also scheduled to commence in 2014 and be completed by 2017.

Notable progress has also been made on rural road construction and rehabilitation. The government, in partnership with AusAID and the International Labour Organization (ILO), has rehabilitated 90 kilometres of roadway, while an additional 150 kilometres is scheduled to be rehabilitated by the second half of 2013.[2] Despite the fact that rural road rehabilitation has achieved just 240 kilometres out of a total of 3,025 kilometres, to some extent this has been critically important as:

---

2   de Sousa, Gastão 9/8/2013. Progress Made during the First Year of the V-Government. Presentation at the Retreat of V-Government, Dili.

over 70% of the population of Timor-Leste are living in rural areas and therefore any progress made will contribute to connect people and communities, encourage agricultural and natural resource development, increase rural incomes and allow for the effective delivery of government services including health care, education and security (RDTL 2011: 70).

Despite the highest priority being given to district roads, this category is recorded as receiving only limited attention, as by August 2013 there were just 70 kilometres maintained. A number of projects for district road rehabilitation are proceeding, but it has been difficult to track progress due to the absence of a reliable data. Most of these works have been undertaken on an ad hoc basis, with improper preparation, and poor adherence to the design and processing requirements necessary to ensure that resources expended will result in the anticipated benefits.

Water supply infrastructure is still recorded as lagging behind. The UN, the new government and its development partners have invested well over US$250 million in the Dili water supply system since 2000. Investments have focused on emergency repairs, operational capacity-building and major infrastructure. Water sources, treatment plants and transmission mains are now in generally good condition, and have sufficient capacity to meet Dili's needs for several years (ADB 2007). An ongoing project for increased water supply for Dili is now progressing well. The project is covering three sub-zones within three different zones, supplying continuous potable water for about 1,600 households/consumers. Works in two additional zones covering about 1,700 households are scheduled to commence in 2014. The *Direcção Nacional de Água e Saneamento* (DNSA; National Directorate for Water and Sanitation) has reintroduced water billing in Dili, particularly within the zones covered by the water supply project co-financed with the ADB. Another government project for Pante Makassar in Oecussi and Manatuto township is now at the procurement stage and is scheduled to commence construction in 2014. A further co-financed project with the ADB to implement the urban water supply is planned in accordance with the SDP.

A public–private partnership (PPP) pre-feasibility study was completed this year reviewing the tariff structure to ensure affordability for the urban poor and effective coverage of operational costs. It also assessed a realistic target date to meet the government's planned level of service expectations and commitments of matching funding. A full feasibility study will be conducted to assess the merits and risks of a PPP before commencing any tender process (Evans & Peck 2013).

There has been some good progress made in rural water and sanitation. One of the key players in this sector is the *Be'e Saneamentu no Ijiene iha Komunidade* or BESIK program (Rural Water Supply and Sanitation Program), financed by AusAID. This program covers all 13 districts and provides access to clean water for over 80 remote villages in Timor-Leste.

Very significant progress has been made in electricity supply. Despite the large investment and achievements made by the recent two periods of government, electricity infrastructure continues to attract conflicting opinions. By June 2013, the government had:

- completed two new power plants with 250-megawatt capacity and nine substations
- connected 506 kilometres of transmission lines out of a planned total of 603 kilometres
- provided 106,072 households with access to electricity; 97,072 households were connected to the grid
- provided 9,000 households with solar panels.[3]

Timor-Leste is heavily dependent on a single national port in Dili for all general cargo imports and exports. The Port of Dili is struggling to cope with the volume of cargo and this situation is likely to worsen as the economy expands. Its limited capacity already results in a berthing backlog of between three and eight ships. To overcome this problem, a new multi-purpose port with a capacity of one million tonnes per year, and catering for commercial cargo and passenger needs will be constructed in Tibar, a few kilometres west of Dili (RDTL 2011: 93–94). The project has reached procurement stage and it will be implemented through a PPP.

The challenges in delivering infrastructures in Timor-Leste

The SDP places state-led capital spending at the centre of its development strategy. To deliver infrastructure as targeted in the SDP would be extremely challenging should there be no change in the current system, procurement practices and institutional arrangements. Timor-Leste lacks capacity both in terms of human resources as well as institutions to deliver SDP targets.

---

3   de Sousa, Gastão 2013. Minister of Public Works presentation at the Timor-Leste Development Partners meeting, Dili, 18–20 June.

The national private sector, particularly in relation to construction, design and supervision, remains low and underdeveloped. The infrastructure to support the development of physical infrastructures needed by the country is limited.

State-led investment in infrastructure development requires the government to perform well in public investment management and public finance management. But this expectation is frequently not met given the continuing capacity constraints.

In addition to limited public sector capacities and capabilities to deliver infrastructure, there are natural impediments for private sector involvement. Timor-Leste can be categorised as a relatively small market for private investment. Its remoteness can result in high costs for doing business. A number of structural factors also constrain private sector investment. These include the weak macro-economic environment, poor governance, extensive state involvement coupled with weak regulation, underdeveloped financial markets, the poor legal and investment policy environment and sensitivity about instability. These combined factors have led to low returns on capital and need to be addressed to establish a reliable and conducive investment environment.

In the absence of private sector in investment, the government has almost no other choice but to stimulate investment directly. The National Electrification Project, the Tasi Mane Project, the Tibar Port Project and the National Road Network Development are major to mega projects selected within the framework to generate future investment while providing basic infrastructure and services. Developing this concept led to an environment in which political economy influences investment logics.

The institutional arrangement for delivering infrastructure is also an issue. Over recent years, the government has established the *Secretariado dos Grandes Projetos* (Major Project Secretariat), the *Agência de Desenvolvimento Nacional* (National Development Agency) and the *Comissão Nacional de Aprovisionamento* (National Procurement Commission) to improve the efficiency and effectiveness of infrastructure planning and delivery. The objective behind the establishment of these agencies is to improve the way in which agencies responsible for planning and implementation can work together to ensure that projects are aligned with SDP objectives, are economically and financially viable, are delivered on time and on budget, and are sustained by the implementation of adequate operation and maintenance arrangements. However, there are overlapping responsibilities between some agencies involved in the infrastructure planning and delivery processes, and there remains a risk that resources are not being used optimally to deliver infrastructure against the objectives set out in the SDP. The current system for prioritising investments is not working effectively, and risks wasting government resources on inappropriate or poorly designed investments.

Two key ministries responsible for implementing infrastructures are the MPW and the Ministry of Transport and Communications; however, with the creation of supporting agencies in the infrastructure sector, these government agencies have, to some extent, overlapping functions. For example, the MPW operates in an external environment of change, political uncertainty and political interference, and with multiple, changing and competing stakeholders.

What is currently lacking in most areas are sector or sub-sector strategies and plans. These would provide an intermediate step between the overall socioeconomic goal and strategy set out in the SDP, and detailed lists of proposed project interventions or macro-level targets. Such strategies and plans would provide:

1. a more fine-grained framework for sector and sub-sector development
2. a set of intermediate goals and sector or sub-sector development indicators that would allow planning and implementing agencies to better measure how individual project interventions are contributing to the realisation of overall sub-sector and sector outcomes.

Realising these objectives will, in turn, contribute to the realisation of the SDP's strategic socioeconomic goals.

The global experience of infrastructure development is that the achievement of efficient investment depends on a number of factors relating to the executing and implementing institutions and their relationships with each other, including clear plans and strategies.[4] Many of these conditions are absent in Timor-Leste, and focusing on some of these areas could be helpful in improving the quality and efficiency of the country's infrastructure investment. Following are some of the most important preconditions for cost-effective and efficient infrastructure investment.

1. Close co-operation is required between all ministries and parastatal agencies involved with infrastructure.
2. There should be a clear separation of political and technical responsibilities. With policymakers setting aspirations and sector priorities, goals and targets, and technicians taking responsibility for deciding how to reach these goals, including determining whether to take in-house responsibility or to execute and evaluate, with delivery delegated to others under contract. Timor-Leste still has major issues in this area with frequent political interference in project selection and delivery.

---

4   Dobbs, R. et al. 2013. *Infrastructure Productivity: How to Save $1 Trillion a Year*. London: McKinsey Global Institute.

3. The government should engage the private sector where it can provide greatest value—including welcoming unsolicited proposals where appropriate. In reality, Timor-Leste is only at the first stage in this process, but understanding what capacity there is in the private sector to take on infrastructure and service delivery roles is an important step.

4. Trust-based stakeholder engagement should be supported by the development of transparent systems and provision of education (including to beneficiaries and stakeholders). This objective includes broad participation in the process, and compensation (or offsets) for those experiencing negative impacts. Again, Timor-Leste is at an early stage in this process, and gaining public trust is the first step.

5. Decisions on investment should be made based on robust and reliable information; this is crucial for sector and sub-sector strategies. Balance-sheet accounting on investments should be made public—to show spending and to promote equity. (Some progress is being made on this with the government's transparency portals in areas such as budget, procurement, expenditure and results.)

6. There should be adequate investment to obtain the required skills—building strong capabilities across the infrastructure value-chain. This goal also highlights the value of focused delivery units—hand-picked teams with a single objective to realise major investments.

Figure 7.1 National road upgrading project.
Source: Antonio Vitor.

Conclusion

Timor-Leste's infrastructure is inadequate and inefficient. The infrastructure built prior to 1999–2000 is deteriorating due in part to age, but largely due to lack of proper maintenance and rehabilitation over the previous decade and more. Most of the key infrastructure, such as ports, airports, major road networks and telecommunications, needs to be upgraded to suit the current and growing demands. There are conflicting views, however, around the selection priorities of infrastructure, given the widespread demand for improvements, and competing economic and political interests. Despite significant investment made so far, the results are yet to meet expectations. To date, the choice has been to invest in transport, telecommunication and the power sectors in order to meet basic infrastructure needs and establish a firm basis for socioeconomic development.

The challenges remain significant. The achievement of efficient infrastructure investment depends upon a number of factors that require effective co-ordination and planning, and the improved capacity of implementing agencies to fulfil their responsibilities and strategic plans.

References

Arthur, J. 2013. *Timor-Leste: Review of ADB Capacity Building Support to Infrastructure Sector*. Dili: Asian Development Bank.

Aschauer, D.A. 1989a. Is Public Expenditure Productive? *Journal of Monetary Economics* 23(March):177–200.

Aschauer, D.A. 1989b. Public Investment and Productivity Growth in the Group of Seven. *Economics Perspective* 13(September/October):17–25.

Aschauer, D.A. 1991. Infrastructure: America's Third Deficit. *Challenge* 34(March–April):39–45.

Brooks, D.H. 2008. Infrastructure and Trade in Asia: An Overview. In D.H. Menon (ed.). *Infrastructure and Trade in Asia*. Cheltenham: Asian Development Bank Institute and Edward Elgar Publishing, 1–14.

Brooks, D.H. 2009. Infrastructure's Role in Lowering Asia's Trade Costs. In D.H. Brooks and D. Hummels (eds). *Infrastructure's Role in Lowering Asia's Trade Costs*. Cheltenham: Asian Development Bank Institute and Edward Elgar Publishing, 1–16.

Darcy, L. 2012. Implementing PPPS in Timor Leste: Institutional Challenges in the Near North. *Public Infrastructure Bulletin* 1(8):1–4.

Evans & Peck 2013. *Dili Water Supply Public Private Partnership Pre-Feasibility Assessment*. Dili: ADB.

RDTL (*República Democrática de Timor-Leste*) 2011. *Timor-Leste Strategic Development Plan 2011–2030*. Dili: RDTL.

CHAPTER 8

Securing a New Ordering of Power in Timor-Leste: The Role of Sub-national Spending

Saku Akmeemana and Doug Porter[1]

A crucial aspect of Timor-Leste's economic performance and political stability in the aftermath of the 2006 crisis has been the way the government has managed a five-fold increase in public spending, and an even more rapid increase in capital spending. While the country's experience has been widely acknowledged as an exemplar of 'buying the peace', less well documented has been the range of unorthodox arrangements adopted by the government to manage this fiscal expansion and to re-order the local political landscape. Sub-national spending was pivotal, despite amounting to only around 3 per cent of the budget. Recent research undertaken by the World Bank,[2] including a joint study with the Government of Timor-Leste of its sub-national development programs, provides empirically grounded insights into how public spending can be used to dynamically trade-off and balance competing technical, social and political priorities in the immediate aftermath of conflict. This chapter's assessment of

---

1 The authors are staff of the World Bank who worked on the study discussed in this chapter, *Sub-national Spending in Timor-Leste: Lessons from Experience* (World Bank, Justice for the Poor, 2014). documents. worldbank.org/curated/en/2014/11/20426607/timor-leste-sub-national-spending-lessons-experience. However, the views expressed in this chapter are not to be attributed to the World Bank, but are the authors' views, based on several years of engagement in Timor-Leste in different capacities. The authors are grateful for advice from Sue Ingram, Bjorn Dressel, Anthony Goldstone and Edio Guterres, and acknowledge comments by participants at seminars at which these findings have been discussed in Canberra (18/4/2013 and 28/11/2013), and Washington DC (25/11/2013 and 23/4/2014).
2 This includes studies of large infrastructure contracts; a political economy analysis of sub-national spending that draws from new qualitative research as well as synthesising existing literature; and a broader contemporary political economy analysis of the country, drawing from an analysis of its history.

public spending provides a lens through which to understand the crafting of political settlements in contexts where securing stability is paramount. The nature of the emerging settlement, in turn, shapes spending outcomes.

Introduction

In the initial post-independence period after 2002, Timor-Leste was heavily aid-dependent and its leaders had few resources through which to pursue policy aims. Over the subsequent years, an exclusivist political dynamic had developed, regional tensions began to run high, and unrealistic expectations fuelled a growing sense of grievance that culminated in the eruption of violence in 2006.[3] The fiscal expansion since 2007 was financed through sharply rising petroleum revenues and utilised government systems to plan and budget, spend and account for results. Annual capital and development spending peaked around US$555 million in 2011 (World Bank 2014: 1). This contrasts with the annual average of US$55 million in the years prior to 2007, which was mostly donor-funded and managed under donor procedures.

This chapter examines one aspect of this fiscal expansion, namely sub-national capital spending. We view the arrangements for sub-national spending in two ways. In the first part of this chapter, we summarise the findings of a World Bank/Banco Mundial and *Ministério das Finanças*' (Government of Timor-Leste Ministry of Finance) evaluation of how different sub-national spending programs performed in meeting immediate policy objectives: stimulating a domestic contractor sector, creating jobs, building infrastructure, avoiding a relapse of conflict in the near term. We then turn to reflect on how these mechanisms contributed to larger, although closely related, 'strategic' purposes, including the imperative to consolidate a new elite bargain by economically empowering previously disenfranchised social and political constituencies. This spending was more than buying the peace in the short term; it was also about a re-ordering of Timor-Leste's political economy that began with the advent of the Petroleum Fund in 2005, control of which has animated politics ever since (Rees 2013).

---

3 The 2006 crisis was sparked by a group of petitioning soldiers (called the 'petitioners'), predominantly from the country's western districts, who charged their army superiors, who were predominantly easterners drawn from the Resistance armed forces, with discrimination in the national army. The subsequent sacking of nearly 600 petitioners by the government led to widespread unrest and violence.

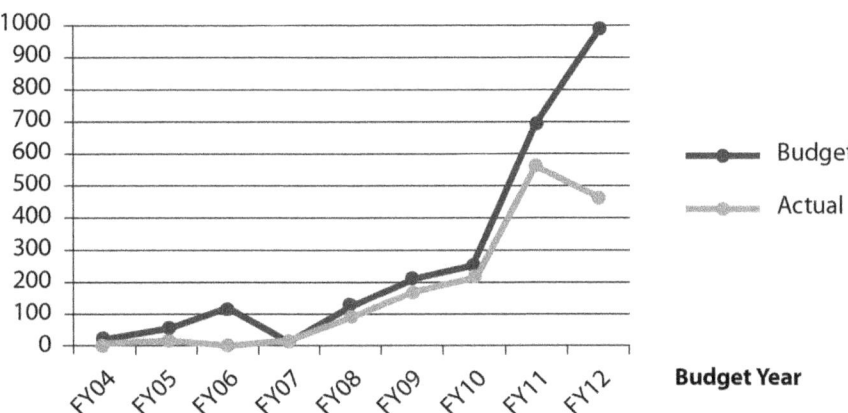

Figure 8.1 Major infrastructure spending FY 2004 – FY 2013 (US$ millions).
Source: World Bank 2014: 1.

Innovations in sub-national spending: the *Pakote Referendum* in brief

The *Pakote Referendum* (Referendum Package), named for the 10-year anniversary of the 1999 independence plebiscite, was announced by Prime Minister Gusmão in a supplementary budget speech in August 2009. In what had been dubbed 'the Year of Infrastructure', the government was struggling to disburse the budget allocation for infrastructure. In August, it reallocated US$70 million of unspent funds to the *Pakote Referendum*. In doing so, it was responding to the demands of an evolving political economy, and the idea of delivering an 'independence dividend' to Timor-Leste's citizenry. The *Pakote Referendum* handled only a modest share of national spending, but it represented a critical effort to address economic, social and political priorities in the aftermath of conflict. Its professed aims were to:

1. create a local entrepreneurial class by capitalising Timorese contractors
2. generate employment
3. deliver quality infrastructure.

These policy priorities were often in tension, and the relative emphasis given to each has shifted over time as the *Pakote Referendum* was refined through subsequent iterations of the *Programa Dezenvolvementu Decentralizado* (PDD; District Development Program). Today they are known as 'PDID projects'.[4]

As a spending modality, the *Pakote Referendum* was risky but innovative. By creating a group known as the *Associação Empresários Construção Civil e Obras Públicas* (AECCOP; Entrepreneurs' Association for Construction and Public Works) at national and district levels, the prime minister embarked on a radical decentralisation of power and authority at direct odds with the logic and prescriptions of 'good governance'. Rather than devolve power to lower level government authorities, the *Pakote Referendum* created market entities and empowered them to handle public expenditure. AECCOP's leadership, closely affiliated with and trusted by senior members of the government, was given responsibility for identifying some 700 small- to medium-sized projects, allocating the funds, awarding projects to their members, and supervising all project implementation. Moreover, during its initial roll-out in 2009, the entire process was not governed by any formal regulations. This bold move was unsurprisingly greeted by a chorus of concerns from the political opposition, civil society and donors about its fiscal sustainability, governance and accountability arrangements. Some donors threatened to pull out of a US$34 million World Bank public financial management reform program, but had yet to grasp that the surge in the country's oil wealth had radically diminished their influence.

The *Pakote Referendum* and its successor programs were part of a suite of measures introduced to respond to the political dynamics following the 2006 crisis. It has been widely acknowledged that Timor-Leste was fortunate in having established a sound architecture for fiscal management in the form of the Petroleum Fund and a reasonably well-defined public financial management system before the surge in oil revenues. Yet these arrangements also placed extraordinary pressure on the minority coalition government—the *Aliança Maioria de Parlamentar* (AMP; Alliance of the Parliamentary Majority)[5]—when it assumed office in August 2007. Unusually for a post-conflict scenario, there were no off-budget rents for government to distribute in pursuit of near-term political and social stability.

---

4   *Planeamento de Dezenvolvimentu Integradu Distritál* (Decree Law for Integrated District Development Planning or PDID) came into effect in January 2012 and now governs a number of different sub-national spending programs.
5   FRETILIN, which had been in government since independence, found itself short of a majority in parliament and unable to secure a majority coalition. Three other parties – *Conselho Nacional de Reconstrução de Timor* (CNRT), *Partido Democrático* (PD) and *Associação Social-Democrata Timorense-Partido Social Democrata* (ASDT-PSD) – formed a majority coalition named the *Aliança da Maioria Parlamentar* (AMP); this was later joined by a further party, *Unidade Nacional Democrática da Resistência Timorense* (UNDERTIM). The durability of this coalition required considerable political and public spending compromises to maintain, many of which were seen in 2008.

Public spending through the existing, but in many respects untested, architecture provided the only means available to stabilise the country and shape the emerging elite bargain—by bringing political opponents and potential spoilers with the capacity to mobilise violence 'into the tent', reward party supporters and allies, and meet the demands for an 'independence' dividend from the broader populace.

Public spending and post-conflict transition— the larger story in Timor-Leste

The 2009 supplementary budget was the government's fifth since August 2007; in rough terms, each of these budgets had doubled the outlays of the one before (Porter and Rab 2010). The government began entering into a wide range of agreements for large infrastructure projects (such as sea and air ports, power and transmission projects, and oil sector equity production arrangements), with the professed aim of increasing annual gross domestic product (GDP) growth beyond 8 per cent and diversifying the economy. To lift the rate of spending, the government opened many new spending lines; more spending powers were delegated to line ministries; and spending increased on goods and services, including subsidies on essential commodities. An expansive social protection scheme was introduced, including universal pensions for the elderly and people with disabilities, conditional cash transfers for school-going children in vulnerable households, support to veterans and survivor families, and ad hoc responses to internal displacement and natural disasters. The *Pakote Referendum* was part of this fiscal expansion.

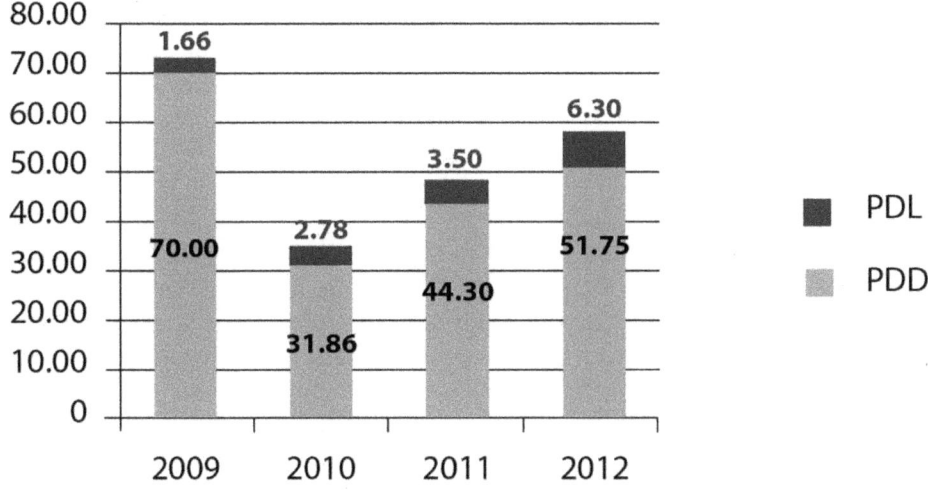

Figure 8.2 PR/PDD and PDL budgets (US$ millions).
Source: World Bank 2014: 4.

Seen through the lens of the post-conflict transitions literature, it could be argued that the government's spending was sending what have been termed 'credible signals of change' to the populace focused on three areas: security (of person and property, but also broader political stability and social order); justice (avoiding egregious exclusion in access to public wealth and economic opportunity); and jobs (a reasonable expectation of a dignified existence and the opportunity to accumulate wealth and assets) (World Bank 2011). The government was signalling that citizens would be protected from the global food and commodity price crisis that emerged in 2008, and they would derive immediate benefits from the surge in oil wealth. Key was the economic empowerment of previously disenfranchised social and political constituencies, including the veterans of the Resistance struggle and their families, disaffected members of the military, and those from western regions of the country who were perceived to be excluded.

Principal among these groups were veterans, particularly those who lived in rural areas, and were not part of the national political or economic discussion. Whether under the Portuguese colonial administration or the Indonesian occupation, the elite bargain was created and held together by a mix of force and incentive. Until 2002, participants in the bargain were few in number. There were few Timorese contractors in the country except for a handful that had collaborated with the Indonesian military, and none at the time with the capacity to execute large-scale contracts. In the post-independence democratic context, the accommodation of the large veterans constituency posed a critical challenge. Until the Petroleum Fund and the surge in oil wealth thereafter, government did not have the means to deal with this fractious and largely impoverished group. The *Pakote Referendum*, among other mechanisms, aimed to economically empower veterans by distributing public contracts to them, thus providing them with a real stake in the new political and economic order that was being constructed and ongoing incentives to participate and co-operate.

The tactical and strategic purposes served by sub-national spending speak to an emerging consensus about what typically occurs in successful transitions out of conflict. Thematically, the World Bank's 2011 survey of experience and scholarship contends that successful regimes need to send 'credible signals' of a break from the past. Longer term legitimacy derives from 'institutional transformation' whereby incentives are created to deliver services inclusively, rather than simply distributing resources to particular actors through forms of patronage that can corrode trust and ultimately exhaust available resources (World Bank 2011). This lens on post-conflict transitions provides one way to frame the challenges faced by the government soon after it came into office. The government had a fragile electoral coalition to consolidate—there was considerable political fluidity, high expectations, and a lively public debate, including through parliament. There was also a palpable threat of instability (Engel and Hanley 2007). Around 150,000 internally displaced people were still in camps close to Dili. While there had been a dramatic economic recovery—8 per cent GDP growth in 2008, after negative 6 per cent GDP growth in 2006—the private sector was stagnating, and private spending was contracting with the onset of the 2008 fuel and commodity crisis. An additional 16,000 youth each year were looking for work and a reasonable expectation about the future. Anecdotal evidence was circulating that poverty and inequality were increasing.[6] There was a sense of injustice among key political constituencies and perceptions of an 'east–west' regional divide. While government had announced a path from 'stabilisation' to 'recovery', its first task was to maintain social order and stability.

In the face of these multiple pressures, the government acted pragmatically. It was not convinced that existing mechanisms to spend public wealth would be able to move quickly enough or enable it to effectively reach key constituencies. This was especially the case with sub-national spending. A mechanism already existed in the form of the donor-supported *Programa Dezenvolvimentu Lokal* (PDL; Local Development Program).[7] The PDL had been initiated in 2004 to respond to a medium-term policy priority of territorial decentralisation. The program was piloted under the aegis of the then *Ministério da Administração Estatal* (MAE; Ministry of State Administration), through building local capacities for administration and political representation, and was subsequently scaled up to all districts.[8] The PDL's approach comprised a system of annual formula-driven allocation of block grants, participatory planning, and competitive procurement. Proposals were generated through consultations at the *suku* (village) level, prioritised by multi-stakeholder groups at subdistrict and district levels, and then implemented under competitive tenders and supervised entirely by subdistrict development committees and district representative assemblies (foreshadowing the potential future role of local government bodies in the form of municipalities). While this local development model had been tested in more than 25 countries,[9] it was, at the time, perceived by government to fall short in several ways. It was believed that PDL's exhaustive participatory planning,

---

6   The issue was not just that one in three Timorese were living in poverty, but the results of the Survey of Living Standards revealed a sharp increase in poverty between 2001 and 2007 (World Bank 2008).
7   It was supported by the UN Capital Development Fund, through funding from the governments of Ireland and Norway.
8   This was not Timor-Leste's first experience in decentralised spending. A prior experience in community-driven development—the Community Empowerment Program (CEP)—had sought to 'strengthen local-level social capital to build institutions that reduce poverty and support inclusive patterns of growth'. As distinct from the citizen–state engagement attempted through the PDL, the CEP favoured community allocation decisions, and was distinct from any government administrative artifice. See further, World Bank Independent Evaluation Group 2006. *Implementation Completion Report Review: East Timor Community and Local Governance Project*.
9   www.uncdf.org/node/325.

competitive tendering and elaborate expenditure controls would hinder the pace of spending and could not be scaled to a national operation as quickly as needed. It was also felt that competitive tendering would favour existing contractors, and weigh against the priority of favouring new entrants, such as the veterans. Finally, it was simply 'too donor driven', when the premium was on electoral claiming through a modality that was distinctively Timorese in conception and operation.

When the *Pakote Referendum* was announced—two years after the AMP Government took office and within a year of attempts on the lives of the prime minister and president—its proponents argued it would have several advantages over the PDL arrangements. It would reduce time and cost, capitalise a new class of contractors, and quickly deliver infrastructure nationwide. The political signalling could not have been clearer, although significant critiques of the *Pakote Referendum*'s efficacy continued. Whereas PDL had a total annual budget at the time of US$3 million, the *Pakote Referendum* was allocated US$70 million in 2009, and nearly US$150 million would be allocated over the next three years in its subsequent iterations.

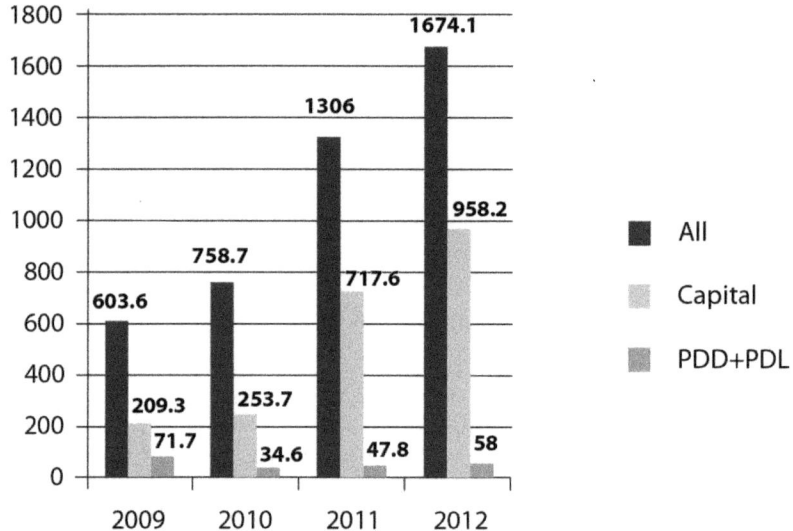

Figure 8.3 PDD and PDL budget compared to public overall and capital spending (US$ millions).
Source: World Bank 2014: 4.

Once the immediate purposes of *Pakote Referendum* had been served, the government made a number of modifications to respond to criticisms about its governance arrangements and efficacy.[10] In 2010, under PDD, new agencies were created at national and sub-national levels (most significantly the *Agencia Nacional do Dezenvolvimento* (National Development Agency)) and refinements were introduced to how projects were planned, and contractors selected and supervised. The *Kommisaun Dezenvolvementu Distrital* (District Development Commission)[11] was made responsible for planning and contracting, and supervising contractor performance. Between 2009 and 2012, the rules governing sub-national spending changed frequently and rapidly—from the radical 'market devolution' of 2009, to a mix of centralised planning and decentralised implementation in 2010 and 2011, to some degree of decentralised planning but a greater degree of central control over implementation in 2012. Over this short period, there has also been a rapid consolidation of several sub-national spending systems under the 2012 *Planeamento de Dezenvolvimentu Integradu Distritál* (PDID; Decree Law for Integrated District Development Planning), the PDL, and a new community-driven development program called the *Programa Nasional Dezenvolvimentu Suku* (PNDS; National Village Development Program). PDID 'defines the rules and regulations applicable on competency, planning, implementation and financing of state projects at the district and sub-district levels'. [12]

---

10   The Head of Parliamentary Committee G, Pedro da Costa of the ruling party, CNRT, was cited in *Suara Timor Lorosae* as saying the referendum projects lack quality and the committee therefore 'has asked the government to establish a system of supervision, monitoring and oversight in order to guarantee good works result'. (*Suara Timor Lorosae* 22/12/2009. Referendum Package Lacks Quality. www.etan.org/et2009/12december/31/22referendum.htm). Earlier, on 18/11/2009, the speaker of the national parliament was quoted in *Jornal Nacional Diario* (quoted in FRETILIN 18/11/2009. Gusmão's Financial Management Questioned from Within. Media release. groups.yahoo.com/group/ETSA/message/9286). The main opposition party, FRETILIN, issued a media release in which the party's Vice President, Arsenio Bano, called the package 'a big disaster' (FRETILIN 27/10/2009. Audit Reveals Gusmão Government's Woeful Financial Management: Action Looms on Referendum Package. Media release. easttimorlegal.blogspot.com/2009/10/fretilin-media-release-audit-reveals.html). The media release of FRETILIN cited all the criticisms of the package from AMP members of parliaments (MPs) and Timorese academics about project quality under the package. A local civil society organisation, *La'o Hamutuk*, states in its 2010 budget submission that *Pakote Referendum* was 'opening up avenues for corruption, waste and poor quality, it prevents proper accountability and sustainability for public works infrastructure projects, which are definitely needed by our people' (*La'o Hamutuk* 18 /11/ 2009. Gusmão's Financial Management Questioned from Within. Media release. groups.yahoo.com/group/ETSA/message/9286).
11   *Kommisaun Dezenvolvementu Distrital* comprised the district administrator, subdistrict administrators, representatives of line ministries at the district, and *suku* chiefs.
12   PDID Decree Law, Art. 1(1).

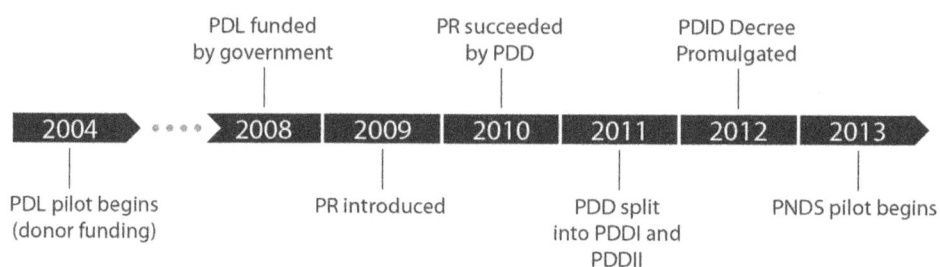

Figure 8.4 Sub-national spending in Timor—a chronology.
Source: World Bank 2014: 7.

The sub-national spending study

The World Bank collaborated with several government ministries in 2012–13 to undertake a comparative evaluation of sub-national spending programs. The prime purpose was to contribute to ongoing efforts to define sub-national spending systems and procedures. It was also intended to speak to political audiences (Timor's parliament and executive, and the donor community) and spark a wider policy and academic discussion about the role of public finance in consolidating elite settlements in the aftermath of violent conflict.

In essence, these policy and academic discourses raise two questions in common. First, in the aftermath of conflict, under what circumstances do elites invest in institutions to order power and what forms do these institutions take? Second, how do these choices to invest in particular forms of institutions impact on the durability, nature and legitimacy of political settlements? Two aspects of these choices appear to be particularly important in determining the scope, depth, and thus durability of a 'successful transition'. One is the ability of elites to impose centralised arrangements to collect and distribute rents (Khan 2010; Slater 2010). Another aspect is the 'ability of central actors and the modalities they use to project authority and distribute resources to places where people live, including them in the settlement by delivering public safety, services, livelihoods and other opportunities' (Craig and Porter 2014). We believe Timor's experience with sub-national spending could be helpful in thinking through these issues.

To address the study's prime purpose, a multidisciplinary team of World Bank staff and consultants and Ministry of Finance officials adopted a 'mixed methods' approach. The team analysed databases on total spending through the PDL and *Pakote Referendum*/PDID mechanisms (2005–13); visited the districts of Baucau, Ermera, Bobonaro and Ainaro (and eight subdistricts); and closely examined a representative range of 22 projects. While chosen to be indicative of the larger picture, the sample for detailed analysis is small, and the results should be approached with due caution. Wide-ranging consultations were held with district and subdistrict administration and line departments, *sukus*, contractors, users of the facilities, non-government organisations (NGOs), and Dili-based government officials. The study provided a comparative analysis of PDD and PDL across five key dimensions:

1. expenditure priorities (rates of budget execution, patterns of spending including links with poverty and geography, achievement of different policy priorities)
2. quality of the assets created (construction standards, durability, 'useability')
3. impact on employment (quantum, quality and equity of opportunity)
4. impact on local contractors and private sector (including short-term and likely medium-term benefits)
5. governance (local stability, disputation, elite capture or inclusivity).

Findings in summary

The full study (World Bank 2014) can only be summarised here. PDL and *Pakote Referendum*/PDD achieved similar results in expenditure priorities and job creation, but diverged considerably on other areas of comparison, such as the quality of infrastructure, the creation of new contractors, and governance-related matters. This is not surprising; each of these mechanisms and the form they took at various times were designed to serve somewhat different priorities. These policy priorities were frequently in tension—at any point in time, one could be ascendant in the minds of policymakers depending on specific political economy considerations.

Table 8.1 Budget execution rates of sub-national as compared to central government investment programs.

	2009	2010	2011	2012
Sub-national programs				
PR/PDD	67%	80%	94%	70%
PDL	93%	103%	98%	99%
Central government				
Government—all capital dev't	85%	86%	81%	46%
Education—capital dev't	n/a	n/a	67%	n/a
Health—capital dev't	n/a	n/a	47%	n/a
Roads—capital dev't	n/a	n/a	27%	n/a

Source: World Bank 2014: 9.

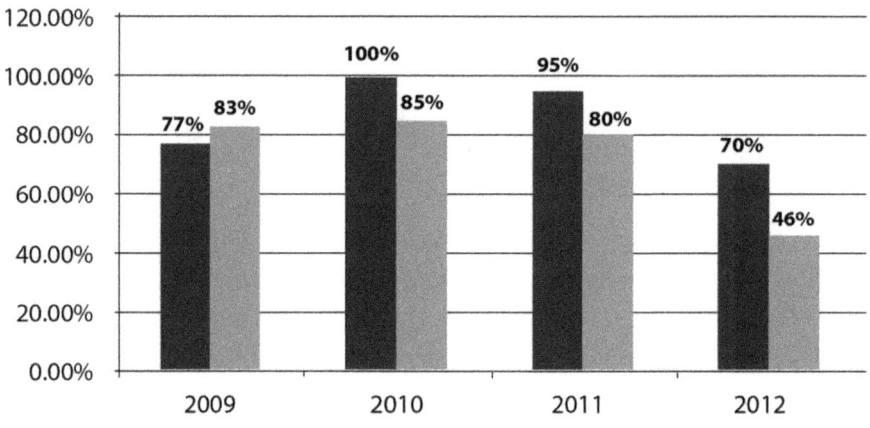

Figure 8.5 Budget execution measures, 2009–12.
Source: World Bank 2014: 10.

Table 8.2: Investment sample—efficiency, quality and useability.

	Total	PDD	PDL
Sample size (n)	19	13	6
Delivery time			
Within year	13	7	6
Extended to next year	3	3	0
Still not completed	3	3	0
Constructed quality			
Acceptable	11	6	5
Barely acceptable	5	4	1
Poor	3	3	0
Useability			
Useable	11	6	5
Partly useable	3	3	0
Not useable	5	4	1

Source: World Bank 2014: 11.

Compared with other government arrangements for capital spending, PDL and PDD both fared very well in terms of *budget execution* and performed considerably better than the rates of execution recorded before 2009—or even now—by most line ministries for infrastructure spending. Spending patterns were broadly (but not entirely) consistent with those for public services prioritised in the government's *Strategic Development Plan* (education, water, health, and agriculture).

Geographical spending equity (measured in terms of dollars spent per capita) under the PDD varied greatly across districts, with the most favoured districts receiving between three to seven times more than the least favoured. No relationship was found between spending patterns and relative need, as captured by poverty head counts—for instance, high per capita allocations were received by Lautem district (with a relatively low poverty rate), whereas low allocations were received by Ainaro (with a relatively high poverty rate).

Table 8.3 PDD allocations per-capita by district (US$ per capita).

Districts	POPN	PR 2009	DDP 2010	DDP I+II 2011	DDP I+II 2012	Total 2011 & 2012
Aileu	45,724	n/a	29	45	63	108
Ainaro	62,407	n/a	24	37	51	88
Baucau	113,748	20	25	18	34	52
Bobonaro	93,787	37	33	29	41	70
Covalima	62,764	51	n/a	63	66	129
Dili	212,469	31	16	24	29	53
Ermera	118,671	15	n/a	12	29	41
Lautem	65,349	33	36	86	45	132
Liquica	69,925	20	31	50	50	99
Manatuto	41,217	57	49	82	87	170
Manufahi	53,995	44	21	40	72	112
Oecusse	67,736	36	23	35	68	103
Viqueque	72,950	40	33	61	75	137
Totals/Means	1,080,742	35	29	39	48	86
Standard Deviation		12.59	8.58	22.17	18.01	36.44
Highest x Lowest		2.90	3.00	7.00	3.00	4.00

Source: World Bank 2014: 12.

As might be anticipated, technical quality and project completion were more robust under PDL than PDD. With the previously mentioned caveats about the small sample size, the quality of PDD investments is mixed: just under half of projects are of acceptable standard and of benefit to users; three exhibit varying degrees of design, construction quality, and usability problems; and four are not usable for the intended purpose without additional investments. A follow-up study of a larger sample was about to commence at the time of writing.

While neither was a specialised labour creation program, the *employment impact* of both PDL and PDD was modest. Compared to the large public works rural investment programs in Asia—such as that established by the National Rural Employment Guarantee Act in India—the share of total investment costs going to unskilled and skilled labour payments under PDD and PDL are low at around

6.5 per cent and 3.5 per cent respectively (specialised labour creation programs range between 50 and 75 per cent). The employment impact depends greatly on the type of infrastructure or investment scheme (for instance, buildings generally employ much less labour than irrigation schemes and erosion protection walls). The programs provided seasonal employment to an estimated 2.5 to 10 per cent of the subdistrict workforce,[13] and it was predominantly the rural underemployed who benefited. Significantly, the benefits were mainly local, and shared widely. For the poorest households, the additional cash injection is a significant proportion of household income.

Discounting the considerable numbers of 'briefcase companies',[14] *Pakote Referendum*/PDD appears to have succeeded in creating a capital base and revenue stream for a *new class of contractors*. The number of registered local contractors has expanded greatly, in the order of a threefold increase since 2009, and a large number of these contractors were each year awarded a PDD contract. However, the fact that contractors were precluded from winning more than one project per year meant there were few opportunities and incentives for contractors to consolidate their businesses and diversify over time. Thus, the expansion in domestic contractor capacity may prove to have been more apparent than real—clearly, a longer time frame and more extensive case analysis would be needed to draw conclusions here.

The *governance dividends* of sub-national spending were mixed. On the one hand, these programs enabled large numbers of Timorese to participate in the allocation of public resources and the production of assets largely in accordance with their priorities. Sub-national spending is best seen as part of a suite of measures the government introduced to support its political, stability and social objectives. Thus, while the way in which these programs enabled government to target important constituencies needed to build stable political settlements should not be underestimated, it would be premature to be conclusive. The *Pakote Referendum*/PDD programs have helped to distribute wealth to rural areas—benefiting a number of constituencies to whom the government wanted to deliver a share of the oil wealth. Nowhere is this more apparent than in the geographical allocations; when the district/per capita allocations are overlaid with a political 'mapping', the pattern of spending is more explicable—an astute use of spending to assuage potential spoilers, broaden political coalitions,

---

13 Extrapolations for FY12 Timorese financial year is the same as their calendar year, suggesting that these programs have created some 1.2 million unskilled and 220,000 skilled workdays respectively. At subdistrict level, this could provide 165 persons with 100 days of employment each, or 740 persons with 25 days each (World Bank 2014: 13).
14 Briefcase companies refer to those that have little by way of capital and no operating site. In the current context, they refer to companies that were awarded contracts and went on to 'on-sell' the contract to contractors with the requisite capacity, taking a percentage of the contract price.

manage dissent in relation to such initiatives as the south coast development, and part of a strategy to win 2012 elections and fracture the unity of the political opposition.

On the other hand, nine out of 13 PDD projects examined closely gave rise to some form of dispute about land, procurement, labour or contractor performance, whereas only one of the six PDL projects gave rise to a dispute (contractor-related). No evidence was found to support the view that sub-national spending mechanisms, compared to centralised spending by line ministries, are vulnerable to 'weak local capacity'. The reasons for variable outcomes are more complex. They lie in the need to frequently modify systems and procedures in response to changing priorities and lessons learned. Several aspects of poor performance may be mitigated in ways anticipated by the PDID Decree Law 2012, including the clarification of assignments of responsibilities (in relation, for instance, to certification and supervision) and by more consistent attention to public communication and accountability arrangements.

The study concluded that, after experimenting with a range of innovative but risky arrangements to deliver public spending and address a series of economic, social and political priorities, the government had largely achieved the initial objectives of *Pakote Referendum*/PDD. It took the decision to 'regularise' the system through the PDID Decree Law 2012 as the point of departure to make several recommendations, including in respect of how budgets are allocated to districts; measures to 'incentivise' better performance; simpler contractor pre-qualification procedures, and competitive tendering to improve contractor performance and create significant cost savings; and reverting to district payments for contractors to break the highly problematic payment bottleneck arising from delays in certification reporting to Dili and in central Treasury payments. Since the study was completed, many of the report's recommendations have been adopted (including competitive tendering and predictable, formula-based budget allocations) or are in the process of being implemented through revisions to the PDID Decree Law. In view of the study's limited sample, government has initiated a further round of analysis of both the quality of assets and the PDID systems and procedures; this will include a study sample of around 200 investment projects.

Broader lessons: institutions for re-ordering power in post-conflict contexts

This chapter has drawn on several empirical sources: new qualitative research; existing data and research on public expenditure (including on the wage bill, large infrastructure spending, an expanded social protection scheme, goods and social services spending); and a broader review of literature. But in drawing wider lessons, it must be noted that the study of sub-national spending on which this chapter draws provides only a thin basis on which to sustain conclusions about how sub-national spending may be transforming the country's political economy.

At face value, Timor-Leste appears to provide a positive example of where domestic elites have used the 'breathing space' given by a peacekeeping operation to forge a locally acceptable settlement that has been sustained hitherto after the departure of foreign troops and police (Akmeemana 2014). The approach that was adopted was politically savvy, targeted at particular constituencies, but also the broader populace. Although the United Nations Integrated Mission in Timor-Leste assumed executive policing responsibilities with one of the largest UN police contingents in the world from 2006 until 2011, the Timorese police force has answered to its own command since 2008 and handled internal threats itself (ICG 2012). In the interplay between a government buoyed by large inflows of petroleum revenues, and a UN mission with a very broad mandate, a settlement with a distinctively East Timorese cast emerged, into which the UN had difficulty in inserting itself (Goldstone 2013: 209–10); but it was one that was locally legitimate, and has thus brought at least near-term stability. A striking characteristic has been the government's ability to reach and 'cater to groups which see it as the focal point for their demands for various forms of recognition (material, political, and symbolic) to which they feel entitled as compensation for losses sustained or services rendered during the struggle for independence and since' (Goldstone 2013: 209). The argument that Timor has moved from a very narrowly based elite bargain in the direction of a more inclusive settlement does not deny that a new economic elite is capturing the bulk of resources in the post-2007 era.

Certainly, the ways in which public spending can be adroitly used to create political capital, pacify populations and consolidate alliances by demonstrating 'commitment credibility' have been well documented, as have the failures to do so and their consequences in the form of violent conflict (Taydas and Peksen 2012; Azam 2001: 435; Burgoon 2006). Recent observers of public spending in Timor-Leste conclude that it 'seems to be enriching elites to a greater degree than before, which is also in line with the expectations of particularist rent distribution associated with clientelist rentier states' (Barma 2014). This may be true, but in respect of the particular case of sub-national spending, this conclusion needs to be nuanced. Certainly, the pace and frequency of changes to sub-national spending arrangements generated confusion and scepticism among officials, local leaders and common citizens. Yet it also provided incentives for certain disaffected groups to co-operate, and thus, while amounting to only 3 per cent of the budget, it has had a much larger political footprint of immediate social and electoral dividends for the incumbent government. It has also arguably underwritten a political assessment that a blend of centralisation and decentralisation offers technically feasible and politically credible ways to consolidate power and project authority to dispersed rural populations, while building upon existing community governance arrangements (which shape social order and collective values for the majority rural population) in order to achieve stability.

Second, the PDD mechanism certainly generated a fair number of localised disputes. This is hardly surprising given the pace of roll-out; the frequent changes in the rules, often year on year; the sheer logistical difficulties of monitoring up to 500 ongoing projects each year; and the fact that local authority figures were largely removed from the process. The comparative evidence from PDL points to the obvious dividends of local participatory processes, of companies prevailing through competitive tendering, and of having local authorities involved— reduced disputes around land, creating incentives for better performance by contractors, and greater local 'ownership' of both process and product.

We would caution against overstating either positive spillover effects of PDD mechanisms, or pessimism that they foster forms of patronage that corrode democratic prospects. The claims that decentralised spending mechanisms are socially generative, including those that invest heavily in popular participation, are routinely overstated and decidedly mixed;[15] there is seldom evidence of positive long-term impact on institutional quality, inclusiveness of decision-making, trust and group formation (Casey et al. 2012; King 2013). On the other hand, the disputes generated by these mechanisms are not necessarily corrosive in the long term, provided that they do not feed larger narratives of grievance and exclusion.[16] Decentralised spending arrangements undoubtedly multiply the number of sites where political contest occurs. But, while these contests might result in small disputes, the overall project that creates local contests about where budget should be spent, by whom and with what expectations can also be a powerful form of political legitimation for the governing regime.

The sub-national spending study—on the basis of limited case examples—did not find that the distribution of benevolent largesse by the state necessarily accentuates existing cleavages. Admittedly, Timor's local landscape is quite different from that in any number of countries emerging from civil war. Social cohesion at the local level is fairly high; local norms generally act as some form of constraint on elite behaviour; and prevalent cultural ideals and

---

15 See King (2013) on the comparative record of community-driven development projects in Afghanistan, Democratic Republic of Congo, Aceh (Indonesia), Liberia and Sierra Leone.
16 Belun's *Conflict Potential Analysis* reports a 'medium level' conflict potential, 'attest(ing) to the gradual stabilisation of the security situation' and, of interest, 'an overall improvement in most indicators describing politically motivated violence' (Belun 2013: 5).

expectations of leadership emphasise community co-operation and have enabled cultural continuity and survival through occupation, hardship, natural disaster, and political upheaval (Brown 2012a: 66; 2012b). Moreover, many of the kinds of conflicts observed around sub-national spending could be ameliorated by measures recommended by the study and appear to have been largely adopted (although their remedial impact is yet to be determined). Further, had it been the case that sub-national spending was projecting political power that was perceived as inequitable, and thus creating cleavages or feeding existing narratives of exclusion, this possibility must be seen against the increased vote achieved by the prime minister's CNRT (*Congresso para a Nacional de Reconstrução de Timor;* National Congress for Timorese Reconstruction*)* party in the 2012 elections—for the first time, it had a higher primary vote than FRETILIN (*Frente Revolucionária de Timor-Leste Independente*; Revolutionary Front for an Independent East Timor)—and commitments by government to further ensconce these arrangements.

While we cannot claim insight into the political strategy of Timor's leaders, it does appear that they are favourably weighing the political and electoral dividends of sub-national spending to date. Since the 2012 PDID Decree, the government has committed a further US$300 million over eight years to a national, village-level spending program in the PNDS, and announced a further, perhaps expanded, round of sub-national spending under revisions to the PDID Decree from 2015. Perhaps more significantly, the Council of Ministers approved the Decree Law on Pre-Deconcentration in August 2013, a new law is being prepared to govern village authorities, and elections for district/municipal assemblies and village councils are anticipated for 2015 and beyond. Looking forward, however, it would be foolhardy for observers to assume that Timor-Leste is set to 'institutionally innovate' along a path toward a liberal form of decentralised government.

Timor's record of fast-tracked, dynamic institutional innovation around sub-national spending mechanisms should interest proponents of 'iterative, adaptive learning' (Andrews 2013). This is instanced by the *Pakote Referendum*'s radical break with convention, the experimentation with hybrid institutional forms, the circling back and forth between decentralised and centralised authority across different elements of the system, through to the routines of administrative rationality suggested by the PDID Decree and the revisions that are currently being drafted. This record also speaks to the conditions under which governing elites will invest in innovative arrangements that break from the past to enhance prospects of regime durability. But, in neither form nor function do these institutional modalities mimic liberal conventions about the desirability of particular models of government at local level.

Conclusion

The current PDID mechanism is a hybrid system that resonates with the broader re-ordering of power in Timor-Leste. It is populist in character, and demonstrably shifts discretion over some aspects of public finance management to lower levels of territorial authority. At the same time, the variable geographically and politically targeted nature of spending points to the salience of a highly centralised political executive (in the form of the annual Budget Review Committee process). It is reliant on capabilities that are alert to and adept in the political art and value in making decisions right down to the project level, on the basis of relationships with local authorities, officials and other targeted constituencies. In light of the experience with *Pakote Referendum*/PDD, the Pre-Deconcentration Decree Law is unlikely to herald a linear trajectory to populist devolution and participatory democracy, but rather its essence will be the extension of the regime's reach into the periphery. With the PNDS also comes the acknowledgement of the *suku* as a point of articulation between locally established governance practices and efforts to render national socio-political order 'legible' from the centre (Brown 2012a: 61).

How do elite choices to invest in particular forms of institutions impact on the durability, nature and legitimacy of political settlements over time? Is the system emerging in Timor-Leste what Terry Karl describes as a 'rentier' system that 'progressively substitutes public spending for statecraft'? (Karl 1997). There might, in closing, be two contending answers to this question. In the specific and narrow terms of the study reported here, one answer may lie in whether political elites follow through on a few key principles—local consultation, competitive procurement, expenditure transparency, and so on—to which they have apparently committed in the PDID Decree. A second, much more speculative response may be found in the wider literature of comparative politics (Slater 2010) and historical institutionalism (Thelen 2004), together with scholarship on the oil curse (for example, Karl 1997; Barma 2014). This might suggest that the flow of oil rents will undermine incentives for elites to coalesce and invest in functional and legitimate public authorities. Among other things, this would mean that follow-through on principles like transparency and competitive procurement might be likely in form, but not in function. Rather, oil will finance what Slater calls a 'provisioning pact', which may be sustained over time; but, over time, the political demands perpetuated by provisioning will exceed available revenue and seriously corrode state capacity (Slater 2010). According to Slater, this trajectory leads to either fragmentation or militarisation (armed groups in control). Such a trajectory might prove to be both crisis-prone as elites battle for control over the prize of oil rents (Tornell and Lane 1999) and, for a time, durable.[17] Durability would rest on two capabilities: patronage through state-sanctioned systems (such as the PDD and PNDS), and coercion to deal with episodic conflict.

The type of system we describe as developing in Timor-Leste faces two key vulnerabilities. Leadership transitions are difficult in systems that are highly dependent on a personalised executive. As with the regimes of Kagame (Rwanda), Museveni (Uganda), and Hun Sen (Cambodia), government since 2007 has been highly dependent on the personalised authority of Prime Minister Gusmão. The first real test of the emerging political settlement and 'mutual dependency' among elites (Phillips 2013) will occur now that the Prime Minister has stepped down. There are clear signals that the transition has been given a great deal of thought. In the 2012 elections, CNRT successfully thwarted FRETILIN's attempts to recapture popular support in the rural base. After the election, it appeared that the FRETILIN leadership, and its Secretary-General Mari Alkatiri in particular, has negotiated a form of 'détente' with then Prime Minister Gusmão. This has been described by some as the beginning of a 'post-political' era in Timorese politics, in which Gusmão and Alkatiri have elected to eschew direct political competition in favour of a form of collaboration, and a consolidation of the patrimonial system (Rees 2013). The second vulnerability is structural: the exhaustion of oil and gas revenues. If the economy does not diversify in the medium term, the country's economic viability will be in question unless new hydrocarbon deposits are found, and may need to be buttressed by significant international interventions—sizeable aid rents along with potential security interventions—in the longer term.

References

Akmeemana, S. 2014. Understanding the Relevance of Political Settlements for the Bank's Work. World Bank blog. blogs.worldbank.org/governance/understanding-relevance-political-settlements-bank-s-work.

Andrews, M. 2013. *The Limits of Institutional Reform in Development: Changing Rules for Realistic Solutions.* Cambridge: Cambridge University Press.

Azam, J.-P. 2001. The Redistributive State and Conflicts in Africa. *Journal of Peace Research* 38(4):429–44.

---

17   Timor-Leste is by no means unique in this scenario. It has become a well-established feature of oil states that while they develop coercive and redistributive capabilities, the general trajectory is both 'crisis prone' and 'durable'. See Peterside et al. (2012).

Barma, N. 2014. The Rentier State at Work: Comparative Experiences of the Resource Curse in East Asia and the Pacific. *Asia and the Pacific Policy Studies*, 257–72.

Belun 2013. Conflict Potential Analysis of Timor-Leste, Trimester XIII: February to May 2013. Dili: Belun.

Brown, M.A. 2012a. Entangled Worlds: Villages and Political Community in Timor-Leste. *Local–Global: Identity, Security, Community* 9:54–71.

Brown, M.A. 2012b. Hybrid Governance and Democratisation: Village Governance in Timor-Leste. *Local–Global: Identity, Security, Community* 11:156–65.

Burgoon, B. 2006. On Welfare and Terror: Social Welfare Policies and Political-Economic Roots of Terrorism. *Journal of Conflict Resolution* 50(2):176–203.

Casey, K., R. Glennerster and E. Miguel 2012. Community-Driven Development in Post-Conflict Sierra Leone. *Quarterly Journal of Economics* 127(4):1755–812.

Craig, D. and D. Porter 2014. Post Conflict Pacts and Inclusive Political Settlements: Institutional Perspectives from Solomon Islands. *Working Paper No. 39, Effective States and Inclusive Development Research Centre*. Manchester: University of Manchester.

Engel, R. and B. Hanley 2007. Timor-Leste On the Brink: A New Way Forward. *FRIDE Comment*. belun.tl/wp-content/uploads/2012/06/TL-Oped.pdf.

Goldstone, A. 2013. Building a State and 'Statebuilding': East Timor and the UN, 1999–2012. In M. Berdal and D. Zaum (eds). *Political Economy of Statebuilding: Power after Peace*. London and New York: Routledge, 209–29.

Hohe, T. 2002. The Clash of Paradigms: International Administration and Local Political Legitimacy in East Timor. *Contemporary Southeast Asia* 4(3):569–89.

ICG (International Crisis Group) 2011. Timor-Leste's Veterans: An Unfinished Struggle. *Asia Briefing* 129. Dili/Jakarta/Brussels: ICG.

ICG 2012. Timor-Leste's Elections: Leaving Behind a Violent Past? *Asia Briefing* 134. Dili/Jakarta/Brussels: ICG.

ICG 2013. Timor-Leste: Stability at what cost? Timor-Leste's Veterans: An Unfinished Struggle. *Asia Briefing* 246. Dili/Jakarta/Brussels: ICG.

Karl, T. 1997. *The Paradox of Plenty: Oil Booms and Petro-States*. Berkeley: University of California Press.

Khan, M.H. 1995. State Failure in Weak States: A Critique of New Institutionalist Explanations. In J. Harriss, J. Hunter and C.M. Lewis. *The New Institutional Economics and Third World Development* London: Routledge, 71–86.

King E. 2013. A Critical Review of Community-Driven Development Programs in Conflict-Affected Contexts. London: UK Aid, Research for Development. r4d.dfid.gov.uk/pdf/outputs/misc_gov/61046-A_Critical_Review_of_CDD_in_Conflict_Affected_Contexts.pdf.

Moore, M. 2004. Revenues, State Formation, and the Quality of Governance in Developing Countries. *International Political Science Review* 25:297–319.

North, D., B. Weingast and J. Wallis 2009. *Violence and Social Orders: A Conceptual Framework for Interpreting Recorded Human History.* Cambridge UK: Cambridge University Press.

OECD 2007. *Principles for Good International Engagement in Fragile States and Situations.* Paris: OECD.

Peterside, S., D. Porter and M. Watts 2012. Rethinking Conflict in the Niger Delta: Understanding Conflict Dynamics, Justice and Security. *Niger Delta: Economies of Violence Working Paper* no.26. Berkeley: Institute of International Studies, University of California. oldweb.geog.berkeley.edu/ProjectsResources/ND%20Website/NigerDelta/WP/Watts_26.pdf.

Phillips, S. 2013. *Political Settlements and State Formation: The Case of Somaliland.* Birmingham, United Kingdom: Developmental Leadership Program, 2013.

Porter, D. and H. Rab 2010. Timor-Leste's Recovery from the 2006 Crisis: Some Lessons. Background paper for *World Development Report 2011: Violence, Conflict and Development.* Washington DC: World Bank, web.worldbank.org/archive/website01306/web/pdf/wdr_2011_case_note_timor_leste.pdf.

Pires, E. 2012. *On the Fragility Assessment in Timor-Leste.* 15 August. Dili. www.mof.gov.tl/on-the-fragility-assessment-in-timor-leste/?lang=en or static1.squarespace.com/static/52117f47e4b01103f3653a0f/t/534f2298e4b0a5b640204290/1397695128390/Timor+Leste+Fragility+Assessment+Report.pdf.

Rees, E. 2013. The Re-ordering of the Political Economy of Timor-Leste. Unpublished manuscript.

Slater, D. 2010. *Ordering Power: Contentious Politics and Authoritarian Leviathans in Southeast Asia.* Cambridge: Cambridge University Press.

Taydas, Z. and D. Peksen 2012. Can States Buy Peace? Social Welfare Spending and Civil Conflicts. *Journal of Peace Research* 49:273–87.

Thelen, K. 2004. *How Institutions Evolve—The Political Economy of Skills in Germany, Britain, the United States, and Japan*. Cambridge: Cambridge University Press.

Tornell, A. and P. Lane 1999. The Voracity Effect. *American Economic Review* 89:22–46.

World Bank 2006. *Implementation Completion Report Review – East Timor Community and Local Governance Project*. Washington DC: World Bank.

World Bank 2008. *Timor-Leste—Poverty in a Young Nation*. Washington DC: World Bank, documents.worldbank.org/curated/en/2008/11/15940689/timor-leste-poverty-young-nation.

World Bank 2011. *World Development Report: Conflict, Security, and Development*. Washington DC: World Bank.

World Bank 2014. *Sub-National Spending in Timor-Leste: Lessons from Experience*. Washington DC: World Bank.

CHAPTER 9

'Empty Land'? The Politics of Land in Timor-Leste

Meabh Cryan

> Our ancestors footsteps are our land, in the past when our ancestors would walk and stop to rest, they would first leave a signal. When they went past a place that had no signal or sign they would place some rocks or plant some trees … If another community wants to use our land for farming or other activities, they must first ask permission because even though the land may seem physically empty it has an owner and eventually we will need to visit it to worship the ancestors, to look for firewood or other things … We use some 'empty land' to bury the dead, when anyone from our clan dies they must be buried on their land … Our land is our body, we will not sell it because if we sold it we would all die.
>
> *Interview with participant from Suku Tutuala (Haburas 2013: 107)*

During the land law consultations of 2009, then minister for justice Sra Lucia Lobato frequently referred to the vast quantities of 'empty land' that needed to be brought under state control in order to drive investment in Timor-Leste. These statements and comments reflect the predominantly top-down, neoliberal paradigm that the Timor-Leste government has adopted in its *Strategic Development Plan 2011–2030* (RDTL 2010). In the government's view of land, there are vast, 'empty' areas of forest, mountain, beach and scrub land that have no owner, and, therefore, can be considered *rai estado* (state land)—a concept in stark contrast to the passage above that underlines the importance of land to local communities. This difference in worldviews cuts to the heart of land politics in Timor-Leste and yet is rarely acknowledged by the political elite and other development actors.

A New Era? Timor-Leste After the UN

Rai mamuk or 'empty land' is one of many such phrases that litter the land rights discourse in Timor-Leste. Language and discourse may seem a strange starting point for a discussion of land rights and land politics, which are often described and defined in more concrete terms. However, in the context of a long legacy of land injustice and displacement in Timor-Leste; the absence of a legal structure for the resolution of land rights; increasing demand for land from the state, domestic and foreign investors, as well as growing urban and peri-urban communities, these seemingly innocent, spatially descriptive words are part of the language of power that individuals, communities and the state tap into in order to influence the validity and existence of land rights in Timor-Leste.

This chapter outlines the politics and exclusion surrounding the 2009 draft transitional land law, which led to an alternative civil society-driven consultation process and eventually to the development of a highly participatory program known as *Matadalan ba Rai* (lit. guide to land). During this process, a team of civil society representatives spoke to communities about their land problems using participatory mechanisms, including village-level community consultation groups, interviews, video, photography, artwork, and storytelling. The large published report speaks to a set of land identities and meanings very different to those put forward by the government and key development actors and donors in Timor-Leste.

Land rights in Timor-Leste: a history

Timor-Leste's vibrant patchwork of customary land rights and uses over 450 years of Portuguese colonisation, layers of displacement and migration, and a violent 24-year occupation by the Indonesian military provide the context for the land issues that the country faces today. Under both the Portuguese and Indonesian regimes, land was taken from traditional owners by force, and through the co-opting of complex local political alliances. By the end of the Portuguese colonial occupation in 1975, 2,843 titles had been issued and land was concentrated in the hands of five principal groups: the Portuguese state; the *mestiço* (mixed race) elite; Timorese *liurai* (traditional chiefs), who had been co-opted by the Portuguese; the Catholic Church; and Chinese traders (Fitzpatrick 2002: 93, 104). During the Indonesian era, some 44,091 titles were issued (Fitzpatrick 2002: 95). Of these, it is estimated that between 10 and 30 per cent of titles were issued corruptly; a further 30 per cent were issued to the 25,000 Indonesian citizens moving to Timor from other provinces of Indonesia under the *Transmigrasi* (Transmigration) program (Fitzpatrick 2002: 66). In 1999, the Indonesia military and militia groups retreated from Timor-Leste, taking with them all land records and destroying over 70 per cent of built infrastructure (CAVR 2006a: 27). Over 68,000 homes were destroyed in the capital city alone (CAVR 2006a: 27).

Land has contributed to, and in many cases escalated, violent conflict in Timor-Leste. Most notably, this occurred during the 2006 crisis, when discontent over housing distribution in the capital, Dili, between groups associated with *lorosa'e* (eastern) and *loromonu* (western) areas of Timor-Leste aggravated the conflict and contributed to extensive property destruction. The haphazard and ad hoc refugee return process post-2006, the failure to deal with urban land ownership issues since independence, as well as a concentration of economic development and opportunities in the capital has further complicated land rights in Dili and beyond.

Significant funding has been poured into efforts to formalise and register land and property rights, most notably three consecutive USAID-funded land law projects costing a total of US$14.5 million. The primary objective of these land law programs was to promote economic development, conflict prevention, economic investment, and the sustainable use of resources. The clearly stated view of these consecutive projects has been that 'a formal property rights system contributes to economic development and facilitates private sector investment in the economy' (*Rede ba Rai* 2013: 23).

Land legislation 1999–2009

Due to the contentious and political nature of land policy decisions, very little was done to regulate land issues during the UNTAET (United Nations Transitional Administration in East Timor) period (1999–2002) other than basic resettlement of internally displaced people and refugees and the minimum amount needed to establish the basis of a functioning administration in Dili and in district capitals. The FRETILIN (*Frente Revolucionária de Timor-Leste Independente*; Revolutionary Front for an Independent East Timor) government's Law No. 1/2003 on The Regulation of State Land provides an expansive definition of state land. It defines all previously designated Portuguese state land and all former Indonesian state land as the property of the Timorese state (irrespective of how it was acquired), and states that all 'abandoned property' should be administered by the Timorese state. While there was almost no consultation on this law during its drafting and approval phases, its implementation has regularly proven contentious. There have been significant objections from communities in Dili and rural areas who feel that their land was wrongly taken from them by previous state action and that they should be provided with some form of compensation from the present government.

Ita Nia Rai and the 2009 draft land law

A third, highly ambitious USAID land law project, branded locally as *Ita Nia Rai* (lit. our land), was launched in 2008. The passage of significant land legislation laying down the basis of all land ownership in Timor-Leste was stated as one of its five core objectives. Other objectives included the establishment of an independent land commission and a national cadastre, and the mapping and registration of over 50,000 land claims.

The program's legal advisor began drafting a policy document in early 2008, which was presented to a drafting committee in September 2008 (Lopes 2008). This document was quickly followed by a draft transitional land law, released for public consultation in June 2009.

Civil society advocates immediately argued that these policy options did not reflect Timorese cultural understandings of land and, given the importance and fundamental nature of land in Timor to identity, spirituality and community life in general, that the law should be based on a broadly consultative land policy. In this respect, they argued that the processes (as well as the outcomes) of drafting land policy were vitally important to resolving land issues in Timor-Leste.

The original Ministry of Justice plan for consultation allowed comments and submissions on the law within a three-month period. After significant lobbying from civil society groups and opposition leaders (most notably Fernanda Borges from *Partidu Unidade Nasional* (National Unity Party)), the ministry agreed that they would hold district-level consultations in each of Timor-Leste's 13 districts. After a significant campaign on the design of this participatory process, further consultations were organised in 27 subdistricts, and the process became one of the most consultative legislative processes in Timor-Leste (aside from the development of the national constitution).

Despite praise, the process turned out to be severely flawed. Copies of the law were handed out on the morning of the consultations but the minister of justice misrepresented the law on multiple occasions, stating that its purpose was to ensure fair distribution of land to all people. Community concerns were dismissed as *beik* (stupid) and rarely, if ever, documented by government officials. The *Rede ba Rai* (Timor-Leste Land Network) and members of a host of national civil society organisations were responsible for the only coherent and public documentation of the process (Wright 2009).

> Although the Minister assured participants that the law would re-distribute land in Timor-Leste, and guaranteed that it would give land to those who currently do not have land rights, many community members left the meeting worried and confused as there are no articles in the law that match the ministers words (Wright 2009).

After some alterations, the law was approved by the Council of Ministers in March 2010. The law lays down the basic principles by which land titles will be recognised and issued in Timor-Leste. This includes a recognition of previous (Portuguese- and Indonesian- era) freehold ownership rights. A complex process of adverse possession is laid down, which is, however, only applicable to those who moved onto land after 31 December 1998. This date is highly significant as it does not allow anyone who began using land during or after the 1999 conflict to formalise their rights. In terms of this chapter, perhaps the most significant element of the law is its broad and wide-ranging definition of state land, which includes all land under state possession, all notional 'empty land' without an identified owner, all properties identified in 2003 by the state as abandoned, and any land that was once used by the Portuguese or Indonesian governments. This effectively creates a presumption in favour of state land that trumps all other claims. A token recognition of community property and community protection zones and a weak protection against eviction for those living in the 'family home' provides only very limited levels of protection *vis à vis* the state.

Perhaps the biggest fear of civil society was that the expansive definition of state land, along with strong powers of expropriation and a top-down, neoliberal state development paradigm, would lead to an erosion of communal and informal rights with little or no due process or adequate compensation.

The *Matadalan ba Rai* project

Aside from the substantive criticisms of various concepts and articles of the transitional land law, a key criticism of the government and USAID drafting process was that there was no overall land policy, and, as a result, it was difficult for communities to understand the core objectives and values of such an important piece of legislation. Civil society consistently urged meaningful consultation to be carried out in order to build consensus on such a fundamental issue. After significant unsuccessful lobbying of the minister for justice and land sector donors, including USAID and the World Bank, civil society actors decided to launch a land consultation process 'of their own'.

> Based on our experiences we [civil society] concluded that the Government and International Agencies working in the land sector are unwilling to hold meaningful consultation with communities about land issues and that they have no will to draft a Land Policy which could help to guide our work throughout this sector. It is because of this that we have organised a separate consultation process (Haburas Foundation 2013: 17).

The consultation process intended firstly to gather a broad sense of the land problems and issues that communities faced on the ground which could be fed in to civil society advocacy work and submissions on the draft land laws, but also to inform civil societies' own work on land issues. The project also hoped to show, contrary to government and donor organisations beliefs, that effective and efficient consultation was possible and could be carried out without unrealistically large budgets and time frames (Haburas Foundation 2013: 18).

A basic consultation process was carried out in 36 *suku* (villages) across seven of Timor-Leste's 13 districts. The consultation process was carried out between April and August 2010, and included a variety of participatory methods to help community groups identify and prioritise key land problems in their respective *suku*. Later, further thematic workshops, interviews and surveys were used to check and add more depth and case study evidence to the data collected during the preliminary consultation process. A total of 1,973 participants were involved in the process.

Land issues identified by community groups were distilled into categories, and the percentage of people selecting these issues as a priority was calculated (see Figure 9.1). The data shows clearly that the largest worry for community groups is fear of a 'state land grab', whereas more localised issues such as 'land conflict between neighbours' were considered a relatively minor issue.

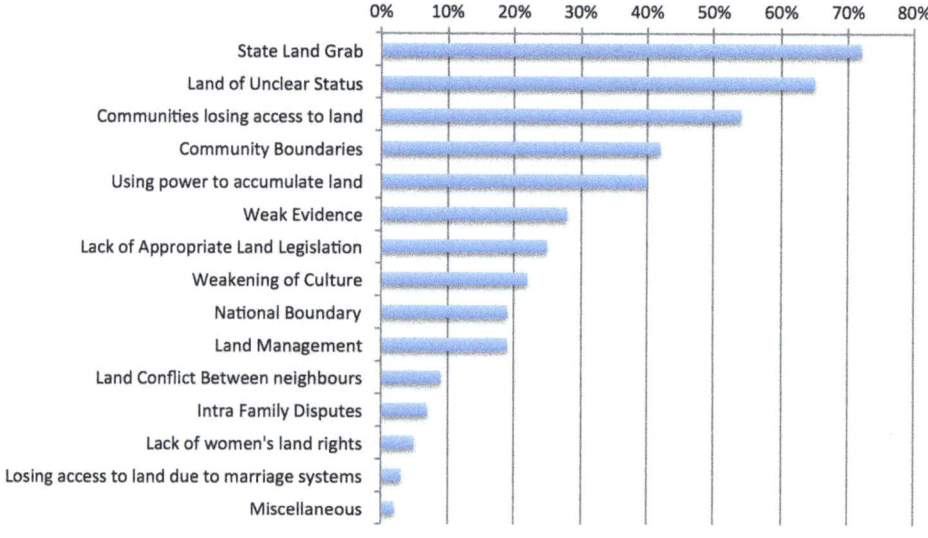

Figure 9.1 Prioritisation of community level land problems.
Source: Haburas Foundation 2013.

Throughout the consultation process, community values and understandings of land came to the fore through narratives, stories, case studies and mapping processes. In writing up the results, 15 separate chapters are dedicated to each of the categories identified above, but three themes recurred throughout the report: the importance of the context and 'social function' of land; the legacy of colonial injustice; and disillusionment with the lack of consultation over land decisions and development processes. All three issues are crucially important to the land rights context in Timor-Leste, but in the remainder of this chapter I will focus on the first to illustrate the extreme divergence between local understandings of the 'social function' of land and government perceptions of its economic value.

Timorese contexts and the social function of land

During the consultation process, an 'imagination and mapping' session was undertaken, where communities described their land and discussed the fundamental question 'what is land?' Discussions and artwork from these sessions shows the multi-layered functions of land. As summarised by the Matadalan report:

> Land is our home, land is where we grow rice and cassava. Land gives us food and a place to open our small stalls. Land is a place to farm and fish and raise animals. Land is a place to get water, to pick firewood and to look for medicine. Land is the basis of our culture because it is here that we see our ancestors footsteps, our sacred stones and our spiritual houses. Land is core to identity, it shows who is our family. Land is a way to share resources and wealth (Haburas Foundation 2013: 35–36).

The drawing below was developed by a community group in Tutuala, Lautem District, in order to illustrate the significance of their land. They show economic areas: a fisherman catching fish to sustain his livelihood, and the food gardens and chickens to the far right. Their land is also an important place for their culture—represented by the sacred symbol *tei* on the far left of the shore. This symbol represents the source of the Tutuala Ratu (clan). They go to the sacrificial altar to pray to the ancestors, to ask for permission to share the land, and to thank the ancestors for the sustenance and strength they derive from the land.

A New Era? Timor-Leste After the UN

Figure 9.2 Explaining the significance of land, Tutuala, Lautem.
Source: Haburas Foundation 2013.

The drawing shows three houses made with traditional materials. A fundamental basis of their identity is the *uma lulik* (spiritual house), which can be seen on the right, and the sacred stones to the far right that mark the *ia mari tulia* (footsteps of the ancestors). This group explained that boats are fundamentally important to their culture and identity because that was how their ancestors first came to these lands. Finally, the group explained that their land was a place of nature, close to the sea, the forest and the mountains, full of wild birds and animals. This explanation and picture is a perfect explanation of the complex layers of function and attachment that land performs at the community level.

During the consultation process, a pilot survey attempting to show how individual households thought about and perceived their land rights was carried out in rural areas. In this survey, instead of asking households whether they owned a particular piece of land, they were asked a number of questions about what activities they could and could not do on a piece of land that they used or had rights to.

Respondents were asked whether they had rights to build a house on their land, farm their land, plant perennial trees, pass on the land as inheritance, build a spiritual house on the land, lease the land to an outsider, or to sell the land.

While the right to farm and build a house are relatively strong 'use' rights, the right to plant perennial trees, pass on land as inheritance, and, particularly, to build a spiritual house on land are traditionally seen as the strongest forms of rights across Timor-Leste. The planting of perennial trees is often described by communities as 'traditional title' because the longevity of trees implies an equally long-term interest in the land.

What can be seen in the data is that many households who perceived themselves as having extremely strong rights (that is, the right to plant perennial trees and the right to pass land on as inheritance) felt that they could not lease land to someone from outside of their community (only 36 per cent agreed they could), and even fewer (17 per cent) felt that they had the right to sell their land.

Conclusion

The *Matadalan ba Rai* report puts together 250 pages of rich case studies and analysis showing and discussing community perceptions of land in Timor-Leste. What emerges is a clear illustration of the importance of the social and spiritual elements of land. The Haburas Foundation team also provides an interesting summary in the report's introduction, stating that land in Timor has many dimensions:

> Land is always linked to people and has many social functions. At Haburas Foundation and Rede ba Rai we follow the principle that land has seven functions: Social, Cultural, Economic, Political Identity, Habitation and Shelter, Ecological and finally as a mechanism for the sharing and distribution of wealth and resources (Haburas Foundation 2013: 35).

This understanding of land rights highlights the disparity between local understandings of land, the government view that 'empty land' is land to be alienated for development, and the donor view that land (once titled) could easily be sold and mortgaged in order to drive investment and economic development.

A fundamental driver and catalyst of this clash of worldviews and understandings of land is the government development paradigm, which prioritises infrastructure and petroleum development with little reference to local values and rights. Over 50 per cent of the 2013 state Budget was spent on infrastructure projects (with only 8.4 per cent and 4.2 per cent on education and health respectively) (*La'o Hamutuk* 2013). The *Strategic Development Plan* clearly echoes the logic and priorities of the land titling programs. Mega projects such as the south coast development plan, urban beautification schemes, and private investments are increasingly driving forced evictions, conflict and disputes between communities and the state.

The *Matadalan ba Rai* project has continued and sparked the creation of Land Defence Groups across eight of Timor-Leste's 13 districts. The program team continues to disseminate information about community land rights, to work against forced evictions, and advocate for more just and consultative land laws as part of the Timor-Leste land rights network. The consultation report acts as a guide and strategic plan for civil society organisation work on land. It was given serious consideration by a number of parliamentarians during the 2011 land law debates and a number of articles were changed during Commission A discussions. The government majority, however, removed any amendments when the law was debated and approved in plenary.

The draft transitional land laws were eventually vetoed by President Ramos-Horta in March 2012, stating (among other reasons) that the laws had been unconsultative and reflected neither Timorese values nor international human rights best practice. While they have been redrafted and approved by the Council of Ministers, it is unclear whether they will be approved by parliament any time soon. Many of the controversial articles remain unchanged, and debate and dissent within parliament seems to have died down. In the absence of any enacted legislation, the land deals, alienation and forced evictions will likely continue unabated. Rather than taking proactive steps to mediate and discuss these divergent worldviews through consultation and constructive policy processes, opposition to even discussing alternative models is becoming entrenched. Top-down economic development that ignores traditional economies, and the spiritual and social realms of communities, remains the dominant worldview amongst the upper echelons of Dili's policy world.

Acknowledgements

I worked as a legal advisor to *Rede ba Rai* (2008–12) and helped to design and implement the *Matadalan ba Rai* consultation process. I would like to acknowledge the fantastic *Matadalan ba Rai* team within the Haburas Foundation and the many communities and individuals who participated with great enthusiasm in the consultation process. Particular thanks to the 37 land rights defenders who carried out this consultation in their various districts and continue to do amazing land rights work in Timor-Leste. Thanks as always to the diverse and vibrant members of the *Rede ba Rai* network in Dili, and, finally, thanks to Ines Martins from *La'o Hamutuk* for all of her work on these issues and for co-presenting this paper at the Timor Update.

References

CAVR (*Comissão de Acolhimento, Verdade e Reconciliação de Timor Leste*; Timor-Leste Commission for Reception, Truth and Reconciliation) 2006. *Chega! The Report of the Commission for Reception Truth and reconciliation in East Timor (CAVR)*. Dili: CAVR, Chapter 7.9.

Fitzpatrick, D. 2002. *Land Claims in East Timor*. Canberra: Asia Pacific Press.

Haburas Foundation 2013. *Communities Voices on Land: The Results of the Matadalan ba Rai Consultation Process*. Dili: Haburas Foundation.

La'o Hamutuk 2013. 2013 General State Budget. www.laohamutuk.org/econ/OGE13/12OGE13.htm.

Lopes, I. 2008. Technical Framework for a Transitional Land Law for East Timor: USAID/ARD Strengthening Property Rights in Timor-Leste. Dili: Ita Nia Rai Project Report. www.mj.gov.tl/files/Policy%20Framework%20for%20a%20Transitional%20Land%20Law%20for%20East%20%20%20%20%20%20%20%20%20%20%20TimorFi3.pdf.

RDTL 2010. *Timor-Leste Strategic Development Plan 2011–2030*. Dili: RDTL.

Rede ba Rai 2013. *Land Registration and Land Justice in Timor-Leste: Culture, Power and Justice*. Dili: Haburas Foundation.

Wright, W. 13/7/2009. Only Brief Thoughts from Baucau Allowed on the New Land Law. Timor Leste Land Studies blog. timorlestelandlaw.blogspot.com.au/2009/07/only-brief-thoughts-from-baucau-allowed.html.

PART THREE
Stability and Peace-building

CHAPTER 10

After Xanana: Challenges for Stability[1]

Cillian Nolan

Introduction

In November 2013, Timor-Leste's Prime Minister Xanana Gusmão announced he would resign before the regular end of the current parliamentary term in 2017. The timing of that resignation remains unclear, but it now looks likely that at the very least he will not run for office again in 2017. When it does happen, it will have important ramifications for political stability. It will mark the beginning of a long-deferred transition of political power from the closed circle of leaders engaged in politics since before the country's 1975 invasion by Indonesian forces. It will also be a key step towards the full demobilisation, in the broadest sense, of the guerrilla independence army that Gusmão effectively commanded from 1981 until 2000.

Since being elected prime minister in August 2007, Gusmão's leadership has been marked by a pragmatic approach to shoring up stability at the expense of deeper institutional development. His election and subsequent decision to merge the defence and security ministries under his own control were instrumental in restoring confidence among many Timorese in the government and its security forces. But by restoring the old military commander as head of government, these steps did little to help develop new leaders or institutions. This is also why Gusmão's resignation will create new pressures from among veterans who

---

1 This paper was written for the 2013 Timor-Leste Update conference held at The Australian National University. It has not been updated to reflect the 2015 resignation of Xanana Gusmão. Please see author's postscript on p.167 regarding this development.

believe their influence may fall once the old FALINTIL (*Forças Armadas da Libertação Nacional de Timor-Leste*; Armed Forces for the National Liberation of East Timor) command and the government are once again made separate.

This chapter examines some of the implications of Gusmão's resignation for stability. First, it looks back at the challenges that have characterised the period since independence, with particular reference to the recurrent, low-grade attacks on the government's legitimacy posed by dissident groups. The chapter argues that because Gusmão, as the former commander of FALINTIL, is both the target and the most effective manager of these challenges, giving him a role outside of government in managing veterans' affairs might help defend the government in the future.

Second, it examines the implications for the country's security sector. Gusmão's unique authority helped temper rivalries within and between the police and the military that could re-emerge after his resignation. A crucial leadership gap remains in the security sector; the search for a successor to an interim police commander appointed from outside the force in 2009 continues, while Gusmão has left himself in charge of the defence and security portfolios he merged in 2007.

The chapter then turns to the political landscape and examines how the path towards Gusmão's resignation was opened by an early 2013 *rapprochement* with his old rival Mari Alkatiri, and greater co-operation between their respective parties, the CNRT (*Congresso Nacional de Reconstrução de Timor;* National Congress for Timorese Reconstruction) and FRETILIN (*Frente Revolucionária de Timor-Leste Independente*; Revolutionary Front for an Independent East Timor). It suggests that a key issue is what the succession will mean for the transition to a younger generation of leaders. None of the candidates who might take over if he steps down in the next two years has the charisma or independent political base to win a future election. Real change will have to wait until the 2017 elections, when many believe that Taur Matan Ruak, the current army chief, is the most likely contender to become prime minister. The FALINTIL–government link would thus continue, but Ruak is a decade younger than Gusmão or Alkatiri and he has shown more interest in grooming a new generation to take over.

Finally, the chapter considers the challenges that will face Gusmão's successor and argues that while the current preference among the leadership may be for a 'consensus' model of governance, more rather than less democratic competition may be the best safeguard of future stability. One challenge will be dealing with potential troublemakers, including dissident veterans, gangs and martial arts groups, and unemployed youth. A second is reducing the capture of resources by the elite that is producing corruption and growing income inequality that itself could become a source of unrest. A third is addressing old social and political cleavages that continue to fester. The broadest challenge will be for Timor-Leste to find a way to emerge from the bind it is now in: that one man's authority is so widely perceived to have been the guarantor of its stability.

Background: a fractured past

Threats to political stability and security in Timor-Leste during its short history as an independent nation have primarily consisted of a series of internal challenges to the legitimacy of the state and its institutions. Within a few years of independence, whatever cross-border threat still existed disappeared as the former militias lost Indonesian support and sanction. Since then, the destabilising influences have been domestic, many of them entailing proxy battles for political influence played out through efforts to control or influence parts of the state's security sector.

One of the root causes behind this volatility lies in the nature of power and influence that developed during the Resistance and how it has been forced to change since independence. The battle for independence was often described as having been fought on three fronts: the armed front, the clandestine front, and the diplomatic front. The latter two included large networks of people active outside Timor—either in other parts of Indonesia, where students and civil servants carried information in and out of Timor and worked with Indonesian pro-democracy movements to strengthen the cause, or outside the region, where members of the diaspora elite lobbied for international attention in New York, Lisbon, Maputo, Sydney, Melbourne, and elsewhere. The dispersed nature of these networks allowed a large number of individuals to develop influence in separate forums. Since independence, that dispersed influence has struggled to fit back into a half-island country of just 1.1 million people.

At home, members of FALINTIL held highly personalised relationships with both their armed subordinates and with members of the clandestine front. These were closed networks of different cells. The central command played an important role in setting overall strategy and co-ordinating efforts, but, at an operational level, the most important relationships were between individual fighters and small groups of followers. These relationships created enduring loyalties that, since independence, have sometimes undermined efforts at institution building (Rees 2004; Hood 2006).

In the early years following independence, a weak security sector provided fertile ground for mobilising old divisions. The most serious problem was how the 2001 demobilisation of the guerrilla army FALINTIL was handled. Some

1,300 ex-combatants were demobilised and enrolled in a reintegration program. Gusmão personally selected 650 fighters to be recruited into the first battalion of the new armed forces; they have since received a regular salary and greater prestige. Meanwhile, the police force—established in 2000 from a mix of 800 Timorese who had formerly served with the Indonesian police and new recruits—struggled in the early years to earn public legitimacy. Those who had served the Indonesian government were often seen as complicit in its crimes, while the rest struggled to learn policing skills.

It was out of the demobilised former FALINTIL, and others who were more loosely associated with the armed front, that many of Timor-Leste's dissident groups were born. They generally share the following characteristics:

- They mobilise support largely in isolated rural populations by drawing on the personal connections and histories of former FALINTIL members.
- They exhibit a parasitic relationship with rural communities, where they collect funds (usually through petty extortion efforts and harassment, and sometimes by raising membership fees or selling uniforms).
- They are protean in nature, tending to strengthen and weaken again over time.
- The divisions between different groups are often unclear, which makes managing them more complex.
- They operate outside the political system, in part because they would likely fare poorly if they entered mainstream politics.

The largest and most consistently active of these groups is the *Conselho Popular pela Defesa da República Democrática de Timor-Leste* (CPD-RDTL; Committee for the Popular Defence of the Democratic Republic of Timor-Leste). The group was established before independence and has been questioning the legitimacy of the state ever since, calling for cancellation of the 2002 constitution and the reconstitution of the security forces. Led by ex-FALINTIL fighter, Ologari Assuwain, who joined Mauk Moruk in the 1984 leadership challenge, it is a mix of a small number of former FALINTIL dissidents and their followers. One of its founding patrons was Abílio Araújo—a man who had headed the FRETILIN External Delegation in the 1980s from his Lisbon home but ultimately switched sides and became one of the Soeharto government's greatest supporters abroad. Since independence, he has been looking for his way back into Timorese politics.

Where these groups have been mobilised to serve the interests of particular political masters, the results have been toxic—both for the development of the security sector and for stability generally. The first interior minister, Rogério Lobato, mobilised various veterans groups onto the streets once it appeared clear he would be passed over for the post of defence minister in the first government (Rees 2004: 51ff).[2] Having proven his capacity to create unrest, he was appointed interior minister, where he set about institutionalising factionalism through the creation of special units with conflicting loyalties, and helped sponsor informal security groups from outside the police, such as a group called *Forças de Base de Apoio* (Resistance Bases), drawn in part from the informal auxiliary support services who had helped FALINTIL.

These brewing tensions came to a head in the 2006 crisis, when a series of complex political tensions crystallised to create destructive disorder in and around the security forces following the dismissal of 591 members of the army known as 'the petitioners'. The crisis led to the collapse of the police command and the death of 31 people, including eight police officers shot by the army. Veterans groups such as Colimau 2000 were mobilised as a way of attacking the legitimacy of the army; the army responded by calling up and arming former FALINTIL members as a reserve force (ISCITL 2006). One legacy of the crisis is that while no one would welcome a return to such violence, many of these informal groups believe that maintaining their access to arms is the only way of thwarting any recurrence.

Tensions within and between the police and the army have largely been kept under wraps since the crisis and the experience of the Joint Command, which saw the police and army working together to flush out the followers of Alfredo Reinado and the remaining faction of the petitioners (Wilson 2009). This is largely because of Gusmão's ability to balance influences within the security forces. By merging the defence and security portfolios and naming himself minister of defence and security, he was able to stave off fears of politicisation.

Challenges for the security sector

Gusmão's resignation as prime minister will also likely prompt the resurfacing of certain tensions within the security services. His personal authority helped dampen tensions within and between the police and the army and reassured a broader public that personal rivalries would not be allowed to fester. But while playing an important role in restoring stability after the 2006 crisis, seven years later the stopgap measure has long been transformed into a significant obstacle to institutional development. The long-deferred appointment of a new police commissioner will be important if the post-crisis reforms are to mean much in the long term. In the army, the appointment of an independent defence minister,

---

2   Lobato had served briefly as defence minister in the FRETILIN administration appointed in 1975, but left the country days before the Indonesian invasion. He spent most of the occupation in Angola and Mozambique.

drawn from outside the ranks of FALINTIL, would be an important step towards marking the independence of government policy from the influence of the former guerrilla army. A key issue for any future defence minister will be how to handle the retirement of former FALINTIL still serving in the army.

The police

The leadership of the police force is an issue that has not been fully resolved since the force's chain of command collapsed during the crisis. In April 2009, the then prosecutor-general, Longuinhos Monteiro, was appointed police commissioner to oversee a two-year transitional period aimed at strengthening the chain of command in the police, including implementation of a new policing law that focused largely on introducing a paramilitary hierarchy and style of discipline. Monteiro, widely seen as a Gusmão loyalist, had few enemies within the force. But pressure has always existed for the appointment of a commissioner drawn from within the institution's ranks. In 2011, Monteiro's term was extended for two years because a number of key reforms, such as the introduction of a new rank structure, were still ongoing. In 2013, his term was extended again, largely because no one from within the institution was seen as a credible replacement. The rank reform has produced a clear field of candidates with the requisite rank, but the concern seems to be that none of them has the authority to prevent the re-emergence of factional tensions.

The reforms that began in 2009 have had a real impact on police professionalism, but there are still areas of serious concern. Increased pay, a more coherent and extensive rank structure, a greater emphasis on discipline, and improved management functions have all contributed to a healthier police institution. The problems include a continued reluctance to improve police accountability, weak investigations, an over-reliance on large-scale special operations (generally featuring military backup), and undisciplined crowd and riot control (ICG 2013). There is still a serious need for improvement.

The army

The army looks in better shape in terms of leadership arrangements, having already experienced a transfer of command in October 2011. That transition followed the resignation of Taur Matan Ruak, who handed over command to his deputy, Lere Annan Timor. Lere is widely seen as somewhat rash of temper and has not always been viewed as politically impartial (he remains a strong FRETILIN supporter). But he is assisted in the job by two well-respected subordinates: Filomeno Paixão, his deputy, who is widely seen as having improved the military's administration; and Falur Rate Laek, the chief of staff.

Two fundamental challenges loom on the horizon. The first is establishing real independent civilian control over defence policy. This cannot be said to fully exist until there is a defence minister drawn from outside FALINTIL. In August 2012, Gusmão proposed Maria Domingas Alves, the former minister of social solidarity, as minister of defence and security. She had developed a strong reputation for management but had no expertise in the portfolio. She would also have been the first woman to hold such a post—something many in the defence forces apparently opposed. Ruak formally rejected the nomination. A second nominee, the head of the intelligence services, was officially approved as minister but never inaugurated; he apparently declined to take up the post believing he did not have Gusmão's real support.

The second challenge will be retiring the ageing contingent of ex-FALINTIL forces who are still serving in the military. The impact of this transition will be more political than operational. Many of the first battalion formed in 2001 are now older than the statutory age of retirement (55); rates of absenteeism among those ranks are understood to be high. Procedurally, their retirement was held up pending the establishment of a civil service statute on retirement, and the legal basis for their retirement (and pensions) has only been in place since 2013. But politically it has also been a sensitive question because it will represent a greater severance of the link between FALINTIL and the state. That is likely to fuel further demands for attention from not just the FALINTIL veterans but also those who have staked their political legitimacy around their ties to veterans. This is one reason why having Gusmão move to lead a forum such as a proposed veterans council could be a key tool for managing tensions.

New configurations of political power

If the question of a leadership transition within the security sector remains a vexed one, the same is true among the country's political leadership. One thing is clear: if Gusmão resigns this year, his successor will not be from the small circle of leaders known in Timor-Leste as the '75 Generation.

The political path to transition has already been opened by a *rapprochement* in early 2013 between Gusmão and his old foe Mari Alkatiri. In February 2013, the two men—whose parties together control 55 of 65 seats in parliament—announced what they called 'a new political arrangement', in which FRETILIN, the sole party in opposition, would play a constructive role on issues of national interest in exchange for a greater role in decision-making. It is likely that the move also involved a consensus on stepping back from leading political roles. It is impossible to imagine Gusmão stepping down if he believed Alkatiri would make another bid for leadership in 2017.

If both men step down, a real transfer of political power from the old guard to a younger generation is possible. But it will likely involve a managed transition—first to a Gusmão protégé to serve out his remaining term, and then to a consensus candidate who many believe will be Taur Matan Ruak.

The old guard

Xanana Gusmão, now 68, and Mari Alkatiri, 64, are the foremost representatives of the '75 Generation—shorthand for the elite that has thus far dominated Timorese politics. After serving as president for five years (2002–07), Gusmão set up CNRT as a vehicle for replacing Alkatiri as prime minister. It is a presidentialist party—established and held together largely as a vehicle for Gusmão—in a parliamentary system. Alkatiri returned in 1999 from exile in Angola and Mozambique, became Secretary-General of FRETILIN—which he had helped found in 1975—and served as the first prime minister from May 2002 until June 2006, when he was forced to step down in the wake of the 2006 crisis. Alkatiri is Secretary-General of the party while Francisco 'Lu Olo' Guterres, a former FALINTIL commander who served largely in non-combat roles, is the party president. José Ramos-Horta, 64, the former president, and Mário Carrascalão, 77, who was governor of Indonesian East Timor from 1983 until 1992, and served briefly as a vice-prime minister from 2009 to 2010, round out the group but have been largely marginalised in recent years following disappointing showings in the 2012 elections.

Discussion of how and when a transition of political power will take place has never been cast as a decision for voters. Instead, it has been framed as an issue for the older generation to determine the 'readiness' of their juniors.

That determination has not been forthcoming, as none has shown much interest in handing over power. A process known as the Maubisse Forum, which began in 2010 with the sponsorship of the Catholic Church, was nominally aimed at discussing the preparation of younger leaders in advance of the 2012 elections. Gusmão, Alkatiri, Lu Olo, Ramos-Horta, and Carrascalão all attended, as did Taur Matan Ruak. It produced few results; an expanded meeting the following year (Maubisse II) pledged only to work towards a peaceful election, with Gusmão suggesting that the younger generation still lacked the authority to lead.

Political parties have not proven effective avenues for the advancement of younger leaders. FRETILIN is widely considered to have the broadest cast of younger, charismatic leaders, many of whom have their own support bases and experience serving as ministers in the first government. But despite their lobbying, there has been little serious discussion of leadership change at party level—a 2011 internal leadership vote was contested only by the incumbents.

CNRT has few obvious potential successors as party chief; the party has staked its electoral appeal so much on the figure of Gusmão himself, and has drawn support from such a disparate range of groups that there are real questions about whether it will survive Gusmão's resignation.

Where younger politicians have risen to important positions, they have struggled to obtain real influence. *Partido Democrático* (Democratic Party) was formed in 2001 in large part to meet the political aspirations of former student activists. Since 2007, the party has tried to get its leader, Fernando 'Lasama' de Araújo, elected as either president or prime minister, but it has been weakened by internal leadership disputes. After Lasama's failure to make it into the second round of presidential polls in April 2012, the party nearly fell apart: his own camp favoured an alliance with FRETILIN and supported Lu Olo in the second round, while others, led by party secretary-general Mariano Sabino, defended an alliance with CNRT. After the election, *Partido Democrático* entered into coalition with CNRT, and Lasama was appointed vice-prime minister. The role has turned out to be largely ceremonial.

The next government

If Gusmão resigns before the 2017 elections, he will choose his own successor. There is no discussion of calling new elections. Under the constitution, the president appoints a person selected by the parties with representation in parliament. FRETILIN—the only other party that could form a coalition government—has made clear that it will not seek to challenge CNRT's 'prerogative', as the party with the most seats (*Tempo Semanal* 2014). Many Timorese commentators have taken to framing the question as who will receive Gusmão's blessing.

This means the next prime minister is most likely to come from within CNRT. There are three leading figures within the party, none of whom has a strong political base independent of Gusmão—one reason why there are questions surrounding the longevity of the party following his retirement. Agio Pereira, the current Minister of State and long-time trusted adviser of Gusmão, is widely considered the forerunner. The other two are Dionísio Babo Soares, the current Minister of Justice and Secretary-General of the party, and Bendito Freitas, the current Minister of Education.

There is, nevertheless, a chance that CNRT could choose to put forward a candidate from outside the party if it were to go into coalition with FRETILIN. The three figures most frequently cited are Rui de Araújo, minister of health in the first post-independence government; Lasama, *Partido Democrático*

President; and Estanislau da Silva, the FRETILIN member of parliament who served briefly as prime minister in 2007 after then Prime Minister Ramos-Horta left office to serve as president.

None of these potential replacements—with the possible exception of Rui Araújo—would herald a real political transition because they do not wield authority independent of Gusmão and are thus unlikely to be re-elected.

Prospects for more lasting change exist following new elections in 2017. Taur Matan Ruak, now President, is the leading contender, although not everyone is convinced he will run. Ruak, who is from Baguia in eastern Baucau subdistrict, was the last FALINTIL senior commander from 1998 to 2001. He then served as Timor-Leste's first armed forces chief from 2001 until his resignation in September 2011 to run for the presidency. He originally struggled to win over voters in the west, but in the second round of the election he beat Lu Olo in every district except Baucau and Viqueque—winning 61 per cent of the overall vote.

Many of Ruak's supporters saw his transition from the military to the presidency as a natural step toward becoming prime minister. His popularity has likely increased since the election. He has made extensive trips to rural communities across the country, promising to act on their concerns in the capital, and positioned himself as the leading constructive critic of government. He has also invested in a core staff of younger advisers who have breathed some new life into the once stuffy presidential staff, indicating he may be more interested in developing future leaders than many of his older counterparts.

If he runs in 2017, Ruak will have to either join an existing party or create his own to enter government. One option would be for him to join CNRT, where he would likely be welcome given that there is no one else strong enough to lead it into an election without Gusmão. He is far less likely to join FRETILIN, but he has generally maintained good relations with the party.

If he establishes a new party, it is likely to draw a considerable number of voters away from existing parties, particularly CNRT (if this happens, the party is unlikely to survive Gusmão's retirement). In any case, he is likely to continue to both attract young voters and promote younger people for party and legislative positions.

Challenges for a successor

Gusmão's successor will face an array of potential security problems, from challenges by armed groups to economic discontent to a possible deepening of old social and political cleavages. None will be new; the difference is that Gusmão will not be in a position to address them.

The main security threats will still be internal. The dissident ex-FALINTIL members and aggrieved veterans have not gone away. Some veterans of the Resistance (a broadly defined constituency) believe they are entitled to a nearly endless stream of benefits, including state pensions, scholarships for their children, preferential access to state contracts, health care abroad and more. It will be in the interest of future governments to decrease these benefits that may have peaked in 2012 at US$109.7 million (or 9 per cent of actual annual state expenditures) but remain a heavy burden on the state.[3] Ruak has become an outspoken critic of the veterans' sense of entitlement and of the poor execution of many small infrastructure projects that they have won through preferential treatment in securing government contracts. Limiting the benefits provided to them, though, will be politically difficult and could cause the kind of mini-rebellion that Mauk Moruk tried to provoke.

A younger generation of spoilers that came to prominence in the 2006 crisis may play a bigger role in the future. It includes a diverse range of army deserters, martial arts groups, and gangs, many of whose members had either joined or co-operated with FALINTIL, in roles such as *estafeta* (messenger) during the last years of the Resistance. They have few political objectives of their own but can be mobilised to support the interests of others. Gusmão's response to the crisis, which saw figures who had played leading roles in the crisis awarded lucrative government contracts, has also arguably established a perverse incentive for causing future trouble.

Timor-Leste's unemployed youth could also be a source of unrest, particularly in a country where nearly 70 per cent of the population is under 30, have limited engagement with the political system established by their elders, and see a small elite benefiting from government contracts and public expenditures projects. Some 95 per cent of the country's revenue is built on oil and gas receipts; a Petroleum Fund established to maximise these earnings has grown to over US$16 billion. The elite that decides how to spend this wealth is small: the finance minister and the natural resources minister are siblings, for example.

---

3   However, see Magalhães in this collection.

Wealth distribution remains markedly uneven, particularly between rural areas and Dili, and is likely growing worse, given that so much of government spending (which makes up the bulk of the non-oil economy) is centred in the capital.

Several old political cleavages that Gusmão succeeded in papering over could also re-emerge. The most important is the old division between former supporters of integration and independence. A significant portion of Gusmão's first and second cabinets were drawn from those who in 1999 had supported continued integration with Indonesia—a strategy that both promoted reconciliation with Indonesia and helped sponsor a boom in investment and construction activities by Indonesian firms. Some Timorese, however, resent that those who once opposed independence are now reaping its benefits. This sentiment is particularly pronounced among members of the army.

A second potential cleavage concerns the favoured position of Portuguese-Timorese *mestiços* (mixed race). A significant portion of Timor-Leste's small political elite is of mixed descent—many born from Portuguese *deportados* sent to its farthest colonial outpost as punishment. Many took part in the Resistance from their exile abroad. No party has publicly tried to mobilise support around the issue, but many admit that quiet resentment exists and that it could grow in the future, particularly if it becomes a proxy for resentment along class lines.

Conclusion

One way or another, the illustrious political career of Xanana Gusmão is drawing to a close. If he does not step down as announced at the end of the year, at the very least it looks clear that he will not run again in 2017. He is one of the few guerrilla leaders who made a successful transition to political leader, and he has been a huge force for stability. Now the reins need to be passed to a new generation. It will not be easy for the country's weak institutions to adapt to a less personalised system of governance, but they will never have the opportunity to develop as long as it remains in place.

The security challenges are daunting, and professionalisation of the security forces remains a work in progress, and needs to be a top priority of a successor. But Gusmão's departure, whenever it takes place, and the replacement of the '75 Generation by younger cadres, should help expand the political elite and make the country less prone to political problems rooted in the feuds and rivalries of the distant past.

The consensus between Gusmão and Mari Alkatiri, if it lasts, is a prerequisite for a workable transition. But it should not come at the expense of open competition between and within the parties—the one pressure most likely to produce a new crop of leaders. The end goal should be a political system that accommodates many voices, grants no special favours to particular groups, including veterans, and does a better job of distributing benefits beyond Dili.

Postscript

On 9 February 2015, more than a year after he publicly announced his intention to resign before the end of his term, Xanana Gusmão stepped down as prime minister. What followed was a negotiated transition of power—just one week later, Rui de Araújo (named by Gusmão in his resignation letter) took over as prime minister, with a slimmed-down cabinet of 34 members. Four others named as possible successors in this essay—leading CNRT figures Agio Pereira and Dionisio Babo, Estanislau da Silva from FRETILIN, and Fernando Lasama de Araújo from *Partido Democrático*—each took on senior roles as ministers of state. The Ministry of Defence and Security was divided into two, with former police commander Longuinhos Monteiro taking over the Ministry of Interior and Cirilo Cristovão the Ministry of Defence. Gusmão himself took on the post of Minister of Planning and Strategic Investment. Araújo's appointment marks an important step in the transition of political power to a younger generation, but the extent to which his tenure leads to a more lasting transformation in Timorese politics will depend in part on how much informal authority Gusmão is willing to cede.

References

Hood, L. 2006. Missed Opportunities: The United Nations, Police Service and Defence Force Development in Timor-Leste, 1999–2004. *Civil Wars* 8(2):143–62.

ICG (International Crisis Group) 2011. Timor-Leste's Veterans: An Unfinished Struggle? Asia Briefing no.129. Dili/Jakarta/Brussels: ICG.

ICG 2013. Timor-Leste: Stability at What Cost? Asia Report no.246. Dili/Jakarta/Brussels: ICG.

ISCITL (Independent Special Commission of Inquiry for Timor-Leste) 2006. Report of the United Nations Independent Special Commission of Inquiry for Timor-Leste. Geneva: ISCITL.

Lusa 6/4/2014. *FRETILIN Explica a Militantes 'Pacto de Regime' com Xanana Gusmão* [Fretilin Explains to its Supporters a 'Regime Pact' with Xanana Gusmão].

Mattoso, J. 2005. *A Dignidade: Konis Santana e a Resistência Timorese* [Dignity: Konis Santana and the Timorese Resistance]. Lisbon:Temas e Debates.

Pinto, C. and M. Jardine 1999. *East Timor's Unfinished Struggle: Inside the Timorese Resistance*. Boston: South End Press.

Rees, E. 2004. Under Pressure: FALINTIL—Forças de Defesa de Timor-Leste, Three Decades of Defence Force Development in Timor Leste, 1975–2004. *DCAF Working Paper* no.139. Geneva: Geneva Centre for the Democratic Control of Armed Forces.

Scambary, J. 2007. Disaffected Groups and Social Movements in East Timor. Unpublished research paper for AusAID.

Tempo Semanal [Tempo Weekly] 31/12/2013. *Horta: Xanana Sai atu Foo Responsabilidade ba foin sa'e ho Remodela V Governu* [Horta: Xanana is Leaving to Pass Responsibility to the Youth through Remodelling the Fifth Government].

Tempo Semanal 27/3/2014. *FRETILIN Respeita CNRT, Sei La Artikula Ba Governu* [FRETILIN to Respect CNRT, Will Not Join Government].

Timor Post 25/6/2012. 'Mai Ita Hamutuk!', Xanana PM Senior ['Let's Be Together!' Xanana as Senior PM].

Wilson, B.V.E. 2009. The Exception Becomes the Norm in Timor-Leste: The Draft National Security Laws and the Continuing Role of the Joint Command. *Issues Paper* 11. Canberra: Centre for International Governance and Justice.

CHAPTER 11

Rethinking Governance and Security in Timor-Leste

Damian Grenfell

Introduction

The social and political turmoil across 2006 to 2008, commonly known as the 'crisis', reverberated through Dili and Timor-Leste, resulting in many deaths and injury, widespread material destruction, and massive internal displacement. With the first fractures emerging from within the newly formed state, an initial split in the military led in turn to a splintering across the security sector, resulting in a massacre of police by the military, attacks on the homes of military leaders and bases, and the arming by ministers of para-militaries and the involvement of parliamentarians in fuelling violence. Rather than being a site of mediation for social conflict, the new state had become a major source of insecurity and societal violence.

Among all the peace-building efforts throughout the crisis, it was striking that one state-led response was a customary-like ceremony held in front of the *Palácio do Governo* (The Government Palace) in December 2006. A generic *uma lulik* (sacred house) was built,[1] and *lia na'in* ('the owners of the word' as interpreters of regulation) from different districts were called upon to enact a *sorumutu* (a ceremonial discussion) to create a binding resolution. Most of the senior political leadership of the country—including those in bitter conflict with one

---

1 The building constructed for the *sorumutu* did not represent any one style; styles vary markedly over the territory.

another—sat together. A *nahe biti*[2] was enacted and there was a sprinkling of coconut juice on a flagpole as a symbol of life.[3] Despite all these elements (or because of them), the event itself had a bizarre quality to it. While attended by the political elite, there appeared very little public engagement and no sense of an outcome, let alone any kind of binding compact between parties. Despite being an event for peace, there was a need for heavily armed security to be present. Moreover, practices important to custom, such as the killing of pigs, needed to be undertaken off-site or substituted for acts that did not offend foreign sensibilities (Braithwaite et al. 2012: 225–28).

The value of reflecting on the event here, then, is not so much directly in terms of what it contributed to peace in and of itself. Rather, the interest here is much more in terms of how this *sorumutu* demonstrated recognition by those at the centre of modern governance that customary social life provided one avenue to shore up the legitimacy of the state. That the event could be seen as 'elite capture' of customary practices still in effect showed a recognition for how important such aspects of social life are to East Timorese society, and, in this sense, serves in this essay as a kind of metaphorical framing for thinking on the challenges of governance and security in a post-conflict and postcolonial state.

On the question of stability, then, this article puts forward two propositions.

The first argument is, perhaps, the more subtle of the two and is made across the chapter as a whole: Timor-Leste security and stability tends to be reproduced or fractured across distinctive patterns of social life, and that modern systems of governance (which are typically seen as central to the reproduction of security) do not exist in some kind of 'perfect isolation' from other forms of social regulation and power.

The second argument is one of analytical frameworks: hybridity has some value when helping adjust analysis for societies who encompass distinctly different sets of social practices (for instance, the customary). However, the constituent parts of the hybrid need to be theorised in order to ensure sound analysis. In doing so, we start to see, for instance, how a hybrid order might become multi-layered rather than implicitly based around two distinct binaries, as is often the case.

In making these two general arguments, there are three sections to this chapter. The first briefly considers the ways in which politics in Timor-Leste is frequently represented as if it is essentially modern in form, rather than taking into consideration a broader definition of politics that encompasses customary

---

2 'The stretching or laying down of the mat as a means to facilitate consensus, or reconciliation' (Babo-Soares 2004: 21).
3 Interview with one of the organisers of the Sorumutu, Dili, 2006.

and traditional systems of power. While there has been increased recognition of the importance of the customary, too often modernity is seen as the exclusive domain for what constitutes politics.

The second section in this chapter argues the value of a term such as 'hybrid political order' as a way of recognising social practices; it means what might otherwise be regarded as 'ungoverned spaces' and drawn into political analysis. These spaces involve different patterns of social regulation, power and authority, as well as playing a vitally important role in terms of the overall sustainability of the polity *per se* (a polity being taken as the broader political community comprised of different social practices). Here, I argue how the constituent parts of the hybrid political order can be theorised; one way of doing so is through the use of ontological categories including the customary, traditional, modern and postmodern.[4] Briefly, what is meant by ontology here is the 'nature of being', of how we understand the world around us in ways that are often based on such deeply grounded assumptions that it can be very challenging to think reflexively about them (time and space for instance). For the moment, though, it is important to note that ontologies are treated as textual devices for analysis—and a product of my own modernity—which, nevertheless, help to understand the relationship between different kinds of practice and meaning-generation.

Building on the prior two sections, the final section of this chapter details what is meant by different ontological categories within my suggested hybrid order model order, and brings the chapter back to why these are important to how we understand questions of governance and security. Such considerations are important, not least because 12 years after formal independence and in the wake of massive efforts to modernise Timor-Leste via local and international efforts, the customary and the traditional remain vital to the social fabric of daily life for many East Timorese. This is not just as a point for academic understanding,

---

[4] This schema is referred to as 'constitutive abstraction' and has been developed particularly by Paul James. See both James, P. 1996. *Nation Formation: Towards a Theory of Abstract Community*. London: Sage; and James 2006. *Globalism, Nationalism, Tribalism: Bringing Theory Back In*, London: Sage. In relation to Timor-Leste, this schema has been applied to understanding the post-independence period in Timor-Leste by Damian Grenfell, see Grenfell, D. and P. James (eds) 2008. *Rethinking Insecurity, War and Violence: Beyond Savage Globalization?* Abingdon: Routledge. One of the challenges of this schema comes with the actual names of its categories. I have used 'customary' here rather than 'tribal' for instance—the problem being that while the 'customary' perhaps suggests a narrower domain, the term 'tribal' has been used in such a pejorative fashion that to employ it here risks distracting from what is actually being argued. Equally, the term 'traditional' can add a layer of confusion, as it is certainly not referring to 'traditional culture' as it might often be used elsewhere. The problem, though, in naming these categories is that the 'modern' is the most accurate, as the term is a product of itself, whereas modernist attempts (such as this one) to name non-modern categories of social being will seem to inevitably jar.

but has relevance to the formation and implementation of modern legal services, democratic forms of governance, as well as administrative systems across various levels of society, resource management, policing, gender programs, and so forth.

Figure 11.1 *Sorumutu*, Dili, 2006.
Source: Damian Grenfell.

'Seeing the modern' in Timor-Leste

From afar, it is easy to conflate the appearance of a country as it is represented on a map with thinking about what life must be like on the ground. As is the norm, Timor-Leste is given a distinct territorial form, a capital, and population. Districts are presented as sub-territories of the national whole, with roads, mountains and place names playing to the same sense of territorial integrity. In CIA Fact Books, Wikipedia and elsewhere, Timor-Leste is categorised in all kinds of ways, including as a democratic country with a constitution, parliament, periodic elections, and a citizenship. For all intents and purposes, Timor-Leste is portrayed only as a modern nation and polity.

This 'seeing the modern' is, to an extent, understandable from a distance. It continues to occur often within Timor-Leste, however, as analysis is made in many different guises (academics, non-government organisations (NGOs), industry and business, government, aid agencies, and so on). In doing so, it is as if an idealised vision of what people think the country should be is presented as if it is already the reality—an imaginary that is brought to life by rendering large parts of social life either negatively, or, almost more powerfully, simply beyond consideration.

To take one example from the most recent elections, the International Republican Institute's (IRI) report *Timor-Leste Parliamentary Elections—July 7, 2012*, covers all the points that one may immediately expect of an election analysis: the objectives of the mission, background, summary of electoral systems, political parties, brief histories, and so forth. On the surface, it all appears fairly innocuous. However, implicitly, the report not only treats politics as narrowly confined to a particular version of modern political systems (constitutional democracy), but there is no sense of how politics outside that system has any significance, even in terms of how they impact on the elections. We are told that 'Timor-Leste is a representative democracy with both the president and parliament directly elected by Timorese citizens' as if that is the full extent of political life (IRI 2013: 13). Measuring the elections against a preconceived form of what democracy should look like, the stated purpose of the study was 'to identify problems, potential issues and areas where efficiency gains could be made to strengthen Timor-Leste's elections framework' (IRI 2013: 7).

Approaches such as this do not recognise the fuller context in which state-building occurs, with one key concern being the potential consequences of measuring democracy via one idealised framework that fails to take into account the diversity of how politics is actually enacted locally. One example from another report by the European Union on the same elections demonstrates such potential limitations:

> The voter register appears to be over-inclusive, especially after the latest updating conducted just before the parliamentary election, and is only sporadically cleansed of deceased people. However, the electoral administration, as well as the political parties and other stakeholders, were comfortable with the inclusiveness of the registration process and did not seem to view the surprisingly large increase in the voting population with concern (EUEOM 2012: 4).

In the first instance, such reports give little sense of the social context for how such decisions might be made. In the report there is a concern that a list does not match reality, and while the 'surprise' might suggest a veiled criticism that a voter registration list had not been 'cleansed of deceased people', it actually shows little sense of why this might be the case. Studies from back in 2002 have shown the importance of ancestors in shaping both leadership in local communities and the potential flow-on effects of engagement with national politics (Hohe 2002: 74), as well as on the voting patterns of the living (Toome et al. 2012: 32–33). It is possible that, in some instances at least, the deceased are expunged only reluctantly, and, in time, from such bureaucratic lists out of respect for how *matebian sira* (souls of the dead) remain central to the lives of the living, and also out of fear of reprisal should the ancestors not be given suitable recognition (Grenfell 2012: 95). Perhaps if there were these kinds of considerations, the nature of the implied critiques may well change.

This chapter does not argue against such a portrayal as found in the above reports *per se*, as there were, of course, elections, and it could be seen as important to measure their success or otherwise within the frameworks from which such systems of governance are conceived. What is being argued, however, is against the way politics is presented as if it is *essentially* modern, and that practices that do not fit the domain of political contestation by political parties are somehow beyond consideration, even where they reverberate upon the broader ability to influence state-building or the political process.

As has been increasingly noted across a range of literature, customary practices remain vitally important when considering the broader condition of Timor-Leste as a 'polity', even with more than a decade of state-building in the territory. For example, the intersection between state and local governance (Cummins 2010; Gusmão 2012; dos Santos and da Silva 2012; Tilman 2012), conflict resolution (McWilliam 2007), the practices of memorialisation (Kent 2011) and reconciliation (Larke 2009), management of natural resources (Palmer 2012), and development practices (Carroll-Bell 2015) all demonstrate the traction that customary life-worlds have.[5]

An important next step then is to develop an analytical framework that ensures that not only is the customary not written out of political consideration, but helps us to understand how these different ontological formations intersect and interweave in ways that rebound on how something such as how systems of modern governance or security can be sustained or undermined.

---

5   This term is originally inspired by Habermas in the sense of shared cultural domains and sets of basic assumptions about the world around us. Pointing to the underpinning dimensions of social life that are in a lived sense taken for granted as 'reality', the concept here is similar to Bourdieu's concept of Habitus, the notion of enduring schema within which practice is situated and socially made sense of.

A hybrid political order

The term 'hybridity' is regularly used in research on conflict and peace, especially in discussions on state-building and security in postcolonial and post-conflict societies (MacGinty 2011; Richmond 2011; Wallis 2012). The term has often been used to identify situations where patterns of governance coexist, inform, contest and intersect with attempts to build a new state, typically with a strong external-international dimension, as discussed below:

> These processes of mutual diffusion lead to a situation of a contradictory and dialectic co-existence of forms of socio-political organization that have their roots in both non-state indigenous societal structures and introduced state structures—hybrid political orders. In hybrid political orders, diverse and competing authority structures, sets of rules, logics of order, and claims to power co-exist, overlap, interact, and intertwine, combining elements of introduced Western models of governance and elements stemming from local indigenous traditions of governance and politics … In this environment, the 'state' has no privileged monopolistic position as the only agency providing security, welfare, and representation; it has to share authority, legitimacy, and capacity with other institutions (Boege et al. 2009: 17).

In the case of Timor-Leste, I will use the term 'customary' rather than indigenous, and 'modern' in place of 'introduced state-structures', so as to begin categorising such social relations in ontological terms. Nevertheless, this quote captures well the key aspects of what is meant here by a 'hybrid political order', particularly that the relationship between ontologies can be marked by sustainable unison, adaptation, as well as contestation. As such, a 'hybrid political order' is a way of speaking on particular polities that comprise differentiated patterns of governance where no one form is clearly in dominance, and assists in correcting the analytical blindness that can occur when sites of conflict are, for instance, rendered 'ungoverned'. As Mallet argues:

> an appreciation of hybrid political orders provides us with a way of: transcending the reductive failed states and ungoverned spaces discourses which so frame much of international politics; locating the often multiple and sometimes invisible governance mechanisms present in post-conflict or 'ungoverned' areas; and understanding their place and role within the broader political community (Mallett 2010: 74).

As discussed, various pieces of research have shown, firstly, the importance of the customary to sociality in Timor-Leste, and, secondly, how different life-worlds sit in relation to each other. This capturing of difference is perhaps less common in policymaking, though can still surface in debates on law as outlined in the following quote referring to the utility of the Law Against Domestic Violence passed by parliament in 2010.

> The current law prohibits customary justice processes from supplanting state justice in resolving domestic violence cases; however, given its prominence in Timorese society, it is a necessary component of a strategy to combat domestic violence. Thus, it is crucial to establish and regulate links between state justice and customary justice systems. While customary justice has weaknesses in the area of domestic violence, it has a role to play if appropriate mechanisms are put into place. A clear and legally established link between the customary justice and formal justice systems would serve to reduce confusion and increase the legitimacy of formal decisions while respecting and reflecting important elements of the Timorese cultural identity (UNDPJSP 2013: viii).

Here, policymakers are being urged to find ways in which two different life-worlds can be brought together to negotiate a complex and pressing social problem. The customary and the modern ('state-law') are being called on to intersect in a way that sustains a process larger than either part, and, in doing so, represents what we are referring to here as a 'hybrid political order'. Some people use 'multiple realities' as a way of acknowledging a simultaneous co-presence of different ways of being (Cummins 2012: 110). Others refer to 'entanglement' so as to speak to 'the co-existence of fundamentally different socio-political cultures and logics of governance' (Brown 2012: 54). Here, the concept of hybridity—and more particularly a 'hybrid political order'—will be drawn upon not dissimilarly, but in a way that allows for a consideration of the condition of the broader polity rather than the more subjective views of people whose lives sit at the intersection of different life-worlds.

To do so, there needs to be considerable care, as terms such as 'hybridity' can be used as labels that result in either concealing more than what they reveal, or worse, in subtle ways inadvertently diminishing the importance and relevance of certain sets of social practices (Grenfell 2014). The use of 'hybridity' here is not necessarily suggesting a syncretic relationship—as in where something new is formed through the amalgamation of two or more existing practices—but rather the holding together of multiple life-worlds or ontological formations in ways that in their sum inform the character of a political community. While it is acknowledged that any society is hybrid in the sense of something generated over time from multiple sources of knowledge and practice, in Timor-Leste it is difficult to identify a dominant life-world within that polity. What remains, however, is a need to be explicit in terms of how we approach the composite parts of such a hybrid order, how they sit in relation to one another, and how such an approach can help us to think about the broader polity.

Social differences and political change

In thinking about what comprises a hybrid order, it is possible that the composite parts could be framed at different levels of analytical abstraction. For instance, at a less abstract level it is possible to draw the practice of *tara bandu* (lit. hanging the law) and NGO peace-building efforts into a form of hybrid relationship (Belun 2013), or the way that different marriage practices are drawn together as part of ceremonial acts (da Silva 2010; Hicks 2012). The emphasis in this article, however, is on establishing a broader model for analysis; it is argued that it is also possible to work at a more abstract level of ontology to frame how we speak of what it is being hybridised.

Briefly, to again give a sense of what I mean by ontology, the term refers to the more basic foundations for how we live. Articles on Timor-Leste are often filled with terms such as 'customary', 'modern', 'traditional' and the like, but if any definitional work is done on them, it tends to only be at the level of practice and often only through empirical explanation. In the process of theorising these ontologies, the customary or the modern are elements of the human condition present in any society, and there are at least four different broad ontological formations that provide a starting place for thinking here: the customary, traditional, modern and postmodern. When treated as analytical categories, each has a distinctive way of comprehending time, space, knowledge and embodiment, and are manifest in practices that are different across exchange, production, communication and organisation. These are analytical categories that help re-engagement with the subject—intellectual devices rather than reified categories.

A key point of difference between each of these categories—customary, traditional, modern and postmodern—is the level of abstraction in terms of social integration. No society comprises any one of these social formations, but it is possible to speak about some societies where one ontological formation is dominant. Timor-Leste is far more ontologically uneven, in that it is more difficult to identify a clearly dominant life-world, hence the relevance of approaching it as a 'hybrid political order'.

To briefly outline the various ontological formations, the modern is taken to be a pattern of social integration demarcated by levels of social abstraction where people are integrated in ways that are highly disembodied (the opposite being face-to-face/embodied extended forms of social integration). All forms of sociality have elements of abstraction to them, as noted by Benedict Anderson at the start of his celebrated treatise on nations. Thus, the argument here is that the modern is distinguished by the way people are held in relation to each other across time and space (to use Anderson's language, the creation of 'imagined communities'). In this regard, the modern is pivotal to the nation, as it is these abstracted means that allow for a commonality to be felt, and for a citizenry to emerge with some sense of connection to one another.

Attempts to modernise Timor-Leste did not only begin in 1999, but it is the extraordinary efforts since that time that are of interest here. As I have said elsewhere (Grenfell 2012), these efforts can be characterised as a lifting of sociality into a modern pattern of social integration in order to sustain the formation of Timor-Leste as a nation. So many of the development projects, infrastructure programs (roads, energy, telecommunications), governance systems, capacity building, and literacy efforts, have been named as part of nation-building and economic advancement, and are driven by the quest for re-calibrating social relations in order to achieve a sustainable modernity.

If we take one mode of practice within a modern ontology, such as organisation, then it is possible, for example, to reflect on state-building practices in the East Timorese context. Under this category, authority is based in constitutions and laws. A prime minister can be removed and a president overthrown. Authority is claimed via the secular and the scientific (rather than the mythological or cosmological) and, in turn, authority tends *increasingly* to be located via those who can claim a particular expertise; bureaucrats, politicians, NGO directors, and even academics become part of a knowledge elite who claim authority based on logic and competency, rather than familial connections or relationship to faith. Again, this is an analytical category, and does not mean, for instance, that the authority of a politician or an NGO director is informed purely at the level of the modern.

The desire for modernity is not just the assumed ontological basis for the acts of many aid agencies and NGOs that have occupied Timor-Leste since independence. For many East Timorese, modernity can be seen as the tangible expression of sovereignty following a war for independence. As such, it is important not to think in terms of the modern as 'outside', and the customary as 'inside', but rather of a far more complex and staggered set of ontological relations that sit in hybrid relation with one another.[6]

The customary is taken as an ontological formation where both subjectively and objectively, social life is framed far more by what we refer to as the face-to-face or 'embodied extended' relations. Social organisation is primarily based in genealogical or affinal ties, where 'kin' is a foundational point for identity and determines one's place in society (McWilliam 2005). Modes of

---

6   In fact, if a modernity was not a significant layer of social life at the time of the Portuguese withdrawal in the early 1970s, it is hard to imagine how a nationalist movement may have succeeded against such extraordinary odds.

communication emphasise the oral (the traditional and the modern moves to print for example), and authority is significantly determined by genealogical relations. Epistemologically, the customary tends to be underpinned by a mythological sense of origin or destiny specific to a grouping of people (destiny shifts in the modern, for instance, to that of the citizenry and the 'birth' and fate of the nation), and the spirit and the human world are often taken to be in coterminous relation.

In terms of Timor-Leste, *lulik* (sacred) and *lisan* or *adat* (custom including the laws that govern the spiritual), or leaders such as *lia na'in* are typical manifestations within a customary ontology, especially in their exclusive application to specific groups and in the connections between the world of the spirits and the living (Marriot 2009: 160). One reason why we can talk about the unevenness of social formations in Timor-Leste is that while some aspects of daily life only hold residually to customary modes of exchange and production (for instance wage labour in urban centres), in a political and ethical sense, the role of *lulik* and *lisan* remains strong. As recognised in the quote on domestic violence above, in many instances customary authority has far greater traction over regulating society than modern forms of authority.

In terms of a hybrid political order, we can then return to the *sorumutu* discussed at the outset. The conference at which this essay was presented acts as a reminder for how the emergent modern state in Timor-Leste remains dependent on alternative ontological formations. It was telling how, at a point of crisis, there was a perceived need to draw on customary forms of leadership (such as the *lia na'in*), lulik practices (the spilling of coconut juice), and through the symbols such as the symbolic use of the chicken, rooster and horns on the roof top of the constructed house). There are many things that could be discussed here, including whether these acts remain customary in such a context. Nevertheless, for the purposes of this essay, what is important is how the state—at a point of crisis—sought to undertake such an act, at least in part as a process of re-legitimising the modern systems of governance. The cultural authority of the *sorumutu* was not only used as part of a way to resolve the intense political competition at the elite level, but also had a nationalising effect at a moment where there was enough concern for the nation's future that the slogan '*Timor ida deit*' (there is just one Timor) became a state-sanctioned mantra.

However, sitting in the background of the *uma lulik*, and on top of the *Palácio do Governo*, were a Christmas tree and star, marking the forthcoming December festivities. The *sorumutu* ceremony itself included priests as the Catholic authority. Albeit briefly articulated here, this suggests a third ontological formation of relevance when thinking on a 'hybrid political order', referred to here as the 'traditional'. In terms of the abstraction of social relations, the 'traditional' speaks to patterns of social integration that are at once more abstracted than the customary, binding people into broader communities via a cosmological order (rather than a secular one as per modernity, or a mythological one as tends to occur in customary society). For instance, authority structures within a traditional ontology tend to be removed from genealogy; the authority of the priest is underpinned by a relationship with a God rather than to ancestors. Hence, and unlike a *lia na'in*, he can be placed into a community from which he has no familial connection (though, and importantly, he is still called 'father'). Epistemologically, and keeping to the relevant example of Catholicism, there is a move from the customary specificity of mythological origin and destiny to a cosmologically based universality of humanity. There is a common fate, and origin and destiny are universalised, even for those who are yet to realise it. In this context, the figure of Christ on a globe reaching out to all of humanity, as it does in front of the Motael Church in Dili, is an impossible claim within customary society, and equally appears an anachronism within modernity (though the universalism remains *sans* faith).[7]

While the point can be made that the Catholic Church is imbued with modernity, and many of the ways in which it has come to organise reflects that, as manifest in aspects of its institutional formation, interventions into community, economic structures and so on. And obviously, even the practices of the most devout Catholics move across different life-worlds. However, at the core of Catholic practice is a belief in God, which is neither customary nor modern in form, and, in turn, is the way in which authority is ultimately prescribed within the Church. The Catholic Church is a tangible example of what is classified here as part of a broader traditional ontology, and as a more abstracted mode of organisation than is typical in customary society.

The argument here, then, is that in Timor-Leste, the hybrid political order is not one based in and around a dichotomised or binary relationship between the customary and the modern, but can actually be analysed around at least three social formations (with the possibility of a postmodern ontology emerging in the consumer-citizenry of Dili and migrants to the capital). Moreover, not only are these not pristine and unchanging categories in and of themselves, but there is a tendency towards the ontological forms drawing each other into a process of reinterpretation and layering (Bovensiepen 2014; Traube 2007). This leads

---

[7] And thus hybridity spans different ontologies, something that we can see in a range or writings including that by McGregor et al. (2012: 1134) when they write that 'Catholic symbols that were placed in sacred spaces, or *lulik*, in an attempt to dispel local beliefs, have been reappropriated to signify the strength of the lulik. Similarly, open-air masses and prayer meetings came to be held on sites of importance to animist belief, such as the 1993 mass on Mount Matebian.' However, given the shortness of space, the concern I have here is that I am creating the sense too strongly that the Catholicism and 'the traditional' are the same thing. Rather, Catholicism is a very relevant example for thinking on Timor-Leste, but in ontological terms is one possible manifestation that occurs with a particular form of abstraction across modes of production, exchange, communication, organisation, and so on.

to constant contradiction and a sense of multiple truths, and the unevenness of social integration can be seen in the multiple meanings found in the most common items of day-to-day life.

Figure 11.2 *Sorumutu* venue, Dili, 2006.
Source: Damian Grenfell.

The concept of a hybrid political order should help us think about locating sustainable practices amidst the intense pressure of social change in Timor-Leste, and to identify why points of tension can emerge in society. Conflict can be caused, for instance, as an attempt to change the social order in Timor-Leste that fails to account for how meaning is reproduced for many people. To return to the crisis discussed at the beginning of this essay (and questions of stability more generally), one way of explaining why some aspects of the violence of that time occurred is that as customary and traditional forms of authority were being supplanted through the institutional formation of a modern state, the societal traction of newer forms of authority was not extensive enough to contain different points of tension. One form of organisation and authority was being displaced while another was yet to form to the extent necessary to replace it. Hence, from this view, the crisis was, in many respects, underpinned by how state-building in the territory had been approached; the process had created fissures for contestation in between the systems of governance that were being constructed, and those that already existed (Grenfell 2008).

In a different way, though, the concept of a hybrid order should also work to alert us to the need to broaden modernist assumptions, both at an ideological level and in daily practice, and it is possible to see how limited the reports on elections discussed earlier are. By way of example, if one thinks of the lack of state integration in many of the rural communities in Timor-Leste,[8] the limited access to policing and government services does not mean that these communities are unsustainable. *Adat* and the Catholic faith remain the normative and regulatory basis for social life—in many respects providing for the resolution of conflict, distribution of resources, as well as the basis for shared identity. In doing so, articulations of customary and traditional social life have, in effect, underpinned the development of the modern state. If such forms of social regulation were not as pronounced or strong, one can imagine that attempts at forging a new state would have been an even more riven affair than it has been to date. The simple resources required to govern at that level and in a uniform way in the post-independence period would have likely been too significant a strain on a state still in formation.[9] The irony of this is that while the state has been reliant on particularly customary systems of governance in order to ensure its development, the modernist prophecy is one where the state becomes the dominant system, with other forms either subjugated or made peripheral.

Conclusion

In order to conclude, I will provide a brief précis of the essay. The main argument has comprised two parts: the first linking stability to governance and security, and arguing that in a polity such as Timor-Leste, both sustainability and conflict are imbricated in the uneven ontological layering of that society. The second argument, as a consequence of the first, has been more a question of approach—one that argues for taking the different ontologies of Timor-Leste into analytical consideration when speaking about major political processes (such as state-building or elections, and to other domains such as security provision, development practices, gender, and so on). The concept of a 'hybrid political order' is helpful, not just in terms of describing the character of polity as it has emerged in an independent Timor-Leste, but also as a way for researchers

---

8   While it can be argued that the state penetrates into all communities via authority structures such as the village chiefs, such positions very often remain primarily connected to the *suku* itself (and informed by alternative authority structures) and in a formal sense remain ambiguous in terms of being formally part of the state. While schools and health clinics can be other manifestations of state penetration, in many rural communities such services remain extremely limited and overall the sense of the state is minimal.

9   Joanne Wallis and others write how the hybrid political order in Timor-Leste is demonstrated by the Government's attempt to govern the state by engaging with and utilising local socio-political practices. This is largely based on a pragmatic recognition of not having the reach or resources to provide for much of the Timorese population (Wallis 2012: 758).

to be thinking and aware of how complex patterns of sociality sit in relation to one another. Moreover, this hybrid order allows for a proper recognition of how the modern features as part of East Timorese society *as one layer of social life*, avoiding any implication or assumption that the outsider (essentially the foreign intervener) represents the modern while the local Timorese somehow represents the customary. Moreover, I have argued that in Timor-Leste the composite parts of the hybrid political order should be expanded so as to include an intermediary category of the traditional, and that this, along with the customary, remain of great social importance in Timor-Leste, not only in rural villages and locations far from the centre, but also for the ways they effect the character and sustainability of modern systems of governance in the territory.

References

Asia Foundation 2013. *Timor-Leste Law and Justice Survey 2013*. Dili: The Asia Foundation.

Babo-Soares, D. 2004. *Nahe Biti:* The Philosophy and Process of Grassroots Reconciliation (and Justice) in East Timor. *The Asia Pacific Journal of Anthropology* 5(1):15–33.

Belun 2013. *The Effective Use of Tara Bandu to Prevent Conflict in Timor-Leste*, Belun, Dili.

Boavida dos Santos, A. and E. da Silva 2012. Introduction of a Modern Democratic System and its Impact on Societies in East Timorese Traditional Culture. *Local Global: Traversing Customary Community and Modern Nation Formation in Timor-Leste* 11:206–20.

Boege, V., A. Brown and K.P. Clements 2009. Hybrid Political Orders, Not Fragile States. *Peace Review* 21(1):13–21.

Bovensiepen, J. 2014. Installing the Insider 'Outside': House Reconstruction and the Transformation of Binary Ideology in Independent Timor-Leste. *American Ethnologist* 41(2):290–304.

Braithwaite, J., H. Charlesworth and A. Soares 2012. *Networked Governance of Freedom and Tyranny: Peace in Timor-Leste*. Canberra: ANU E Press.

Brown, A.M. 2012, Entangled Worlds: Villages and Political Community in Timor-Leste. *Local Global* 11:54–71.

Carroll-Bell, S. 2015, Development Alternatives in Timor-Leste: Recasting Modes for Local Engagement, *Bijdragen tot de Taal-, Land- en Volkenkunde* (Journal of the Humanities and Social Sciences of Southeast Asia) 171(2-3), forthcoming.

Cummins, D. 2010. Democracy or Democrazy? Local Experiences of Democratization in Timor-Leste. *Democratization* 17(5):899–919.

Cummins, D. 2012. Multiple Realities: The Need to Re-Think Institutional Theory, *Local Global* 11:110–122.

Cummins, D. and M. Leach 2012. Democracy Old and New: The Interaction of Modern and Traditional Authority in East Timorese Local Government. *Asian Politics & Policy* 4(1):89–104.

da Silva, K. 2010. *Foho* versus Dili: The Political Role of Place in East Timor. In P.C. Seixas (ed.). *Translation, Society and Politics in Timor-Leste*. Porto: Universidade Fernando Pessoa.

Dale, P., K. Himelein, D. Nikitin, A. Bexley and G. Moniz da Silva 2010. *Trust, Authority and Decision Making: Findings from the Extended Timor-Leste Survey of Living Standards*. Dili: World Bank.

EUEOM (European Union Election Observation Mission) 2012. *Final Report: Parliamentary Election 2012*. Brussels: European Union.

Grenfell, D. 2008. Reconciliation: Violence and Nation Formation in Timor-Leste. In D. Grenfell and P. James (eds). *Rethinking Insecurity, War and Violence: Beyond Savage Globalization*. London: Routledge.

Grenfell, D. 2012. Remembering the Dead from the Customary to the Modern in Timor-Leste', *Local Global* 11:86–108.

Grenfell, D. 2014. Diversity and the Discourses of Security and Interventions. *Sage Handbook on Globalization*. London: Sage.

Gusmão, A. 2012. Electing Community Leaders: Diversity in Uniformity. *Local Global* 11:180–191.

Hicks, D. 2012. Compatibility, Resilience and Adaptation: the *Barlake* of Timor-Leste. *Local Global* 11:124–37.

Hohe, T. 2002. Totem Polls: Indigenous Concepts and 'Free and Fair' Elections in East Timor. *International Peacekeeping* 9(4):69–88.

IRI (International Republican Institute) 2013. *Timor-Leste Parliamentary Elections July 7 2012*. Washington DC: International Republican Institute.

James, P. 1996. *Nation Formation: Towards a Theory of Abstract Community*. London: Sage.

James, P. 2006. *Globalism, Nationalism, Tribalism: Bringing Theory Back In*. London: Sage.

Kent, L. 2011. Local Memory Practices in East Timor: Disrupting Transitional Justice Narratives. *The International Journal of Transitional Justice* 5:434–55.

Larke, B. 2009. '… And the Truth Shall Set You Free': Confessional Trade-Offs and Community Reconciliation in East Timor. *Asian Journal of Social Science* 37:646–76.

MacGinty, R. 2011. *International Peacebuilding and Local Resistance: Hybrid Forms of Peace*, Hampshire: Palgrave Macmillan.

Mallet, A. 2010. Beyond Failed States and Ungoverned Spaces: Hybrid Political Orders in the Post-Conflict Landscape. *eSharp: Uniting Nations: Risks and Opportunities* 15:65–91. www.gla.ac.uk/esharp, viewed 15/5/2015.

Marriot, A. 2010. Leaders, Lawyers & *Lian Nains:* Sources of Legal Authority In Timor-Leste. In M. Leach, N.C. Mendes, A.B. da Silva, A. da Cota Ximenes and Bob Boughton (eds). *Proceedings of the Understanding Timor-Leste Conference 2009*. Melbourne: Swinburne Press.

McGregor, A., L. Skeaff and M. Bevan 2012. Overcoming Secularism? Catholic Development Geographies in Timor-Leste. *Third World Quarterly* 33(6):1129–146.

McWilliam, A. 2005. Houses of Resistance in East Timor: Structuring Sociality in the New Nation. *Anthropological Forum* 15(1):27–44.

McWilliam, A. 2007. Restorative custom: Ethnographic Perspectives on Conflict and Local Justice in Timor. *The Asia Pacific Journal of Anthropology* 8(1):1–8.

Palmer, L. 2012. Water relations: Customary Systems and the Management of Bacau City's Water. In A. William and E.G. Traube (eds). *Land and Life in Timor-Leste: Ethnographic Essays*. Canberra: ANU E Press.

Richmond, O.P. 2010. Post-Colonial Hybridity and the Return of Human Security. In D. Chandler and N. Hynek (eds). *Critical Perspectives on Human Security: Rethinking Emancipation and Power in International Relations*. Abingdon: Routledge.

Siapno, J. 2012. Dance and Martial Arts in Timor-Leste: the Performance of Resilience in a Post-Conflict Environment. *Journal of Intercultural Studies* 33(4):427–43.

Tilman, M. 2012. Customary Social Order and Authority in the Contemporary East Timorese Village: Persistence and Transformation. *Local Global* 11:192–205.

Toome, E., D. Grenfell and K. Higgins 2012. *Local perspectives on political decision-making in Timor-Leste: A short report on the 2007 Presidential and Parliamentary Elections in Dili and Venilale*. Melbourne: Globalism Research Centre, RMIT.

Traube, E.G. 2007. Unpaid Wages: Local Narratives and the Imagination of the Nation. *The Asia Pacific Journal of Anthropology* 8(1):9–25.

UNDPJSP (United Nations Development Programme Justice System Programme 2013. *Breaking The Cycle of Domestic Violence in Timor-Leste: Access to Justice Options, Barriers, and Decision Making Processes in the Context of Legal Pluralism*. Dili: UNDP.

Wallis, J. 2012. A Liberal-Local Hybrid Peace Project in Action? the Increasing Engagement Between the Local and Liberal in Timor-Leste. *Review of International Studies* 38(4):735–61.

CHAPTER 12

Building Social Cohesion from Below: Learning from the *Laletek* (Bridge) Project 2010–12

Catharina Maria

Introduction

By the end of 2009, most people in Timor-Leste who were internally displaced by the 2006–07 violence had returned to their communities. Nonetheless, many unresolved grievances remained, suggesting that genuine reintegration had not automatically taken place. Multiple small-scale conflicts continued to afflict a number of communities in and around Dili. In response, Catholic Relief Services and the Diocesan Justice and Peace Commission of Dili implemented the *Laletek* (Bridge) Project, a two-year peace-building initiative aimed at rebuilding social cohesion. The project adopted a multi-pronged, evidence-based approach that encouraged opposing groups to learn about one another's experiences, focusing on what connected them, and supported them to collaborate on issues of mutual interest. This chapter reflects on some of the lessons learned from the project. It identifies a number of challenges as well as the tools and preconditions necessary for successful and sustainable peace-building in the complex urban environment of Dili.

Background

While Timor-Leste is often called a 'post-conflict' country, those involved in peace-building work understand that as human beings we cannot avoid conflicts—it is a fact of life. As individuals and groups we deal with conflicts many times each day as we negotiate our different needs, expectations and interests (Caritas Training Manual 2006: 58). Conflict is not necessarily a bad thing as long as it is not expressed through violence. It is through conflict that unjust relationships and structures are often challenged. Conversely, the absence of war or violent conflict does not necessarily mean that there is 'peace'. Rather than labelling Timor-Leste as a post-conflict country, it may be more appropriate to consider it a 'post-war' country that has recently emerged from 25 years of brutal Indonesian military rule. This experience of war and occupation may have contributed to a sense in which, for many Timorese, violence continues to be understood as a legitimate means of resolving conflicts. For the first 10 years after the 1999 Referendum, Timor-Leste experienced numerous violent incidents where grievances were expressed through the burning of houses and attacks upon those perceived as the enemies. This crisis peaked in 2006–07 when over 150,000 people left their homes (ICG 2008: 2), mostly in the capital of Dili, to seek refuge in churches or other public spaces.

After successful parliamentary and presidential elections were held in 2007, the Fourth Constitutional Government of Timor-Leste designed a comprehensive National Recovery Strategy (NRS) that was launched on 19 December 2007 and chaired by the vice prime minister. The NRS consisted of five interlinked pillars—housing, stability, socioeconomic development, trust building, and social protection—to encourage and facilitate internally displaced people (IDP) to return to their homes. The process was co-ordinated by the government, involving the local government, community leaders, various international and local non-government organisations (NGOs), religious leaders, bilateral and multilateral donors, and United Nations agencies. From the time of the launch of the NRS to the closing of the last big IDP camp in Metinaro at the end of July 2009, there was regular and effective co-ordination and division of responsibilities.

Despite the success of the program, the repatriation of IDPs to their homes occurred very swiftly. This did not allow for meaningful processes of reintegration to take place between IDPs and their local communities either before or after their repatriation. To strengthen the Trust Building Pillar (*Hamutuk Hari'i Konfiasa*) of the NRS, the Catholic Relief Services (CRS) and the Diocesan Justice and Peace Commission (DJPC) of Dili designed and implemented the *Laletek* (Bridge) Project.

Design of the *Laletek* Project

The *Laletek* Project was implemented from 15 March 2010 to 14 March 2012. It was designed to achieve the goal of social cohesion by bridging divides between adversary groups while at the same time empowering community members to engage with decision-makers to access services and participate in decision-making processes.

At the time of the project's development, the CRS Team was supporting government efforts to ensure that IDP's could be reintegrated safely back into their communities and live in safe and dignified conditions. The DJPC was also actively engaged in a number of Dili-based communities through its youth engagement and human rights program. Utilising CRS and DJPC's in-depth knowledge about the different communities in Dili, consultations were conducted with the *Ministério da Solidariedade Social* (MSS; Ministry of Social Solidarity), civil society organisations working in peace-building and/or in the capital, as well as government officials and community leaders at the subdistrict and village levels in order to avoid duplication, ensure complementarity of approaches, and leverage resources. Twenty-two conflict-prone *aldeia* (hamlet/sub-villages) in six *suku* (villages)—Becora, Camea, Mascarinhas, Bidau Santa Ana, Fatuhada and Comoro—were selected as the target areas of the *Laletek* Project based on incidents of past, current and ongoing violent conflict.[1] These 22 *aldeia* also had a high number of 'spoilers' who exhibited tendencies to engage in communal conflict and prevent, or actively sabotage, local development efforts.

---

1   Bairo Pite and Vila Verde were also identified during the assessment but were not selected as other organisations, including BELUN and CARE International, were working in those areas.

Figure 12.1 Liliana Amaral, *Lalatek* Technical Advisor, leading a mapping exercise in Fatuhada.
Source: CRS Timor-Leste.

Baseline study

The next phase of project development involved conducting a baseline study.[2] A thorough baseline study was conducted in the six target *suku* using participatory rural appraisal techniques.[3] Twenty local facilitators were trained to conduct 23 focus group discussions and 30 key informant interviews with a total of 267 respondents, 42 per cent of whom were women. Baseline studies were not common practice in peace-building projects in Timor-Leste at this time. CRS was of the view that this lack of in-depth analysis had led to the creation of generic projects that risked targeting the wrong people. The generic nature of these projects also made it hard to measure impacts that could be attributed to project interventions.

---

2   The baseline study was conducted after the Office for Conflict Mitigation and Management of the United States Agency for International Development had agreed to fund the *Laletek* Project to the order of US$600,000, and an additional US$84,000 was provided from CRS.
3   The baseline study utilised a participatory rural appraisal (PRA) methodology. In this approach data was gathered from and analysed by community members using diagrammatic tools. The data was then verified by sharing the research findings with community members, who then helped formulate an activity plan for the duration of the project. Semi-structured interviews, FGDs, Venn diagrams, timeline and community mapping were among the main tools selected for this PRA, which focused on collecting conflict- and development-related data and stories of the most significant change (MSC).

The baseline study found that 42 per cent of a total of 192 respondents from the six *suku* had experienced violence in the last six months, 10 per cent of respondents had experienced violence directly in 2010, while 32 per cent knew someone who had experienced it. The Becora, Comoro and Fatuhada percentages were quite high at 56–67 per cent. Camea also had a rate of violence, at 41 per cent, while the other two villages, Bidau Santa Ana and Mascarenhas, stood at 27 per cent and 13 per cent respectively. The types of violence experienced or witnessed included physical and verbal abuse within households and schools, stone throwing and fighting using sharp objects between different youth groups, mostly members of martial arts groups.

The baseline study also found that only 55 per cent of respondents believed that groups within their *aldeia* had developed better relationships with each other since 2007. However, there were still tensions in the community. For example, IDPs had yet to be completely accepted back into the community, especially in Becora, Camea and Mascarenhas; two to three fights per week occurred between martial arts groups in Comoro and Fatuhada, and there were tensions between newly elected community leaders and former leaders in Bidau Santa Ana.

Furthermore, 35 per cent of the respondents said that conflicts could be resolved at the local level depending on the nature and the scale of the conflict, while conflicts involving large numbers of people or those that involved the killing or serious injury of someone needed to involve the police, MSS Dialogue Team, and the justice system. The baseline data also showed that most infrastructure projects implemented at the village level by institutions such as the International Organization for Migration (IOM), the United Nations Development Programme, and directly by the government (such as the MSS for the disaster response and *Ministério das Obras Publicas* (Ministry of Public Works) for road, water and sanitation) were planned in consultation with local leaders in order to identify needs. However, the implementation of the projects was contracted out and did not involve the local population and leaders.

How the baseline informed the strategies

The baseline study provided *Laletek* Project staff with a good understanding of the variety of different conflicts taking place in each *suku/aldeia*, and the frequency with which violent incidences occurred, their locations and the actors involved—whether individuals or groups. It also provided information about the local actors involved in peace-building and existing conflict resolution mechanisms. This exercise helped the project staff to identify the barriers and enablers of peace in order to tailor the project activities, as well as the timing and targets of project activities.

At the time that *Laletek* was implemented, there were numerous government and NGO-led peace-building initiatives in and around Dili involved in various conflict mitigation and resolution activities. Their programs emphasised activities such as skills development for local leaders and youth engagement, women's empowerment, and the identification and resolution of macro causes of conflict or individual cases of conflict. While each might have contributed to a more peaceful Timor-Leste, they did not focus explicitly on building trust and developing healthy relationships. This became an explicit focus of the *Laletek* Project as, based on CRS's previous peace-building experience, without overcoming the animosity that divides opposing groups and spurs violence, communities would continue to experience violent conflict.

The *Laletek* Project also complemented other peace-building efforts by working at the lowest possible level—the *aldeia*—using a people-to-people approach to strengthen intra-communal relationships, as well as engaging various groups in the maintenance and management of new community infrastructure projects. The project activities built on pre-existing and past trust-building efforts, and attempted to benefit the community as a whole rather than focusing on one target group.

The baseline data showed that *suku* Bidau Santa Ana had an existing social contract based on the *suku* law written by the local leaders. This *suku* law, which bound all community members, listed the sorts of behaviours that were unacceptable to the community and the punishments for those who violated them. Similarly, *suku* Camea, Becora and Mascarenhas, which had conducted a subdistrict *tara bandu*[4] ceremony shortly before the baseline study, had also signed a *tara bandu* law as a binding social contract. This was an initiative by the local government supported by The Asia Foundation through their Community Policing Project. However, when a violent incident took place four days after the ceremony between Camea and Becora, some youth and *aldeia* leaders said that they had not been involved in drafting this law and did not know what its content was. The *Laletek* Project saw an opportunity to strengthen the impact of these existing social contracts by supporting local leaders to socialise the and *suku* laws in their *aldeia* and accompanying them to utilise these laws in resolving local conflicts. In several *aldeia* in Manleuana in *suku* Comoro, which had yet to develop a written social contract, the project supported the local

---

4   *Tara bandu* is a traditional ceremony that is aimed at regulating people-to-people relations, people-to-animal relations, and people's relationship to the environment (Belun and The Asia Foundation 2013: 4). It is done with an sacred animal sacrifice where the blood is drunk or splattered and oath is taken by parties involved, witnessed by their ancestors.

leaders and the MSS to bring together community and conflicting martial arts groups—*Perguruan Silat Setia Hati* (PSHT) and *Kmanek Oan Rai Klaran* (KORK)—into a peace agreement.

The *Laletek* Project was also committed to addressing the root causes of the conflicts in different localities through dialogue and mediation. By ensuring that those involved in the conflicts were present, and that local leaders were in charge, the project helped to strengthen local peace-building capacities. For example, the population in the *aldeia* of Fatuk Francisco, Camea, accused people of the neighbouring *aldeia*, Buburlau, of stopping their water supply by cutting a water pipe, leaving the community with no access to clean water. The pipe was fixed by the IOM after the IDPs returned; however, because the Buburlau community received no water from the pipes passing their *aldeia*, the pipes were cut again. The mediation provided by the *Laletek* Project brought 40 people from both *aldeia* together, resulting in an agreement that both communities would have access to clean water. Following this agreement, once the pipe was fixed, the water supply was not cut again.

The *Laletek* Project also gave opposing groups, different ethnic groups, neighbouring *aldeia* members, and leaders who had a history of conflicts training in 'active non-violence' to equip them with the tools and skills to identify, analyse, and resolve their common problems. The training courses provided a safe venue for members of conflicting groups to share how the conflicts have affected them and to explore ways forward. Conflict maps were used as a visual aid to help participants analyse and identify the root causes of conflicts and to identify lasting solutions. The *Laletek* Project also implemented other activities, including annual traditional dance competitions among *aldeia*, and sporting events in Bebonuk, which carefully selected participants to ensure that each team comprised opposing groups.

Furthermore, the project engaged everyone in the community, including the spoilers, to work together to do something tangible for the community through small community infrastructure projects. This was done when the opposing groups in the community felt ready to collaborate. They identified their needs together using a community resource map developed by the project; they listed all the needs and prioritised one that could be developed as a joint project and would facilitate dialogue and co-operation. *Laletek* Project staff accompanied the participants closely, facilitating activities when requested by the local leaders, and providing small grants of US$1,000–4,500 for the rehabilitation or construction of community infrastructure water taps, public toilets and *aldeia* meeting venues.

What worked?

The *Laletek* Project applied the Lederach Four Dimensions of Conflict Transformation framework (Lederach, Neufeldt and Culbertson 2007: 18–22) to analyse how conflicts have changed the community in personal, interpersonal, structural and cultural dimensions; to define the root causes of the problems, and establish the changes sought. The four dimensions helped in gaining an understanding of how conflicts affect individuals personally, how they impact trust and relationship patterns, how the systems and structures are organised, and how conflicts disturb the patterns of behaviours. These four dimensions are linked and considered as equally important; therefore, the *Laletek* Project analysed the four to see how each contributed to the *aldeia*-level conflicts in the target areas. The main emphasis of the *Laletek* Project was the relational dimension—to build healthier relationships between opposing groups—as this was the main challenge to preventing sustainable reintegration after the 2006–07 crisis.

The following strategies were adopted to address these factors driving conflict identified in the baseline survey.

Personal	**Relational**
Conflict changes individuals personally, emotionally, spiritually	Refers to people who have direct face-to-face contact. When conflict escalates, communication patterns change, stereotypes are created, polarisation increases, trust decreases
Structural	**Cultural**
Conflict impacts systems and structures — how relationships are organised and who has access to power — from family and organisations to communities and whole societies	Violent conflict causes deep-seated cultural changes, for example, the norms that guide patterns of behaviour between elders and youth, or women and men

Figure 12.2 The four dimensions of a conflict transformation framework.
Source: Lederach, Neufeldt and Culbertson (2007).

Understanding the complexity of local conflicts: *Laletek* did not take for granted what were perceived to be the main fault lines of conflict in Timor-Leste like the 'east–west' divide, or disputes between martial arts groups. Instead, the project invested time and effort in learning about the realities in each *aldeia* in order to develop an in-depth understanding of the relational tensions between different groups, and how personal, structural and cultural issues exacerbated these. For instance, the stone-throwing in the *aldeia*, along the river dividing Becora and Camea *suku*, was commonly seen as a conflict between easterners who just came back from the IDP camps and the westerners who stayed behind during the conflict. One of the main issues identified during the baseline study, however, related to who had access to the very limited water in the river. Project staff facilitated the *aldeia* people of Culau Laletek and Mota Ulun, Becora, and Fatuk Francisco, Camea, in finding a solution. The tap water system destroyed in 1999 was rebuilt, bringing water to their respective homes, and violent stone-throwing between the *aldeia* stopped. In the process, all parties got to know each other and learned to work together.

Staying focused: Part of *Laletek*'s success was that it did not lose sight of its key goal, which was for opposing groups to sit together, discuss their problems, and find a common resolution. Activities were carried out not for their own sake, nor according to pre-determined schedules, but only if and when they contributed to the project goal of bringing opposing groups together. This meant that if opposing groups were not ready to work together in a training or community project, the team would step back and find a different entry point and opportunity. For instance, in the first few meetings in Bidau Santa Ana, only those living close by the *suku* office and well acquainted with the newly elected *suku* chief were involved. As it turned out, there were tensions between the outgoing *suku* council and the newly elected ones. Therefore, the local youth suggested a team-building exercise at the beach, to which members of both *suku* councils were invited to discuss their *suku* development informally, share meals together, and make a joint statement to the community. While this was a very simple activity, it showed to the community that the two leaders were working together.

Community ownership: The strength of *Laletek* was the degree of community ownership the project was able to create. Community ownership drove the project, rather than pre-determined project plans and schedules. Team members were consistent in encouraging communities and leaders to take the initiative in addressing their own issues. This was demonstrated throughout the project, including in conflict mapping and monitoring, reconciliation dialogue, and small infrastructure project planning. At the beginning, there was some resistance when those asked to get involved demanded payment. Thus, the staff spent a lot of time working with the informal and formal community leaders to get their support for the project, and to develop their understanding that the project was supporting their existing efforts. This meant that there were no payments for participation, except for reimbursement of transportation costs when meetings were conducted outside a leader's *aldeia*. The fact that the DJPC Dili was embedded in the community through the Catholic Church also helped to revive the volunteerism spirits of the community.

Vertical relationship-building was also fostered with leaders at the sub-national and national level through accompaniment of local leaders during preparation and implementation of any community reconciliation or community infrastructure projects. For instance, the project worked with the secretary of state for art and culture to provide mentoring to community groups in preparing for the traditional dance competition. Another example is Camea community leaders proposing the building of a water pipe system; the project invited the subdistrict officials and the Department of Water and Sanitation to be involved to ensure there was no overlap with their development plan. When there were violent incidents that were outside the local leaders' authority, these issues were referred to the police and the Department of Peace-Building and Social Cohesion (DPSC) of the MSS.

Committed and dedicated staff: Another strength of the project was that it employed committed staff who understood and believed in what they were doing. After receiving training on conflict transformation skills, they were closely mentored to accompany local leaders and help them resolve existing and emerging conflicts. The staff employed effective community engagement strategies to realise project objectives. For instance, given that the project was designed to bridge particular opposing groups, staff ensured that only those who were directly involved in conflicts were selected for each project activity. These activities included Active Non-Violence Workshops, traditional dancing competitions, mediation and dialogue, as well as community infrastructure rehabilitation or building activities.

Challenges of implementation

The project faced various challenges during its implementation. A few of the critical ones are discussed below.

Lack of readiness for peace: The fact that the project was implemented soon after a major crisis that drove half of Dili's residents out of their homes, and led to the destruction of properties and loss of lives, was a particular challenge. A number of groups and individuals still held grudges towards each other and were not ready for peace when the project started. The most challenging area was Bebonuk, which had a protracted conflict involving four to five *aldeia*. Martial arts leaders simply said 'no' to the project, stating that they wanted war and revenge for the death of one of their members during the crisis. Project flexibility helped here as staff just took their time and worked separately with the two groups. Eventually, in the second year of the project, it was possible to bring the groups together as the project team decided to take a different approach, asking locally based, respected nuns and a priest to do a house-to-house visit, talking to each of the main leaders involved in the conflict and their parents. This personalised approach managed to open their minds and hearts. This led to various joint activities, including the rehabilitation of the Bebonuk Youth Center.

Lack of participation of local leadership: As the Timor-Leste community is very hierarchical, the blessings and support of local elected leaders is crucial for projects to succeed. *Laletek* staff put a lot of effort into cultivating good relationships with *aldeia* and *suku* leaders; nevertheless, these attempts were not successful in all 22 target *aldeia*. Throughout the project, the *aldeia* chiefs of Culau Laletek and Mococo Mate of Becora *suku*, for example, refused to be involved in the project. In other *aldeia* and *suku*, community leaders were too busy with full-time jobs to be involved. Nonetheless, in some cases *Laletek* staff managed to convince local leaders to appoint someone in their place to liaise with project staff.

Politicising of local leadership: The fact that some community leaders were representatives of political parties and that the project was implemented soon after the *suku* election (when new *aldeia* chief took over the old ones in 14 of the 22 *aldeia*) created additional problems. In most *aldeia*, the names of those newly elected leaders were unknown by the community members and they had not yet met their *aldeia/suku* leaders and council members. Some of the newly elected *aldeia* and *suku* chiefs did not feel that they had the authority to call the conflicting parties together to resolve an issue. The project staff worked to empower the new *aldeia* and *suku* chiefs by accompanying them in preparing and leading meetings with the community, and conducting and mediating a conflict.

Expectation for payment for involvement: At the beginning of the project, both community members and community leaders had high expectations that they would be paid for participating in the project. To address this issue, project staff spent a lot of time and effort highlighting that the project was, in fact, supporting local community efforts. This also contributed to strengthening community ownership of the project. The fact that the DJPC was the implementing partner of the project also helped as the project was seen as coming from the Catholic Church so the community were willing to participate with no financial incentive. Nevertheless, a mediation dialogue between two conflicting schools in Fatuhada and Aimutin was cancelled as a teacher based at one of the schools expected a payment for participating in this event.

Conclusion

There are a few lessons that can be learned from this two-year project for successful future peace-building works. First, it is important to understand the context well by conducting thorough research, instead of simplifying the conflict based on what appears on the surface. A baseline study is a good way to gain a picture of the situation, including those involved in conflicts, those involved in peace-making, and the sources of local conflicts. This information can be used as an entry point for project activities. It can encourage the local population to work together, and strengthen the potential for conflict resolution and transformation.

Secondly, as mentioned earlier, conflicts are part of day-to-day interactions between people and between groups. Given that conflict is not a one-off occurrence, it is important for any project-based interventions to empower local leaders to resolve their own problems, to support them to network with other organisations, and advocate for assistance from the sub-national or national government, rather than doing it for them. The project will come to an end, but those leaders will remain in the community and can continue to transform any violent incidences constructively beyond the life of the project.

Third, a great deal of thought and preparatory work is needed to ensure that the right people are involved in the project. This includes those involved directly in the conflicts and those who can or have the potential to resolve communal conflicts. In working with spoilers, project staff have to tread carefully so as not to reward bad behaviour by singling those individuals out from the rest of the communities and solely targeting them in all project activities. Instead, spoilers should be treated as members of their community, who, like other citizens, are responsible for maintaining peace in their neighbourhood.

Given that the *Laletek* Project was a small, two-year project implemented in an urban setting, further study is needed to see how it can be replicated in a rural setting where there may be more entrenched violent conflict.

References

Belun and The Asia Foundation 2013. *Tara Bandu: Its Role and Use in Community Conflict Prevention in Timor-Leste*. Dili: Asia Foundation.

Bishop, J. 2011. Final Evaluation Report: Strengthening Early Recovery for Comprehensive and Sustainable Reintegration of Internally Displaced People (SERC) Project. Dili: United Nations Development Programme.

Catholic Relief Services 2010. *Laletek (Bridge) Program Baseline Study Report*. Dili: CRS/Timor-Leste program.

Catholic Relief Services, United States Conference of Catholic Bishop 2011. *Social Cohesion and Youth Learning Document*. Cairo: CRS.

Catholic Relief Services 2013. *Laletek Project Manual: Strategic Community Peace-Building in Practice*. Baltimore: CRS. www.crsprogramquality.org/storage/pubs/peace-building/strategic-community-peace-building-in-practice.pdf.

Globalism Research Centre, RMIT University Melbourne 2009. Understanding Community: Security and Sustainability in Four Aldeia in Timor Leste—Luha Oli, Nanu, Sarelari and Golgota. Melbourne: Globalism Research Centre.

Gusmão, X. 1/3/2011. Timor-Leste: Goodbye Conflict, Welcome Development. Address by the Prime Minister and Minister of Defense and Security of Democratic Republic of Timor-Leste at Johns Hopkins University, Washington DC.

ICG (International Crisis Group) 2008. Timor-Leste Displacement Crisis. *Asia Report* 148.

Lederach, J.P. 2003. *The Little Book of Conflict Transformation*. New York: Good Books.

Lederach, J.P., R. Neufeldt and H. Culbertson 2007. *Reflective Peace-Building: A Planning, Monitoring, and Learning Toolkit*. Indiana: The Joan B. Kroc Institute for International Peace Studies, University of Notre Dame.

Paffenholz, T. 2009. Summary of Results for a Comparative Research Project: Civil Society and Peace-Building. *Centre on Conflict, Development and Peace-Building (CCDP) Working Paper* Geneva: CCDP.

Paffenholz, T. and C. Spurk 2006. Civil Society, Civic Engagement, and Peace-Building. *Social Development Papers: Conflict Prevention and Reconstruction* 36(October). Washington DC: Conflict Prevention & Reconstruction Social Development Department, The World Bank.

RDTL (*República Democrática de Timor-Leste*) 19/12/2007. 'Hamutuk Hari'i Futuru': A National Recovery Strategy. Office of the Vice Prime-Minister Media Release, Dili. Reproduced by East Timor and Indonesia Action Network. www.etan.org/et2008/6june/22/19hamutuk.htm.

Scambary, J. 2012. *Laletek Project Final Evaluation: Final Report*. Dili: CRS/Timor-Leste Program. www.dmeforpeace.org/learn/laletek-project-final-evaluation.

Scambary, J. 2013. Conflict and Resilience in an Urban Squatter Settlement in Dili, East Timor. *Urban Studies* 50(10):1935–50.

PART FOUR
Citizens, Inequalities and Migration

CHAPTER 13

A Social Movement as an Antidote to Corruption

Adérito de Jesus Soares

Introduction

Corruption has become a very complex and intractable problem facing the world. Billions of dollars earmarked for the poor, including vital education and health sector assistance, ends up in the pockets of a relatively few corrupt people every year (OECD 2014: 2). Studies by the OECD, for example, have estimated that corruption may cost 5 per cent of global gross domestic product, which, according to the World Bank, represents up to US$1 trillion paid in bribes every year.

Various entities at regional, national and international levels have been attempting to tackle corruption. But it remains well entrenched and is even on the rise in some countries, particularly among those in the developing world. Of course, corruption also occurs in developed countries, but they generally have stronger legal frameworks and mechanisms in place to tackle it. By contrast, many developing countries, such as Timor-Leste, lack effective institutional capacity to deter corrupt practices.

Timor-Leste as a post-conflict society is confronting the problem of corruption and putting in place a number of mechanisms to address problems of accountability and transparency. Central to these efforts has been the establishment and implementation of the *Comissão Anti-Corrupção* (CAC; Anti-Corruption Commission) in 2010. But while efforts have been made to tackle the growing problem of corruption in Timor-Leste, there remain a number of significant factors that make Timor-Leste at least potentially prone to corruption. Among these factors are the fledgling nature of the state institutions, and the legal framework that remains a work in progress and weak. There is a growing business sector that lacks a culture of accountability, while high unemployment and widespread economic hardship loom large as real challenges.

I argue in this chapter that given the faults of its legal system and the weakness of enforcement in this post-conflict Timor-Leste society, it would be a serious mistake to rely solely on legal mechanisms to fight corruption. This is even more the case given that Timor-Leste has inherited cultures of corruption from two previous colonial regimes that continue to influence contemporary practice. In this context, I argue that comprehensive efforts to combat corruption must go beyond legal measures to involve raising public awareness in the community at large.

There is a very simplistic understanding on the public's part about the capacity of legal mechanisms to counter corruption. It is simply more dramatic and attractive for the public to see alleged corrupters arrested, prosecuted and sent to jail; and it is important to have legal mechanisms that can enable this if due process is followed. However, more comprehensive, non-legal strategies also need to be developed, so that both strategies can be combined to effectively address the issue of corruption.[1]

Thus, this chapter is divided as follows. I first describe the state of corruption in Timor-Leste, past and present. This is followed by a discussion of some common challenges facing anti-corruption commissions around the world, and a review of Timor-Leste's efforts in dealing with corruption. I then describe efforts to raise public awareness on this issue, followed by an account of the role of the private sector in economic development and its vulnerability to corrupt practice.

Corruption in Timor-Leste at a glance

Timor-Leste has experienced the ill effects of corruption, from the Portuguese colonial period to 24 years of illegal occupation by the Indonesian regime (1974–99). During both of these dark periods, corruption became entrenched within the colonial architecture and machineries of state.

From the 17th century, the Portuguese imposed a *finta* (collective tax) on the population of Timor-Leste. *Finta* were collected in different forms including corn, rice, cattle, honey, sandalwood and gold (Castro 1867: 375–76). Portuguese soldiers and officers were tasked with collecting *finta* from

---

1   I have elaborated this line of argument elsewhere (see Soares 2013: 85–97).

the villagers and various petty *reino* (kingdoms) that encompassed the great majority of the population. But this process was prone to corruption, and the amount of *finta* that eventually reached the capital, Dili, was always less than what had been collected. Although Timor made a relatively minor contribution to the coffers of the Portuguese treasury, petty corruption among the Portuguese officers was widespread across the land. Colonial documents note that corruption was rife in the customs sector. It not only involved Portuguese officers and soldiers, but to some extent the Timorese elite—*regulo* (kings) and *suku* (village) leaders—were also involved in the cycle of corruption that affected the majority of Timor's people. History has shown that various rebellions by the Timorese were frequently triggered by resentments over the collection of *finta*, which was often obtained through coercion and the use of violence (Roque 2010: 10).

During the 24 years of the Indonesian occupation, the experience of corruption in Timorese society was perpetuated and solidified. Indonesian military and senior government officers were involved in massive corruption while running Timor-Timur—as it was known during the occupation—as a branch of the Indonesian company, P.T. Denok Hernandez International. This company had the monopoly on coffee exports from East Timor and was used by the Indonesian military as a cash cow for the generals (Taylor 2000: 125). In addition, the top Indonesian civilian officers emptied the public purse by diverting Jakarta's money into their own pockets (Carrascalão 2006: 145–49). The web of corruption became wider as many Timorese elite, who were in positions of power, also benefited directly from corruption with their Indonesian patrons. The culture of corruption in the public sector became entrenched in daily life.

Both petty and grand corruption flourished during the occupation. Thus, the attempt to integrate Timor-Leste into the Republic became, among other things, a project of massive plunder throughout the territory, quite apart from the human rights atrocities widely documented elsewhere. Even General Kiki Syahnakri, the then military commander in Timor-Leste, lamented that Timorese people rejected the politics of integration into Indonesia because of the massive corruption committed by both military and civilian leaders in the territory (Syahnakri 2013: 346). Of course, Syahnakri's comment is only partly correct, as there were more fundamental reasons for the Timorese to oppose integration, but his criticism did put corruption at the centre of the Indonesian's administrative machinery in Timor-Leste at the time. The same observation came from Mário Viegas Carrascalão, the then Indonesian-appointed governor in Timor-Leste. According to Carrascalão, during his tenure, the central government used to appoint one high-level military retiree as the 'Pimpro' (*pimpinan proyek*; project leader), who had the task of granting government contracts to individuals preferred by the regime, without any proper procurement mechanisms.[2]

In post-independence Timor-Leste, there is no doubt that corruption is on the rise. For a start, there is more cash floating around, especially in the public sector, while the oversight mechanisms that are in place remain very weak. Timor-Leste is one of the most oil- and gas-dependent countries in the world. State revenues from oil and gas exceed 90 per cent. This also makes the country vulnerable to corruption, like the experience of many oil-rich countries in the world where the public sector's culture of accountability is still very underdeveloped. The dramatic increase in the annual state budget since 2007—even though the capacity to execute the budget remains highly constrained—has opened more opportunities for corruption by public servants in collusion with the private sector. Although Timor-Leste has one of the best oil and gas trust funds in the world, designed with Norwegian advice following independence, the issue of expending substantial quantities of this fund in the state budget raises serious questions.

Tensions between time and expectations

The experience of many anti-corruption commissions established around the world shows that there is a very high public expectation when the commission is first established. The public often expects the commission to work quick miracles in combating corruption. They expect the commission to act quickly in the shortest time frame possible, putting additional pressures on the commission. However, such expectations are bound to be unmet if state support for a new commission is insufficient. State support can manifest through strong political will, the provision of a sufficient budget, a judicial system that is truly based on the rule of law, and so forth. Support from the public can be expressed in various ways, including an abhorrence of bribery, encouraging people to inform relevant institutions about instances of suspected corruption, and support for anti-corruption campaigns.

The Independent Commission Against Corruption of Hong Kong and the Corruption Prevention and Investigation Bureau of Singapore are successful because they had these conditions in place. However, Ghana, Malawi, Tanzania, Uganda and Zambia have all established anti-corruption commissions but failed to combat corruption because they lacked these safeguards (see Doig et al. 2005).

---

2   See 'Saya Bukan Pengkhianat' [I am not a traitor], Tempo's interview with Carrascalão. setiyardi.wordpress.com/2009/04/03/mario-viegas-carrascalao-saya-bukan-pengkhianat/.

It is one of the paradoxes of combating corruption in post-conflict countries that on one hand, the legal system is generally weak (including the judiciary), but on the other hand, public expectation is very high, and to some extent unequal to the efficacy of that country's legal system. This is understandable, as the public is anxious about social ills (corruption) that have negative impacts on people's lives. The public want to see swift, tangible results, such as imprisoning criminals. Therefore, to be successful in combating corruption, there should be realistic support measures in place and an anti-corruption push that should not be monopolised by any anti-corruption commission. Instead, there should be a widespread social movement across the country. Today, with the expansion of global capitalism, organised crime has also expanded. For this reason, efforts need to be expanded beyond state borders. Timor-Leste's endeavours in fighting corruption post-independence illustrate this paradox very well.

Anti-corruption efforts post-independence

During Timor-Leste's transition to independence from 1999 to 2002, the United Nations established the Office of the Inspectorate General (OIG), which still exists under the auspices of the Timor-Leste government. The main task of the OIG is to conduct internal audits of alleged maladministration and corruption in the public sector. It submits its reports to the prime minister, who has the discretionary power and the final say on whether there should be further investigations, whether to impose administrative sanctions, or to archive the cases. Following the establishment of the *Provedor de Direitos Humanos e Justiça* (PDHJ; Human Rights Commission) in 2006, the OIG has worked side by side with the PDHJ in the area of good governance. Both institutions have the power to carry out investigations: OIG for internal administrative audits; the PDHJ for independent non-criminal investigations, which it submits to the *Ministério Público* (Office of the Public Prosecutor). The mandate to investigate corruption was removed from the PDHJ when the new CAC was established in 2010. The CAC was given a broad mandate of conducting criminal investigations and as well as awareness-raising (Soares 2013). However, the CAC, as in the case of the PDHJ, has to submit its final investigations to the prosecutor. The prosecutor then decides whether to pursue cases should they demonstrate strong admissible evidence.

There are still areas of overlap in this institutional arrangement. For instance, it is hard to avoid allegations of corruption being investigated simultaneously by two state institutions in the early stages of a case. This is partly because of confusion created by the laws governing the mandates of these institutions.[3]

---

3   An analysis of the legal framework is of utmost importance; however, it is not the focus of this chapter.

Some of this confusion emerges from weak institutional leadership and, to some extent, competition between the institutions. This occurred in the case of the relationship between the CAC and the *Ministério Público*. Given that the prosecutor's office controls and supervises all criminal investigations under Timorese law, this institution has the discretionary power to decide which cases it investigates and which can be delegated to the CAC.

With the establishment of the Audit Court in 2012, which is mandated to audit all government expenditure, another institutional player has been added to the list of oversight in this country of a little over one million people.

The imperative of awareness-raising

Since its inception in 2010, the CAC has been very active in raising awareness about the causes and consequences of corruption in public life. The CAC's vision was to 'create a strong culture of rejecting corruption' in Timorese society. As such, awareness-raising was central to realising this objective, given the dark trajectory of corruption in modern Timorese society. As the inaugural CAC commissioner, I believe that combating corruption can only be successful if it becomes a widespread social movement involving all segments of Timorese society (Soares 2010).

It is important to note that prior to the establishment of CAC, awareness-raising about corruption had been carried out by other institutions, including some non-government organisations (NGOs), albeit in an unsystematic way and with a much smaller audience than the one CAC managed to reach. According to a commissioned survey, 52.5 per cent of respondents did not understand what was meant by the term corruption (CAC 2011). Only a very small percentage of respondents knew how to report corruption cases to the proper authorities. According to the survey, over 60 per cent of respondents agreed that the CAC had to intensify its public outreach.

In 2013, more than 7,000 people attended the CAC's public outreach meetings and seminars across the country (CAC Annual Report 2013), with a much larger audience reached via media reports on these meetings. Apart from the objective of encouraging the public to report corruption cases to the CAC or other competent authorities—such as the *Ministério Público*—the other important objective of this outreach was to inspire the civic spirit of citizens, and encourage them to join anti-corruption efforts, to help them understand the consequences of corruption, and to prevent them from becoming involved in corrupt behaviour. Target audiences at public outreach events varied from youth groups to community leaders, district governance officers, women's groups, and students from primary school to university. The CAC reached out to all 13 districts in Timor once it began effective operations in January 2011.[4]

The CAC conducted outreach programs in collaboration with other entities such as NGOs, youth groups, schools, universities, and religious organisations, especially the Catholic Church. The form of public outreach varied. For instance, the CAC organised essay and speech competitions with various schools and universities. It also disseminated basic information about corruption to community leaders and public servants in various districts.

As for public servants, the CAC combined two approaches: disseminating basic information; and discussing preventative strategies with them. One example of successful public outreach was the celebrations of 9 December for International Anti-Corruption Day. Since 2010, CAC has held large events on this day. For instance, in 2013, in collaboration with the *Comissão da Função Pública* (CFP; Public Service Commission), the CAC organised a one-day conference, attended by 1,500 people, including all directors general and heads of department from the civil service. The country's leaders also attended and addressed the forum.

The CAC encourages the public to report any allegation of corruption across Timorese society. As a result, in 2011, CAC received 103 reports from the public. The number declined a little in 2012 with 60 reports, followed by 75 reports in 2013 (CAC 2014). However, these reports did not all necessarily translate into potential corruption cases. Indeed, only a small percentage of the reports were followed up by the CAC. On investigation, many of these reports were found to be unrelated to corruption but linked to other issues, including human rights violations and civil cases such as divorce.

Public awareness-raising and monitoring activities carried out by NGOs and the media are of the utmost importance in this context. However, Dili-based NGOs and media need to focus their attentions more at the district level, particularly as development and high-value infrastructure projects are increasingly taking place at the subdistrict and district levels. In order to broaden the network of security, it is also important to break the 'exclusivity' of NGO agendas by involving communities at the local level.

---

4   CAC was established with the swearing-in of its first commissioner in February 2010, however, its effective operation only commenced in January 2011. The first year (2010) was basically used to establish infrastructure and recruit staff and investigators, as well as to train the first recruits.

With the increasing roles of the private sector in Timor-Leste's economy, in conjunction with the presence of substantial foreign private sector enterprise—many of which do not have good reputations on transparency and accountability, a cautious look at these actors is also required.

Private sector fetishism and the need for raising public awareness

No one could deny the importance of the private sector in a modern liberal economy. However, caution is needed in post-conflict societies such as Timor-Leste. It is noticeable that from independence to the present, the government has prioritised the private sector—in this case, mostly national contractors who rely on government projects—to fuel economic development and job creation. On the other hand, the government also has been trying hard to convince international/foreign investors to invest in Timor-Leste. One example was the strategy of lowering company tax to attract foreign investors.

This fetishising of the private sector in development can result in favouritism towards certain businesses, bypassing laws and procedures, and lead to corruption. For instance, the government has awarded infrastructure projects through single source mechanisms to a small group of national contractors known as the *Consorcio Nasional de Timorense* (Timorese National Consortium) that has strong connections with those in power. These apparent conflicts of interest have evoked some public criticism as potentially leading to corruption.[5] From independence to the present, there have been many government projects awarded to individual businesses through the single source process. Thus, this discretionary power of leaders in terms of awarding government projects has created the perception of corruption, if not actual collusion.

Favouritism shown to the private sector by the government could also jeopardise the economy of Timor-Leste. This is because most of the private sector lacks the interest or capacity to invest in alternative areas such as agriculture and fisheries, but relies instead and almost solely on government (infrastructure) projects. At the same time, many have also become brokers to foreign investors who have taken part in many of the state's recent multimillion-dollar project tenders. This dependency could create a networking of patron–client relationships

---

5   See Tempo Semanal, *PM Eskolta Samuel-Xanana Protetor Koruptor* [PM escorted Samuel-PM protected corruptor]. www.temposemanal.com/nasional/pm-eskolta-samuel-xanana-protetor-korruptor. *Consorcio Nasional de Timorense* is composed of several Timor business groups such as Tinolina Lda, owned by Agostinho Gomes; Suai Indah Ltd, owned by Americo; Marabia, Lda, owned by Jorge Serano; Jonice Ltd, owned by Nilton Gusmão; Hidayat Lda, owned by Ahmad Alkatiri; and Montana Diak Lda and GS Lda.

across the Timorese economy. Fetishising the private sector could also lead to a marginalisation of other groups, such as farmers, and the informal sectors that also have great potential to contribute to equitable economic development.

Engaging the private sector from the outset in activities directed to awareness-raising is crucial in combating corruption. This has not happened to any extent in Timor-Leste. In early 2014, the CAC in collaboration with the Timor-Leste *Câmara de Comércio e Indústria* (Chamber of Commerce and Industry), held a one-day conference to consider ways to prevent corruption. The seminar attracted a small number of participants compared to other public awareness-raising initiatives. Thus, a serious dialogue with the private sector on how to combat corruption is needed, as they have strong leverage in terms of capital and are well connected to local power-holders and influential elites.

Conclusion

I have briefly discussed the current state of corruption in Timor-Leste and the opportunities for combating it. I have highlighted the importance of awareness-raising in order to create social movements to combat corruption. I have also raised some notes of caution in relation to the private sector's role in the economic dynamics of post-conflict societies like Timor-Leste.

A weak legal system and continuing fragile state institutions could be compensated by a massive public education campaign against corruption. Combining two approaches could well thwart corruption at the outset. The power of social movements and vocal public criticism, combined with a swift investigation, is a more thorough antidote to combat this ill.

References

CAC (*Comissão Anti-Corrupção*; Anti-Corruption Commission) 2011. *Corruption Perception Survey*. Dili: KAK. cac.tl/wp-content/uploads/2011/11/CP-Survey-Report_TL11-12.pdf.

CAC 2013. Relatorio Annual CAC, Dili 2013. File with author.

CAC 2014. *Kompilasaun Relatoriu Annual 2010–2014* [Annual Report Compilation]. Dili: CAC.

Carrascalão, M.V. 2006. *Timor Antes do Futuro* [Timor-Before the Future]. Dili: Livraria Mau Huran.

Castro, A.D. 1867. *As Possessões Portuguezas na Oceania* [The Portuguese Possessions in Oceania]. Lisbon: Lisboa Imprensa Nacional.

Doig, A., D. Watt and R. Williams 2005. *Measuring 'Success' in Five African Anti-Corruption Commissions: The Cases of Ghana, Malawi, Tanzania, Uganda & Zambia.* Bergen: u4 Anti-Corruption Resource Centre and Chr. Michelsen Institute. www.u4.no/publications/measuring-success-in-five-african-anti-corruption-commissions/.

OECD (Organisation for Economic Co-operation and Development) 2014. *The Rationale to Fight Corruption.* Paris: OECD. www.oecd.org/cleangovbiz/49693613.pdf.

Roque, R. 2000. The Unruly Island: Colonialism's Predicament in late Nineteenth-Century East Timor. *Portuguese Literary & Cultural Studies* 17/18:300–30.

Syahnakri, K. 2013. *Timor-Timur: The Untold Story.* Jakarta: Kompas.

Taylor, J.G. 2000. East *Timor: The Price of Freedom.* London: Zed Books Ltd.

Soares, A.de J. 2013. *Kombatente versus Kontraktor versus Koruptor* [Combatant versus Contractor versus Corruptor]. *CAC Bulletin* no. 5. File with author.

Soares, A.de J. 2013. Combating Corruption: Avoiding Institutional ritualism. In L. Michael and D. Kingsbury (eds). *The Politics of Timor-Leste.* Ithaca: Cornell University Press.

Soares, A.de J. 2010. Address to the National Parliament on February 22nd, 2010. File with author.

CHAPTER 14

The Veterans' Valorisation Scheme: Marginalising Women's Contributions to the Resistance[1]

Lia Kent and Naomi Kinsella

As women, we are offended and upset that on national days the leaders mention all the heroes' names to honour them, but forget our women leaders who gave their lives to liberate this nation

Maria Tapó, Bi Lear, We-We, Muki, Soimali, Mariazinha, Bi-Doli-Mau and others.

It is now ten years since we have restored our independence but the leaders have forgotten the contribution and values [that women brought to the independence struggle]. Will it be that these women's participation ended with their deaths? Or for those who are still alive, that they will only receive recognition as the wife of a deceased combatant or cadre? If so, this is unfair, particularly when we want to create a complete history of our people.

Secretary General Lourdes Maria A.M. Alves de Araujo, Organização Popular da Mulher Timorense (*OPMT; Popular Organisation of East Timorese Women*).[2]

---

1 Some of the material in this chapter has been published as Lia Kent and Naomi Kinsella, A Luta Kontinua: The Marginalisation of East Timorese Women in the Veterans' Valorisation Scheme. *International Feminist Journal of Politics* (2014).
2 Speech of the OPMT Secretary General, Lourdes Maria A.M. Alves de Araújo at a fundraising event for the OPMT documentation project, 6 August 2010.

Introduction

It is well known that East Timorese women played critical roles during the 24-year Resistance struggle (the Resistance) against the Indonesian occupation. As large numbers of men took up arms against the Indonesian military and were imprisoned and killed, women took on new responsibilities. Some hid in the mountains and forests with FALINTIL (*Forças Armadas da Libertação Nacional de Timor-Leste*; Armed Forces for the National Liberation of East Timor)—the military wing of FRETILIN (*Frente Revolucionária de Timor-Leste Independente*; Revolutionary Front for an Independent East Timor)—where they played important logistical roles: they collected food, cooked, mended clothing, took care of the wounded, acted as guards, and managed munitions. When under fire, women guerrillas would prepare supplies for removal in case of retreat, or salvage ammunition, weapons, or other supplies from the bodies of dead soldiers on both sides. Women were also engaged militarily against the Indonesian forces and took part in raids on Indonesian security posts and exchanges of fire (Alves, Abrantes and Reis 2003: 25–27; Conway 2010). More commonly, women were involved in the *frente clandestina* (clandestine front)—the network of civilians based in the villages and towns that supported, and greatly outnumbered, the FALINTIL forces. It has been estimated that women comprised 60 per cent of *clandestinos* (Cristalis and Scott 2005: 39), acting as couriers, supplying those on the frontlines with food and other necessities, seeking support within the church and local communities for the independence struggle, and hiding senior members of the Resistance. Women were also active in the diplomatic front of the Resistance. Urban-based student activists often living in exile worked with international solidarity and women's networks to raise awareness about human rights violations, and to ensure the outside world did not forget their struggle. Members of FRETILIN's *Organização Popular da Mulher Timorense* (OPMT; Popular Organisation of East Timorese Women) and the *Organização da Mulher Timorense* (OMT; Timorese Women's Organisation) played a critical role in the lead up to the 1999 referendum for self-determination, providing civic education in preparation for the referendum (CAVR 2005a: part 3, para 514–16).

Through a case study of the veterans' valorisation scheme (veterans' scheme), this chapter argues that women in independent Timor-Leste have been insufficiently recognised for their diverse and critical contributions to the Resistance. Specifically, it shows that the scheme, established in 2006 to provide symbolic recognition and material benefits to veterans of the 24-year Resistance, has discriminated against women. Given that the veterans' scheme has become a key nation-building pillar, consuming a significant amount of state resources and helping to shape social, political and economic status in independent Timor-Leste, this has significant implications for East Timorese women and, indeed, for the society as a whole.

Drawing on interviews with politicians, veterans and representatives of women's organisation, along with a close reading of the veterans' legislation and pension statistics, we shows the scheme's increasing orientation towards meeting narrowly defined 'stability' goals has been to women's detriment.[3] We then demonstrate that the scheme's emphasis on rank and time served within the Resistance has marginalised women's contributions, while provisions within the scheme—particularly those relating to remarriage, second wives and vulnerability criteria—add another layer of discrimination. We then make some suggestions as to how the veterans' scheme could be adapted to better recognise women's roles in the Resistance, acknowledging that any attempts to widen its existing parameters are likely to encounter significant opposition from powerful male veterans. Nonetheless, we argue that the marginalisation of women within the scheme represents a lost opportunity to recognise women's agency in the Resistance struggle, and, in doing so, to potentially improve women's social and economic standing and status in society. The marginalisation of women's contributions also has consequences for the nation as a whole by narrowing the way the Indonesian occupation is remembered and represented, and further promoting a militarised construction of citizenship.

Background to the veterans' scheme

The marginalisation of women within the veterans' scheme can be traced to the establishment of a series of commissions by the then President Xanana Gusmão from 2002, to identify and register veterans of the Resistance. The commissions were intended to avoid the improper use of veteran credentials to obtain political and material benefits, to placate the growing number of disaffected members of the Resistance who were threatening to rearm, and fulfil the constitutional requirement to valorise the Resistance (Rees 2003). The first two commissions—the *Comissão para os Assuntos dos Antigos Combatentes* (CAAC; Commission for the Issues of Former Combatants) and the *Comissão para os Assuntos dos Veteranos dos FALINTIL* (CAVF; Commission for the Issues of FALINTIL Veterans)—were established in September 2002 to register veterans of the armed struggle. Only 13 women (out of a total of 36,959 names) registered with the CAAC and CAVF during the initial registration phase, and these 13 names were then omitted from the final list. At the time, the justification given for the exclusion was that they had acted in support roles to FALINTIL and that they had held political (as opposed to military) positions within the Resistance structure. While this may have rankled with women who had spent years as an

---

3   Interviews were conducted by Naomi Kinsella, Natalia de Jesus Cesaltino and Manuela Leong Pereira in 2011.

integral part of FALINTIL in logistics and intelligence collection roles, there is evidence to suggest that the women were placated by President Gusmão, who instructed them to wait for a third commission, which would register veterans involved in the clandestine front (Ospina 2006: 24).

The *Comissão para os Assuntos dos Quadros da Resistencia* (CAQR; Commission for Matters of Cadres of the Resistance) was established in 2004 to register former *clandestinos*. It was far more successful than the previous commissions in gaining women's participation; indeed, 25 per cent of those who initially registered their names with CAQR were women. At the completion of the various presidential commissions' mandates, a total of 76,061 former members of the Resistance had been registered.[4] This included 10,337 women (13.5 per cent of the total).[5]

Following the completion of the first phase of registration, an ad hoc parliamentary commission was established to develop legislation on 'valorising' the Resistance. Unfortunately, the draft law was completed in July 2005—before CAQR had finished its work. This meant that the commission involving the largest number of women had little impact on veterans' policy formulation. The 2006 Statute of the National Liberation Combatants defines a 'National Liberation Combatant' (NLC) as a Timorese citizen who participated in the independence struggle for more than three years (or less than three years if killed due to their participation in the struggle), and was 'part of the structures or organizations of the Resistance'. Benefits for NLCs under the legislation include various forms of symbolic recognition, including medals, the right to funeral honours, and presidential decorations. NLCs, their spouses and children also have the right to access state health and education services free of charge, and a later decree law has established scholarships to assist with uniforms, books and tertiary education fees for veterans' children.

The valorisation process also provides for entitlements to pensions for a select group of veterans. Initially, pension eligibility was based upon 'vulnerability' criteria. Elderly and disabled veterans were prioritised, while widows, orphans, elderly parents, or tortured siblings of deceased veterans were eligible for a 'survival pension'. Later revisions to the law have, however, raised pension amounts and shifted the beneficiary emphasis. It is clear that length of service and rank within the Resistance structure are now key factors in determining

---

4   Two different technical commissions were created in 2004 and 2006 to respectively verify the previous commissions' data and consolidate it into a single database. See the press release, H.E. President Kay Rala Xanana Gusmão has sworn in the Commission of Verification of Data's (CVD) Monday, 15 November 2004; Presidential Dispatch 1/2006, Extension of the Mandate of the Data Consolidation Commission (CCD) of the Timorese Resistance and National Liberation Combatants, 9 December 2006.

5   March 2011 statistics from the Secretary of State for National Liberation Combatant Affairs.

pension amounts.[6] A combatant's years of service are considered to be the sum of all periods of deportation, detention and work in 'exclusive dedication' to the Resistance ('exclusive dedication' meaning that individuals were not engaged in study or regular waged labour).

The manner in which the scheme attributes monetary benefits has led to tensions between the clandestine front and FALINTIL. A key issue concerns the requirement for 'exclusive dedication' to the struggle, which makes it extremely difficult for former *clandestinos* to gain access to pensions. This is because clandestine front activities were often only possible by concealing one's activities behind study or work, or using one's position within the Indonesian Government, police or military to pass on intelligence to the Resistance. This definition has also excluded large numbers of women, not only because there were more women in the clandestine front than FALINTIL but because women tended not to hold official positions or titles within the Resistance structure despite carrying out important clandestine work. Other tensions have emerged due to difficulties in verifying who is a legitimate veteran for the purpose of the scheme. Despite the establishment of special committees to 'verify' veterans' claims, complaints of exaggeration or under-recognition of years of service are common, in some cases giving rise to violent disputes (see Belun and CICR 2013; ICG 2011).

Rising pension amounts

Since the introduction of the veterans' valorisation scheme, veterans' pension payments have risen steadily. In 2010, US$23.1 million (3 per cent of the state budget) was allocated to veterans' affairs, most of that for the payment of benefits (RDTL 2010). By 2011, this amount had risen to US$82.7 million, or 6 per cent of the 2011 state budget (RDTL 2011). Although payment amounts may have peaked in 2012 at US$109.7 million (or 9 per cent of the budget), they remain a significant allocation of state resources (IPAC 2014: 12). As Wallace (this volume) observes, more money is now spent on veterans than on health or education, and the lowest veterans' payment of US$276 per month is many times higher than the average East Timorese income.

---

6   Law 3/2006 as amended by Law 9/2009 of 29 July 2009, Article 26 'Special Retirement Pension', Article 25 'Subsistence Pension', Article 28 and Article 29. Veterans with more than eight years of full-time dedication to the struggle are eligible for monthly pensions, those with four to seven years' full-time service can apply to receive a one-off payment and a superior pension has also been created for a small number of 'prominent figures' within the liberation struggle. The family of deceased veterans can receive either a survival pension or one-off payment depending upon their relationship with the veteran. The survival pension is payable to only one heir, with the spouse receiving first priority followed by parents, children and siblings who have suffered torture as a result of the veterans' militancy. Once this individual dies, the right to a pension is extinguished.

The significant size of the veterans' pensions indicates that the Timor-Leste Government has relied on the scheme as a means of 'buying' political stability. In the wake of the security crisis of 2006–07, for instance, the veterans' scheme has been used as a means of placating those who could become potential threats to the state (UNHCHR 2006). This, in turn, makes it difficult to reign in pension amounts. In January 2008, for example, when the government attempted to reduce pension amounts due to budgetary constraints, the opposition party accused the government of 'insulting veterans' and the proposed reductions were never made.[7] The orientation of the scheme towards meeting narrowly defined stability goals also means there is likely to be little interest among the political leadership in making it more inclusive of women.

What is clear is that, at the time of writing, the primary beneficiaries of the scheme are men who can claim to have been high-ranking and/or long-serving combatants. In addition to pensions and recognition of their past roles, these men are being rewarded with significant respect and power. Veterans' views carry weight in parliamentary debates, election campaigns and within local politics. Veterans are also benefiting financially through the preferential allocation of government contracts (IPAC 2014: 13), and continue to play a variety of informal security roles, such as intelligence gathering and personal protection (ICG 2012: 14). All of this suggests that the veterans' scheme is bolstering the power and influence of a militarised male constituency—an issue that is problematic, not only for East Timorese women but for the society as a whole.

Problematic assumptions within the veterans' scheme

Behind the marginalisation of women in the veterans' scheme is the implicit assumption that the Resistance was an overwhelmingly male struggle. A prevailing view held by prominent male Resistance figures is that given men were the primary participants in the armed front, a program to valorise veterans will necessarily include a higher proportion of men than women. While readily agreeing that women played an invaluable role in the struggle, and suffered in gender-specific ways as a result of this contribution, a number of senior Resistance figures interviewed for this study suggested that the valorisation scheme was intended to recognise a persons' contribution to the struggle regardless of whether they were a man or woman, and was, therefore, non-discriminatory.[8]

---

7   *Timor Post* 8/1/2008. Government Asks the Parliament to Alter the Veterans' Law, Fretilin: AMP Insults Veterans.
8   Interviews with the Secretary of State for National Liberation Combatant Affairs, Marito Reis, 21 March 2008; Parliamentarian Cornelio Gama (*nom de guerre* L7), 12 April 2011; Parliamentarian Faustino dos Santos (*nom de guerre* Renan Selak), 13 April 2011; former Resistance member and member of the CAAC and CAVF, Andre da Costa Abel (*nom de guerre* L4), 26 March 2011.

While this argument appears logical on the surface, a deeper reading suggests that it is based on erroneous and gender-stereotypical assumptions about the roles of East Timorese women. Key among these is the implicit view that women's contributions to the Resistance were not as important as the roles of male combatants. This view ignores the way in which the Resistance effectively operated. As is well known, FALINTIL relied heavily upon the clandestine network for its survival, and civilian-led demonstrations, diplomacy and advocacy were vital to the ultimate success of the independence struggle.

Assumptions that downplay women's agency as political and military actors are reflected in criteria upon which veterans gain access to pensions under the scheme. Roles such as bearing arms against the enemy are elevated over the contributions women made to the Resistance as logisticians, couriers, cooks, nurses, *clandestinos* and international activists. The reliance on tallying up the years of 'exclusive dedication' to the struggle and a person's formal position within the Resistance hierarchy in determining access to decorations and pensions further excludes women. While this definition also excludes men who made non-armed contributions to the Resistance, women are particularly disadvantaged because they are far less likely than men to have held formal positions within the Resistance hierarchy and be able to prove an uninterrupted, full-time period of service.

Specific provisions in the veterans' scheme further discriminate against women. For instance, one provision precludes spouses of deceased veterans from receiving a pension if they have remarried. The implicit assumption behind this provision seems to be that women should have been 'loyal' wives awaiting the return of their men from the battlefront. It also seems to reflect a view that women are not independent persons but the property and responsibility of their husbands. The deeply entrenched nature of this assumption was evident during the parliamentary debate on the 2006 NLC statute, when some women parliamentarians raised a motion to amend the law, allowing widows of Resistance members to be entitled to pensions regardless of whether they had remarried or not. They argued that in many cases these women were left vulnerable to sexual abuse by the Indonesian security forces and their militia after their husband disappeared, died or fled to the jungle. Remarriage was often the only way they could avoid this abuse. The motion was defeated as former male commanders, with the support of a number of female parliamentarians who were widows of FALINTIL, argued that these women should have been loyal to the memory of their deceased husbands and demonstrated the same strength as other women who had not remarried.

The veterans' scheme also excludes women who suffered sexual violence as a result of their work for, or connections with the Resistance. Although the veterans' scheme is not intended as a reparation program for victims of human rights violations during the conflict, it does purport to support veterans and their immediate family who were left vulnerable as a result of their contribution to the Resistance. Factors such as an individual's age, disability, and their experiences of detention and torture are, therefore, taken into account within the scheme. The issue of sexual violence, however, never entered into parliamentary discussions on the veterans' legislation. This is despite the fact that women associated with the Resistance were particularly vulnerable to rape and sexual abuse during the occupation, and often became proxy targets for male family members who were fighting in the mountains or who had fled abroad (CAVR 2005: ch. 7; see also Carey 2001: 258–59).

Another aspect of the veterans' legislation that discriminates against women is its neglect of second wives. It is well known that many male FALINTIL fighters took on second wives—often referred to as *feen ailaran* (bush wives)—while remaining legally married to their first wives. Under the NLC legislation, the survival pension must be equally divided among heirs with equal claims, such as the veteran's parents or his/her children. Although spouses receive priority over parents and children in relation to receipt of a survival pension, in the event that multiple wives come forward to present their claims only the legally married spouse is entitled. This ignores the reality that former Resistance fighters had multiple relationships and children with women who they subsequently abandoned. It also serves to reinforce the gendered stereotype that these 'bush wives' were women of low morals and not legitimate wives as they had been 'living rough' with male FALINTIL fighters in the bush. The extent to which 'bush wives' continue to be held in low regard was reflected in the attitudes of policymakers interviewed for this study. The prevailing view expressed was that it was up to the woman herself to negotiate with the legal wife on sharing the pension. A 'bush wife' who seeks to claim veterans' benefits is, therefore, dependent upon the largesse of a woman and family with whom she has no links and, therefore, no leverage.

This is not to suggest that the veterans' scheme has not benefited some women. At the time this study was conducted, 38 per cent of those in receipt of a veterans' pension were women. However, of these women, 97.5 per cent were receiving a Survival Pension, which means they were not receiving a pension in recognition of their own contribution, but that of a family member. This means that the underlying gendered assumptions about women's roles during the conflict are not being challenged. Nonetheless, that a significant percentage of pension recipients are women suggests that, in theory, the scheme has had some empowering possibilities for those who were widowed during the conflict. Given the tenuous position widows occupy in society, particularly those without the support of extended families, more research is needed to gauge the extent to which women are truly benefiting from the survival pension.

Towards a more inclusive veterans' scheme?

At a purely technical level, a greater recognition of women's contributions to the Resistance could be accomplished relatively easily. Possibilities could include amending the legislation to allow second wives to claim a part of their former husband's pension and allowing remarried spouses to claim the pension. There is also scope within the existing veterans' legislation to award the title of National Liberation Combatant (NLC) to women who provided logistical support, medical services or intelligence to FALINTIL or the clandestine networks for a minimum of three years. It would also be relatively easy and affordable to award women the honorific title of 'Supporter of the National Liberation Struggle' if they do not have the necessary years to qualify as an NLC, but they did provide valuable support to the Resistance. A special award could be created to recognise *women's* roles within the Resistance, as was done for young people who were involved in the Santa Cruz demonstration of 1991.

Of course, given what is at stake for existing male veterans in terms of financial and symbolic power, any attempts to broaden the parameters of the veterans' scheme are likely to encounter significant resistance. Little is likely to be accomplished without the active involvement of women's NGOs and women parliamentarians. None of the male former Resistance figures interviewed for this study saw it as their role to advance the interests of their female *camarada* (comrades), and, at the time of writing, women's NGOs had been noticeably absent from any debates surrounding veterans' policy and legislation. One notable exception was the successful attempt by women's groups to advocate for honorary military decorations, including 'The Order of the Guerilla' to be bestowed upon women who were stationed with FALINTIL in the jungle. Although the women maintain political rather than military titles, that this award recognises them as part of the armed front is significant. Yet, even this relatively modest initiative has encountered resistance. One former senior member of FALINTIL complained that women 'who just sat there' have been provided with the same level of symbolic recognition as men who directed military strategy.[9] Given the powerful nature of the veterans' lobby, it might be necessary for women parliamentarians, OPMT, OMT and women's NGOs to form a strategic partnership to enable women to exert more influence over veterans' policy. Insisting on women's representation from FALINTIL and the clandestine and diplomatic fronts, and within the proposed Consultative Council of NLCs, could be the first challenge of this partnership.

---

9   Interview with former senior member of the Resistance, 21 March 2011.

Of course, for those seeking to promote gender equality in Timor-Leste, it may also be problematic to place too much faith in a strategy that seeks to recognise more women as veterans. What is clear is that the veterans' scheme is bolstering a vision of citizenship that is based upon a militarised identity. It perpetuates the idea that a person's role in the (armed) Resistance is a key factor in determining their status to speak as a 'legitimate' East Timorese and, consequently, their access to political and economic power. East Timorese women's organisations and others pursuing a gender equality agenda need to carefully consider the extent to which they want to 'buy in' to this vision of citizenship or seek to promote a more inclusive vision. Energies might be better spent, for instance, advocating for an expansion of the existing social safety net system to address the needs of vulnerable East Timorese regardless of whether they participated in the struggle.

Conclusion

The marginalisation of women within the veterans' scheme has consequences not only for East Timorese women but also for society as a whole. It means that the economic benefits that flow from the veterans' scheme are accruing mainly to men. Second, given that social status in Timor-Leste is inexorably tied to an ability to establish one's credentials within the Resistance, women are missing out on the respect that is accorded to veterans and the social capital that accrues from this. In this sense, the veterans' scheme represents a missed opportunity to promote women's agency and strength, and to help improve their social status. Third, the elevation of the role of armed men is further privileging the voices of former male combatants above others, and, in doing so, contributing to a militarised construction of citizenship. This construction of citizenship also fosters an environment in which violence against women is condoned. Finally, the representation and remembrance of the conflict as an armed (and predominantly male) struggle against the Indonesian occupiers represents a missed opportunity to create a national narrative that is inclusive of the diverse and complex experiences of men, women and young people. To do justice to these experiences, and to work towards gender equality, it would seem that long-term and creative efforts are required both within and beyond the veterans' scheme.

References

Alves, M., L. Abrantes and F. Reis. 2003. *Hakerek ho Ran* [Written with Blood]. Dili: Office for the Promotion of Equality, Prime Minister's Office.

Belun and CICR (Center for International Conflict Resolution) 2013. The Social Impact of Veterans' Payments Processes. *Early Warning and Response Policy Brief* VI. Timor-Leste: Belun and CICR.

Carey, P. 2001. Challenging Tradition, Changing Society: the Role of Women in East Timor's Transition to Independence. *Lusotopie* 2001:255–67.

CAVR (*Comissão de Acolhimento, Verdade e Reconciliação de Timor-Leste*; Timor-Leste Commission for Reception, Truth and Reconciliation) 2006. *Chega! The Report of the Commission for Reception Truth and Reconciliation in East Timor (CAVR)*. Dili: CAVR.

Conway, J. (ed.) 2010. *Step by Step: Women of East Timor, Stories of Resistance and Survival*. Darwin: CDU Press.

Cristalis, I. and C. Scott 2005. *Independent Women: The Story of Women's Activism in East Timor*. London: Catholic Institute for International Relations.

ICG (International Crisis Group) 2011. Timor-Leste's Veterans: An Unfinished Struggle? *Asia Briefing* 129. Dili/Jakarta/Brussels: ICG.

IPAC (Institute for Policy Analysis of Conflict) 2014. Timor-Leste after Xanana Gusmao. *IPAC Report* 12. Jakarta: IPAC.

Myrttinen, H. 2009. Poster Boys No More: Gender and Security Section Reform in Timor-Leste. *DCAF Policy Papers* 31. Geneva: DCAF (Geneva Centre for the Democratic Control of Armed Forces).

Ospina, S 2006. Participation of Women in Politics and Decision Making in Timor-Leste: A Recent History. *Report for the United Nations Development Fund for Women*. Dili: UNIFEM.

Rees, E. 2/9/2003. The UN's Failure to Integrate Falintil Veterans may Cause East Timor to Fail. *Online Opinion: Australia's E-Journal of Social and Political Debate*. www.onlineopinion.com.au/print.asp?article=666.

RDTL (*República Democrática de Timor-Leste*; Democratic Republic of Timor-Leste). 2010. *State Budget, Book 3*. Dili: RDTL.

RDTL 2011. *State Budget, Book 4*. Dili: RDTL.

UNHCHR (United Nations High Commissioner for Human Rights) 2006. Report of the Independent Special Commission of Inquiry for Timor-Leste. Geneva: UNHCHR.

CHAPTER 15

Rural–Urban Inequalities and Migration in Timor-Leste

Andrew McWilliam

Introduction

Inequalities between urban and rural Timor-Leste have been a persistent feature of the social landscape from colonial times. Many of these disparities reflect the asymmetric political and economic dynamics that distinguish urban centres of power and financial influence, especially the capital Dili, from the scattered, impoverished countryside where near subsistence agriculture and inevitably limited state services prevail. Socially, too, under Portuguese rule, the old status distinctions between *assimilados* (*civilizados*; assimilated)[1] and *indígenas* (natives) or worse (*salvagem;* savages) spoke to a perceived social gulf between advanced and educated urban modernity over and against the primitive and unenlightened rural hinterland (Roque 2012). If today these regimes of place-making between *cidade* (town) and *foho* (country) have been reworked and revised under Indonesian occupation, and the subsequent achievement of independence, echoes of these discriminatory spatial categories are, nevertheless, reinscribed through differential access to economic opportunity and services of state (Silva 2011).

These persistent inequalities can also be measured in statistical terms. In 2012, for example, the population of Timor-Leste stood at 1,154,625, and 70.4 per cent of citizens were classed as rural dwellers. They include a majority of the

---

1 As Silva (2011: 159) notes, 'assimilated' were those who adopted Christianity, spoke Portuguese and consequently were considered free from the taint of *usos e costumes* (custom and traditions).

vulnerable 50 per cent of the population living on less than US$2 per day—most of whom are highly dependent on the marked seasonal variations of the tropical monsoon climate. By contrast, some 57.8 per cent of urbanites in Dili occupy the highest wealth quintiles compared to just 8.7 per cent in rural areas (National Statistics Directorate (Timor-Leste) 2010: 27–28). As a result, some 91 per cent of urbanites enjoy safe drinking water, while just 57 per cent of their rural counterparts receive a similar level of service (National Statistics Directorate (Timor-Leste) 2010: xx). Rural areas have high rates of child mortality (8.7 per cent of children under five years of age) and much lower literacy levels (44 per cent of those >15 years) (National Statistics Directorate (Timor-Leste) 2010: xvii). Children in urban areas are almost four times more likely to be enrolled at secondary school than their peers in rural areas (National Statistics Directorate 2011).

In recent years, funding efforts by the national government to improve living standards beyond the urban concentrations have had positive impacts. New schools; well-stocked village health clinics; the roll-out of electricity transmission services; and the expansion of social payments to pensioners, veterans and village labour projects have made substantial contributions to improving rural household well-being. But inequalities persist, and one visible response to endemic levels of rural poverty has been a sustained rural–urban drift, both from the hinterland to district townships and from the remote uplands to the buzz and bright lights of the city, especially to Dili, the national capital, and especially by young people disenchanted with the prospects of a lifetime of subsistence agriculture and the overly familiar confines of home communities.

Some of these hopefuls move in search of better education opportunities and vocational training. Others respond to the lack of rural employment opportunities, and the drudgery of swidden agriculture.[2] All embrace their youthful desires to engage and consume the attractions of modernity, away from prying eyes of parents and neighbourly kin. This migratory trend can be appreciated in the 33 per cent increase of the Dili population (58,296) since 2004—a figure that represents 40 per cent of the overall population increase of the Timor-Leste population over that period (National Statistics Directorate (Timor-Leste) 2011). The lure of the city and the perceived freedoms and possibilities it presents has been a striking feature of post-independence East Timor, and one that is unlikely to diminish anytime soon.[3]

---

2   The lack of support for agricultural development has meant that in the 2014 national Budget just 2.2 per cent (US$34 million) has been allocated to the sector, undermining its economic and agronomic prospects.
3   Indeed, internal migration has been a sustained feature of the history of Dili, especially from the early 20th century. Guterres (2003: 4) notes that on the eve of the Second World War and the subsequent Japanese invasion, the population of Dili was just 12,000 people, which grew to 30,000 by 1975, and over 100,000 during the Indonesian occupation. See also Ranck (1977), who argued that Dili was a migrant city even before the Indonesian invasion in 1975, with as much as 75 per cent of the population composed of rural migrants.

As in the past, migration pathways to the city are closely associated with kinship and broader affinal networks, which rural householders draw on in urban centres to access temporary accommodation and networks of patronage (see Ranck 1977; Field 2004). This trend was given greater impetus in the months and years following 1999, when thousands of squatters took up residence in abandoned Indonesian housing, especially in the western parts of Dili. Over time, the sustained pattern of urban drift has seen the emergence of a distinctive residential make-up in the capital, as Scambary makes clear:

> East Timor's patterns of rural–urban migration over the past three decades have produced diverse hybrid micro-societies, in that they maintain aspects of traditional village systems such as clusters of kinship groups and vestiges of traditional authority, but in abbreviated form, sharing space with other kinship groups in highly heterogeneous societies reminiscent of more established urban and industrialised societies (2013: 3).

These concentrations of familiar social relations built around extended networks of kinship and alliance to source communities in the rural hinterland have been an important enabling mechanism to facilitate migration to the city and corresponding circular patterns of return.[4] But the reality of urban life for most young migrants is frequently disappointing, and despite inclusion in urban networks of support and patronage, youthful aspirants still face the reality of inconsistent itinerant work, endemic, high youth unemployment, and strong competition for a limited number of jobs. The absence of manufacturing industries with constrained private sector investment leaves little room for absorbing the steady stream of high school graduates who enter the employment market every year—an impact estimated to be more than a quarter of the youth population aged 15–29, or nearly 15,000 young people per annum (Thu and Silva 2013). The result is a complex urban dynamic of competitive adaptation among socially aligned networks, the rise of youthful political discontent, the spread of opportunistic petty crime, alcohol consumption, drug use and gang hooliganism (see Scambary 2012; Kostner and Clark 2007).[5]

In this challenging environment, there are opportunities for bright and connected young people, but similarly, there are, perhaps, many more who struggle to secure pathways to successful urban livelihoods, and whose dreams end in disillusion and failure. As Guterres (2003: 192) has observed in his study of Timorese migrants to Dili, some of whom found the transition eventually untenable: '(r)ural life may not be exciting, but it is relatively easy and provides

---

4   Scambary (2013) has highlighted the dynamic, mobile and heterogenous character of the membership of many urban communities, as seasonal factors and continuous visits between hinterland settlements and the city by school students who may return for vacations, or people who participate in religious and ceremonial events.
5   The impact of these dynamic processes reaching a destructive high point in the 2006 crisis in East Timor when the fragility of the new nation was exposed (Scambary 2009).

a safety net for those who fail in the city'. It is noteworthy in this respect that, despite the continuing movement of people to the towns and cities, the rural population of East Timor itself continues to grow. At an estimated average growth rate of around 2.5 per cent per annum, the rural population is projected to top one million by 2020. This compares with nearly double the rate of urban population growth (4.83 per cent) to over half a million (UNESCP 2010).

International migration

The possibility of realising aspirational futures among young rural migrants to the city remains elusive and a significant challenge for government policy and Timorese society alike. However, since the historic achievement of independence, a growing cadre of young Timorese have found new pathways to comparative prosperity through international labour migration. Some of these pathways have been promoted and sponsored through bilateral government programs with regional countries such as Malaysia, South Korea and Australia. In the case of South Korea, for example, East Timorese labour migrants are included among the 15 countries that have signed a memorandum of understanding with South Korea to take up temporary labour opportunities, mostly for unskilled employment, and all subject to annual quotas (Yoon and Jung 2013: 16). In 2012, for example, 485 East Timorese obtained work contracts, but these numbers are dwarfed by migrant workers from other countries in Asia for the same year, such as Indonesia (6,110), Vietnam (6,853) and Cambodia (8,047) (Yoon and Jung 2013: 17).

Timor-Leste has also been included in Australia's Seasonal Worker Programme, directed mainly at Pacific Island communities. It is designed to enhance employment opportunities for low-skilled, unemployed workers, and to satisfy demand in the horticulture and tourism sectors for low paid, seasonal workers (DEEWR 2013). The pilot program was initiated in 2012, and some 50 East Timorese have participated in work placements, which is a reasonable beginning. But recent evaluations suggest that regulatory complexity for approved employers, and cost advantages of employing European backpackers on working holidays over East Timorese workers, limits the effectiveness and scope of the present program (Thu and Silva 2013). That said, for participants, the exercise has been rewarding. According to Thu and Silva (2013), in 2012–13, a sample of Timorese seasonal workers earned between AU$10,000 and AU$18,000 in their five- to six-month period of contractual labour in Australia. These figures are well above any comparable remuneration that they may have secured in Timor-Leste. Reportedly, these earnings provide a range of livelihood benefits to participants and their families back home.

Formal work exchange agreements enacted through bilateral agreements clearly offer labour opportunities for young, low-skilled East Timorese workers, but in terms of addressing problems of domestic under-employment, the results to date have been underwhelming and limited in scope. Far more significant has been the dramatic rise of informal temporary labour migration of young hopefuls who have left Timor-Leste seeking shiftwork and low-skill factory jobs in Western Europe, especially the United Kingdom (UK). Key to this unexpected and surprising development over the previous decade has been the ability of East Timorese to secure Portuguese passports and thus eligibility to work in the European Union. The origins of what is now a thriving chain of migration derive from the pioneering travel of former student activists in the 1990s, who gained political asylum through embassies in Jakarta to escape state persecution following the repercussions of the Santa Cruz Cemetery massacre of students in Dili (1991). Following the remarkable achievement of independence and the decision by the Government of Portugal to automatically recognise all East Timorese born before 20 May 2002 as Portuguese citizens with associated entitlements, a path was opened to international travel and access to employment in the European Union (McWilliam 2012).

Since the end of Indonesian occupation, large numbers have accessed the migration pathway to the UK, drawn from many corners of Timor-Leste, including the rural hinterlands and towns where family networks and contacts in Portugal have been instrumental in sponsoring initial participants (see McWilliam 2012). Estimates of the number of participants are difficult to gauge. Shuaib (2008), in one study, estimated that up to 800 young Timorese were leaving for overseas work every year, and while his study was undertaken when the Global Financial Crisis (GFC) was beginning to be felt in Europe, the flow of Timorese labour migrants heading overseas has continued unabated. Young men make up the majority of travellers, but young women are well represented—many joining their brothers or cousins along well-versed networks of kinship and family. These days, thousands of East Timorese workers are dispersed around the UK, employed in a variety of low-skill jobs: shiftworkers in food packing factories (for example, Tesco and Sainsburys) and manufacturing, meat processing in Northern Ireland, cleaning, security and night porter work, car detailing, and restaurant services. Most live in group houses, sharing expenses and experiences, and keeping in touch with distant relatives and friends through the modern miracles of Skype and social media such as Facebook. The streams of Instagram images exchanged among relatives and friends in cyberspace offer insights into a cosmopolitan modernity involving travel and adventure, which encourages younger siblings and their friends back home to emulate their success. And if, in reality, the images often mask less desirable and unfulfilling aspects of life in the UK—the cold, grey weather, homesickness, isolation, gambling losses, and discrimination—there is no shortage of would-be labour migrants waiting for news of their passport and support from sponsors who might facilitate their journey to a 'better' life.

Remittance livelihoods

For most young Timorese migrants, the primary goal of overseas work is to generate savings to support their families in Timor-Leste and to build a financial stake to secure their own futures back home. Deirdre McKay (2007) has referred to the practice of remittance payments as monetised expressions of care and obligations to family, and the evidence is clear to see in certain contemporary settlements in Timor-Leste, where the bulk of new house construction is funded directly through remittance transfers from sons or siblings diligently putting away a sizeable portion of their wages to support their families at home. Los Palos in Lautem District is a case in point, where large numbers of its young people are now working and living in the UK, and, in certain areas of the town, such as the Aldeias of Ira Ara and Lere Loho, there is a widespread building and renovation boom underway (McWilliam 2012). Financial transfers from committed savers are enabling many young families to fast-track the construction of new cinder block housing and signal their success to their neighbours and wider community. Maria Da Costa, for example, while living with her parents and young daughter, has been able to construct a completely new house to lock-up stage in just over 12 months, using the money her husband, Marito, transfers each month (US$500) from his job in a local library in Oxford. His proficiency with English and a tenacious savings ethic has achieved something they didn't think possible when he embarked on his journey. There are many similar stories, and they highlight one reason for the popularity of international labour migration to Europe for young East Timorese.

Not all people who make the journey are disciplined savers, of course, and there are numerous stories of migrants and *suaka politiku* (asylum seekers) who have spent years overseas but fail to generate savings or send proceeds of their efforts to their families in need. Gambling, partying and spending-up means that there may be little left over to remit back home. Across the UK, including the towns and cities where East Timorese settle for work, there are typically numerous gambling and sports betting outlets (Ladbrokes, 888sport, Elite and Skybet, among others) that are more than ready to relieve bored shiftworkers of their weekly incomes. Gambling for young Timorese has a strong social aspect—they can gather after their shifts to put a few pounds through the digital roulette machines, bet on the results of English football matches, or chance the quick-pick lotteries. Rumours of big wins among Timorese players that circulate among migrant groups and local Timorese networks is often enough to keep young people feeding the machines.

For those who sustain their commitment to family and their savings targets, the flow of remittances through Western Union wire transfers are making significant contributions to community livelihoods. Funds are regularly directed to support everyday expenses and contributions to lifecycle rituals of kin and affines. In addition to new house construction and improving the material conditions of life, savings and capital are also directed to supporting parents, siblings, spouses and children for everyday consumption needs and associated costs. Where possible, participants also seek to build a financial stake for future trading or microenterprises on their return home. According to Shuaib's study of those receiving remittances, some 45 per cent of households used the transfers to support daily household consumption, 41 per cent for housing improvements, 30 per cent for school fees, and 10 per cent for loan repayments. Most were also saving a portion of these funds to direct to education expenses (75 per cent), housing improvements (35 per cent), weddings and funerals (18 per cent), and business investment (10 per cent) (Shuaib 2008: 209). These findings are highly consistent with more recent personal research on which this chapter is based, and point to a growing significance of remittances for livelihood support and everyday consumption.

The role of remittance in supporting the education of younger siblings to attend high schools in Dili and further afield in neighbouring Indonesia is a further important feature. This objective has long been a factor in Timorese rural–urban migration, as Ranck pointed out in his survey of Dili in the 1970s. Then he noted that urban adaptation through education was a key element of migration success, and 'all the network sets show an obviously over-riding concern for education' (1977: 235).

Furthermore, and despite Timor-Leste's tumultuous past, Indonesia has become an increasingly attractive destination for young East Timorese seeking to secure vocational training and educational qualifications. Drawing in part on earlier pathways for education forged by young East Timorese during the Indonesian period (Bexley 2009), the new transnational education migration is driven by a pragmatic parental assessment of relative costs and benefits, as well as the familiarity of Indonesian educational institutions, language and attendant cultural values. Although supporting children in school or university in Indonesia is expensive for the average East Timorese family, lower living costs in Java and the perceived quality of education services can make the total package a cost-effective option. Bexley has noted, in 2009 at least, that the Timor-Leste embassy in Jakarta estimated there were some 3,500 East Timorese studying in Indonesia, and the number is likely to have increased since then (Bexley 2009).

Young East Timorese appear to be enthusiastic participants in the process, related in part, no doubt, to the popularity of Indonesian pop music and *sinetron* (televised soap operas) that have huge followings in Timor-Leste and contribute in no small way to contemporary experiences of modernity and the shaping of youthful values and aspirations (see also Ostergaard 2005).

Patterns and prospects for labour migration

In his 2008 survey of 105 East Timorese households receiving remittance flows, Shuaib made a number of striking observations that speak to the growing importance of transnational labour migration and the export income it generates. Among these findings, he noted, for instance, that:

1. 'Households with members working overseas are better off financially by many multiples than households pursuing local employment'.
2. Western Union electronic transfers remitted some US$370,000 per month into Timor-Leste (2008), predominantly from the UK. This amounted to an estimated US$5 million per annum in 2008 now likely to be significantly higher.[6]
3. The value of inward remittances to Timor-Leste makes migrant labour the country's second largest non-oil export after coffee.

These observations point to the growing importance of this livelihood option for many young East Timorese disillusioned with unemployment and the limited livelihood options in their hamlets of origin or on the dusty streets of the towns and cities. Labour migration to the distant UK is providing a bounteous and unexpected source of income and remittance flows to thousands of beneficiary households, whose member's lives have been materially enriched through the practice. Despite the impact of the GFC, especially in Western Europe, the slowdown has had limited effect on the outward flow of Timorese recruits. Their willingness to tackle low-skilled, menial and factory line work means that they can still access the comparatively higher wage opportunities on offer in the UK. If the macro-economic impact of these remittances remains relatively small in an economy so heavily dependent on oil revenues—estimated to be just 1.4 per cent of non-oil GDP in 2006 (Shuaib 2008: 195)—the revenue flow is only likely to grow, and, over time, contribute a sustained source of economic support for multiple Timorese households with members overseas. Like its regional neighbours in the Pacific and Southeast Asia, labour migration is likely to provide an important and continuing source of supplementary

---

6   The sum included transfers of funds through the established banks in Dili, such as ANZ Bank and the Portuguese *Caixa Geral de Depositos* trading as BNU.

income for many years to come.[7] Its broadly democratic nature also contributes to expanded education opportunities for many young Timorese and to breaking down the historical class inequalities that have persisted between rural and urban residents for generations.

References

Bexley, A. 2009. Getting an Education: Links to Indonesian Schools and Universities Remain Strong in East Timor. *Inside Indonesia* 96(Apr–June). www.insideindonesia.org/getting-an-education.

DEEWR (Department of Education, Employment and Workplace Relations) 2013. Seasonal Labour Mobility Initiative with Pacific Island Countries and East Timor for Development Purposes: Regulation Impact Statement. Canberra: DEEWR.

Field, A. 2004. Places of Suffering and Pathways to Healing: Post-Conflict Life in Bidau, East Timor. PhD thesis, James Cook University.

Guterres, A.S.C. 2003. Internal Migration and Development in East Timor. PhD thesis, Massey University, New Zealand.

Kostner, M. and S. Clark 2007. Timor-Leste's Youth in Crisis: Situational Analysis and Policy Options. Washington D.C.: World Bank.

McKay, D. 2007. Sending Dollars Shows Feelings, Emotions and Economies in Filipino Migration. *Mobilities* 2(2):175–94.

McWilliam, A.R. 2012. New Fataluku Disaporas and Landscapes of Remittance and Return. *Nation-Formation, Identity and Change in Timor-Leste*, special issue *Local–Global: Identity, Security, Community* 11:72–85.

National Statistics Directorate (NSD) [Timor-Leste], Ministry of Finance [Timor-Leste] 2011. 'Highlights of 2010 Census Main Results in Timor Leste', *Timor-Leste Population and Housing Census* 2010. Dili: Timor-Leste [produced in conjunction with the United Nations Population Fund (UNFPA)].

National Statistics Directorate (NSD) [Timor-Leste], Ministry of Finance [Timor-Leste] and ICF Macro 2010. Timor-Leste Demographic and Health Survey 2009–10. Dili, Timor-Leste: NSD [Timor-Leste] and ICF Macro.

---

7   In this regard, Shuaib (2008: 195) highlights the significant contribution of inward remittances to regional neighbours such as Sri-Lanka and the Philippines (both 10 per cent of GDP), Samoa (26 per cent), Tonga (42 per cent) and Fiji (7 per cent).

Ostergaard, L. 2005. Timor-Leste Youth Social Analysis Mapping and Youth Institutional Assessment. Dili: World Bank.

Ranck, S.R. 1977. Recent Rural–Urban Migration to Dili, Portuguese Timor: a Focus on the Use of Households, Kinship, and Social Networks by Timorese Migrants. MA (Hons) thesis, Macquarie University.

Roque, R. 2010. *Headhunting and Colonialism: Anthropology and the Circulation of Human Skulls in the Portuguese Empire 1870–1930*. New York: Palgrave Macmillan.

Scambary, J. 2009. Anatomy of a Conflict: The 2006–7 Communal Conflict In East Timor. *Conflict, Security and Development* 9(2):265–88.

Scambary, J. 2013. Conflict and Resilience in an Urban Squatter Settlement in Dili, East Timor. *Urban Studies* 50(10):1–16.

Scheiner, C. 2013. Rights and Sustainability in Timor-Leste's Development. Paper presented at ANU SSGM seminar, 27/11/2013.

Shuaib, F. 2008. *East Timor Country Report*. Canberra: Department of Foreign Affairs and Trade. aid.dfat.gov.au/Publications/Documents/etimor_ study.pdf.

Silva, K. 2011. Foho versus Dili: The Political Role of Place in East Timor National Imagination. *Revista de Estudos Anti-Utilitaristas e PosColoniais* 1(2):144–65.

Thu, P.M. and I.M. da Silva 2013. The Australian Seasonal Workers Program: Timor-Leste's Case, *SSGM Briefing Note* 13. Canberra: State, Society and Governance in Melanesia, The Australian National University.

UNESCAP (United Nations Economic and Social Commission for Asia and the Pacific) 2010. Online Statistical Database. www.unescap.org/stat/data/swweb/DataExplorer.aspx.

Yoon, A.O. and J. Jung 2013. *Determinants of International Labor Migration to Korea*. Seoul: Korean Institute for International Economic Policy.

CHAPTER 16

Assessing the Implementation and Impact of Timor-Leste's Cash Payment Schemes

Joanne Wallis

Introduction

In 2013, Timor-Leste ranked 134 out of 186 countries in the United Nations Development Programme's Human Development Index (UNDP 2013). In 2012, 37.4 per cent of its 1.17 million citizens lived on less than US$1.25 per day, and 68.1 per cent of its population lived in what the UNDP defines as 'multidimensional poverty'—that is, they experienced multiple deprivations at the individual level in health, education and standard of living (UNDP 2014). However, since 2005, Timor-Leste has had access to relatively large revenues from the Bayu-Undan and Kitan oil and gas fields. It may also receive additional future revenues from the Greater Sunrise field and from other fields yet to be explored (UNESCAP and UNDP 2003). Some projections predict that these revenues could run out by 2025 (*La'o Hamutuk* 2014), and questions of how the government should use these revenues to address the country's development challenges remain subject to debate. The cash payment schemes that the government introduced in 2008 should occupy a leading role in this debate, as while they play a role in peace-building and social protection, they also contribute to rising levels of government spending. Therefore, it is important for long-term development to assess who these programs are targeted at, how they are implemented, what impact they have, and what alternatives may be available.[1]

---

1   Research for this chapter was in part performed in 2010 with Alexandra Gillies and Mericio Akara under a consultancy for the Revenue Watch Institute.

Payments to veterans of the resistance and their survivors

The most extensive cash payment scheme comprises four pension schemes for veterans of the resistance to Indonesia's invasion and occupation. Superior Pensions are for veterans distinguished 'for their outstanding contribution to the resistance struggle'. Special Subsistence Pensions are for veterans with at least eight years of full-time participation in the struggle, or who are incapable of work due to physical or mental disabilities resulting from their participation in the struggle. Special Retirement Pensions are for veterans with at least 15 years of full-time participation in the struggle. Survivor Pensions are for the surviving spouse, orphans (regardless of age), parents or siblings of 'National Liberation Veteran Combatants' who died 'as a result of their participation' in the struggle, or who were beneficiaries of either the Special Subsistence or Special Retirement Pensions and have since died. The order of preference among survivors is: surviving spouse, children, parents and then siblings. If there is more than one rightful claimant (such as multiple children), the pension 'shall be divided equally between claimants'.[2]

Payments to internally displaced persons (IDPs)

The second cash payment scheme targets the approximately 100,000 persons who were internally displaced during, and in the aftermath of, the April and May 2006 security crisis. In late 2007, the government launched its National Recovery Strategy, *Hamutuk Hari'i Futuru* (Together Building the Future). One of the strategy's five pillars, *Hamutuk Hari'i Uma* (Together Building Homes) (ICG 2009; Lopes 2009; OVPMRDTL 2007), aimed to facilitate the return or resettlement of IDPs by providing compensation for damage caused to their houses. The payments varied according to the level of verified damage: internally displaced persons (IDPs) whose houses had been totally or largely destroyed received US$4,500, IDPs whose houses were severely damaged but still standing received US$3,000, IDPs whose houses were less severely damaged received US$1,500, and IDPs whose houses needed only minor repairs received US$500. Most payments were made in 2008. In late 2009, the government also compensated IDPs for possessions damaged in the crisis. As it was too difficult to assess on a case-by-case basis, each family was given US$500.

---

2 Decree Law on the Pensions of the Combatants and Martyrs of the National Liberation no. 15/2008.

'Petitioner' payments

Following the security crisis, the government also used cash payments to resolve the case of the 'petitioners'—a group of 591 disgruntled soldiers who had helped to instigate the crisis. As the government perceived the petitioners as a potential source of insecurity, in early 2008 it introduced a demobilisation program that consisted of payments of US$8,000 each to reintegrate into civilian life (ICG 2013).[3]

Support allowances for the elderly and disabled

The third cash payment scheme also aimed to assist other vulnerable groups under the National Recovery Strategy. Accordingly, in 2008 the government introduced a Support Allowance to meet the 'basic needs' of the elderly and disabled.[4] Individuals that receive other types of benefits (such as veterans) are ineligible. The amount of the Support Allowance 'shall not exceed one third of the minimum wage accorded for the current year to civil service employees and shall not be lower than the previous one'. The initial amount of the allowance was set at US$20 per month, which was equivalent to 20 per cent of the national minimum wage for civil servants. However, in 2010 the allowance was raised to US$30 per month in recognition that incomes had risen (RDTLMSS 2008, 2009).

Bolsa de Mãe program

The fourth cash payment scheme, the *Bolsa de Mãe* (Mother's Purse), was also introduced in 2008 in accordance with the National Recovery Strategy. It provides the neediest female-headed households with a monthly subsidy to assist them to feed and educate their children. This payment is conditional on children receiving good grades at school and the amount of the payment varies according to the education level of the child: US$5 per month for primary school, US$10 per month for junior secondary school, US$20 per month for senior secondary school, $25 per month for university within Timor-Leste, and $30 per month for university overseas (RDTLMSS 2008, 2009).

---

3   Decree on the Integration of Ex-Soldiers into Civilian Life no. 12/2008.
4   Decree Law on the Support Allowance for the Aged and Disabled no. 19/2008.

Implementation

The implementation of the cash payment schemes has faced a number of administrative challenges, primarily relating to the identification of recipients. In order to identify veterans who should receive pension payments, the former President Xanana Gusmão established veterans' commissions, who worked during 2003–05 to register veterans and their survivors (Fundasaun Mahein 2011).[5] In 2009, their data was verified by the *Comissão de Homenagem* (Homage Commission), which compiled the initial lists of veterans to receive payments.[6] A separate tribunal, the *Comissão de Homenagem, Supervisão de Registo e Recurso* (Commission for Homage, Supervision of Registration and Appeals), was created to hear appeals about the registration process.[7] However, although the process of identification has been relatively thorough, individuals have made false claims of being veterans (ICG 2011).[8] The identification of wives, children and siblings who claim the Survivor Pension has also proved difficult, as many have difficultly verifying their relationship to the deceased veteran in the absence of reliable birth or marriage records during the Indonesian occupation.[9]

Similar difficulties arise with respect to the IDPs payments. In order to claim these payments, IDPs registered with the *Ministério da Solidariedade Social* (MSS; Ministry of Social Solidarity), and then MSS estimation teams worked with the *Ministério das Infraestruturas* (Ministry of Infrastructure) and village chiefs to verify the reported damage. To cheat the system, some non-IDPs took up residence in IDP camps and tried to register to receive payments, some IDPs from the same household each claimed payments, while other IDPs duplicated their electoral cards to claim multiple payments.[10] A portion of these fraudulent claimants are likely to have received payments, as the process for verifying the damage to IDP houses was labour-intensive and rushed.[11] Identification problems also arise with respect to the Elderly and Disabled Support Allowance, as it can be difficult to identify who qualifies as elderly, because electoral cards

---

5 Interview with a government official, 30/9/2010.
6 First Amendment to Law No. 3/2006 of 12 April no. 9/2009.
7 Statute of the National Liberation Combatants.
8 Interview with a government official (a), 27/9/2010; interview with a government official, 30/9/2010.
9 Interview with a government official, 30/9/2010.
10 Interview with a member of Timorese civil society, 26/9/2010; interview with a member of Timorese civil society, 27/9/2010; interview with an international humanitarian worker, 27/9/2010; interview with an international humanitarian worker, 28/9/2010.
11 Interview with an international humanitarian worker, 30/9/2010.

often contain unreliable age data.[12] There are fewer problems with the *Bolsa de Mãe* program, as recipients are currently identified by village chiefs and MSS child protection officers assess applicants and mediate claims.[13]

Making cash payments is also a logistical and security challenge, particularly in rural areas where effective banking and mail systems are underdeveloped.[14] While most cash payment schemes are administered by the MSS, the *Ministério das Finanças* (Ministry of Finance) makes the actual payments. Many payments have been paid in cash, although there are plans to make more payments into bank accounts. In most cases, Ministry of Finance officials travel with the cash from Dili to district administration offices, and then work with MSS officials and village chiefs to ensure payment.[15]

Collusion and corruption is another challenge. For example, in the case of the IDPs payments, some MSS officials are said to have overstated the damage to IDP houses in order to secure a larger payment for the IDPs and subsequent kickbacks for themselves.[16] There is also said to be manipulation in the administration of allowances to the elderly and disabled: in some cases, recipients had died yet their names remain on the recipient list so that others could claim their money.[17] One member of civil society cited a case where a subdistrict administrator asked a village chief to sign a blank list of recipients, which the administrator would later complete.[18] There is anecdotal evidence of MSS officials demanding payments from elderly and disabled recipients for fictional 'administration costs' before they could be paid or given their identification cards.[19] One member of parliament (MP) argued that the commissioners who vetted veterans' registrations 'handpicked those they deemed to be veterans and blocked those who they did not like'.[20]

Related to this, there appears to be insufficient oversight of the cash payment schemes. This is partly explained by the fact that Timor-Leste is still a young state experiencing capacity and resource shortages. Census and other citizen registration data is often unreliable, particularly identification documents from Portuguese colonial times or the Indonesian occupation. The cash payment

---

12   Interview with a village chief, 28/9/2010; interview with an international humanitarian worker, 29/9/2010.
13   Interview with a government official, 28/9/2010.
14   Interview with a government official (b), 27/9/2010; interview with a government official (a), 29/9/2010.
15   Interview with a government official (a), 29/9/2010.
16   Interview with a member of Timorese civil society, 26/9/2010; interview with a member of Timorese civil society, 27/9/2010; interview with an international humanitarian worker, 27/9/2010.
17   Interview with a member of Timorese civil society, 26/9/2010.
18   Interview with a member of Timorese civil society, 1/10/2010.
19   Interview with a member of Timorese civil society, 1/10/2010; interview with a member of parliament (b), 30/9/2010.
20   Interview with a member of parliament (b), 30/9/2010; interview with a member of Timorese civil society, 1/10/2010.

schemes were introduced 'very quickly', and it was a 'massive job to set up procedures, administration and distribution systems'.[21] Accountability structures are also in their infancy, such as the *Comissão da Função Pública* (Civil Service Commission), *Escritório do Inspetor-Geral* (Office of the Inspector-General), *Comissão Anti-Corrupção* (Anti-Corruption Commission), and the *Tribunal Superior Administrativo, Fiscal e de Contas* (High Administrative, Tax and Audit Court).

More promisingly, there are impressive examples of genuine efforts to improve the system. For example, the MSS is working with international donors to create a registry of all vulnerable families. This will allow the MSS to use reliable socioeconomic data and proxy means testing to target *Bolsa da Mae* (Mother's Purse) and other payments to the neediest households.[22] Efforts are also being made by the Ministry of Finance to examine whether mobile banking facilities can facilitate payments.[23]

Peace-building

The most important impact of the cash payment schemes has been their role in peace-building since the security crisis, which displaced almost one-tenth of the population and resulted in violence and widespread tensions. In order to facilitate peace-building, it was important to return or resettle IDPs, and the IDP recovery packages played an important role. International Organization for Migration (IOM) surveys of communities who received IDPs indicate that their return or resettlement was largely (although not entirely) peaceful and that societal tensions have subsided (IOM 2008a; 2008b; 2008c; 2009a; 2009b). However, there is concern that the IDP recovery packages merely 'bought peace', and that longer term solutions are required to ensure that former IDPs successfully reintegrated.[24] In particular, there were instances of jealousy between recipients and non-recipients.[25] Some tensions were diffused through mediation or customary ceremonies; others by IDPs making payments to village members (such as the temporary occupants of their house) (Impact Alliance 25/2/2010; RDTLMSS 2009).[26] Complaints also arose from those who lost their

---

21 Interview with an international development adviser, 30/9/2010.
22 Interview with a government official, 28/9/2010.
23 Interview with a government official, 29/9/2010.
24 Interview with a member of Timorese civil society, 26/9/2010.
25 Interview with a government official, 29/9/2010; interview with an international humanitarian worker, 28/9/2010; interview with an international humanitarian worker, 29/9/2010; interview with an international humanitarian worker, 30/9/2010.
26 Interview with an international humanitarian worker, 27/9/2010; interview with a member of Timorese civil society, 27/9/2010.

belongings or assets during the crisis but were not compensated because they had not fled.[27] A former IDP commented that 'those who did not flee are also victims'.[28]

The veterans' pensions also play a peace-building role. Certain veterans groups contributed to escalating the security crisis, as they expressed resentment about their treatment since 1999.[29] When they were officially 'demobilised' in February 2001, only 650 out of 1,950 veterans were recruited into the new army, with the rest given small packages to assist their reintegration into the community. Demobilised veterans mostly missed out on jobs in the civil service and the new police force, and many faced unemployment and significant hardship. Consequently, veterans groups formed and began to conduct parades and operate as political lobby groups. Several became increasingly strident and were perceived as threatening the stability of the state (World Bank 2008). The decision to rapidly introduce the veterans' pensions in 2008 can be understood partly as a response to this pressure. However, there are questions over the sustainability of the government effectively buying peace from the veterans. There is concern that veteran groups may pose a threat to stability should their demands (including for further payments) not be met. One MP cautiously observed that veteran groups remain 'waiting in the mountains, ready to come back down to Dili and cause problems'.[30] While no one questions the esteem in which veterans are held, ordinary people are concerned about the role that some veteran groups have played since independence, particularly during the security crisis.[31]

Similarly, the payments to 'petitioners' reflected their potential danger rather than any particular need. These payments did encourage these former soldiers to demobilise and reintegrate into society. However, there is a perception that the petitioners had been 'rewarded for causing trouble', especially since they had technically broken the law by abandoning their barracks, and, beyond being dismissed from the army, had not faced sanctions for their actions during the crisis.[32]

---

27 Interview with a member of Timorese civil society, 27/9/2010.
28 Interview with a former IDP, 28/9/2010.
29 For a discussion of the treatment of veterans following the withdrawal of Indonesia in 1999, see Conflict, Security and Development Group (2003).
30 Interview with a member of parliament (b), 30/9/2010.
31 Interview with a member of Timorese civil society, 26/9/2010; interview with a member of Timorese civil society, 1/10/2010.
32 Interview with a member of Timorese civil society (a), 27/9/2010.

Dependence and expectation of future payments

The cash payment schemes may also have generated a degree of dependence and expectation of future payments. The recovery packages for IDPs and payments to the 'petitioners' risk setting a precedent that victims, or those who threaten the peace, deserve financial compensation. For example, following the introduction of the IDPs payments, youth groups in IDP camps pressured the government and ended up receiving 'student packages' of US$200 apiece.[33] Several people whose houses were destroyed during violence in 1999, or during the Indonesian invasion, have tried to make claims for IDPs payments. A prominent victims' advocate even suggested on national radio on 20 July 2008 that 'it's better if we 1999 victims just organise ourselves and go and live in a refugee camp' in order to receive state assistance (quoted in Kent 2010: 194). Veterans have also mobilised for greater payments, leading to the expansion of the eligibility criteria for veterans' pensions, as well as the one-off veteran payments. Similarly, whether members of the extensive network of civilians who supported the independence struggle, referred to as the *frente clandestina* (clandestine front), also deserve payments now features more frequently in public discourse.

A stark example of escalating demand is the draft Reparations Law, which seeks to initiate a memory and reconciliation process for the conflict between 1974 and 1999, and to empower and support 'vulnerable victims' (Amnesty International 2012).[34] One MP argued that it 'is not intended to be a big social assistance program. It is just about finding and helping the most vulnerable and traumatised people'.[35] Others see the law as an effort to create another cash payment scheme aimed at a very amorphous and difficult-to-identify group. One civil society representative saw it as a symptom of a new culture where there is 'competition to be victims because people have seen that that is how people benefit'.[36] An MP expressed concern that 'the compensation train is steaming out of control', and if the Reparations Law creates extensive cash payment schemes, 'the floodgates will open' for further demands.[37]

---

33   Interview with a government official, 29/9/2010; interview with an international humanitarian worker, 27/9/2010.
34   Draft Law Establishing the Public Memory Institute. www.laohamutuk.org/Justice/Reparations/Organic15JunEn.pdf, accessed 19/9/2010; Draft Law Establishing a Framework for the National Reparations Programme. www.laohamutuk.org/Justice/Reparations/Reparations15JunEn.pdf, accessed 19/9/2010.
35   Interview with a member of parliament (b), 30/9/2010.
36   The proposed Reparations Law raises the broader issue of the role that the discourse of 'victimhood' plays in determining an emerging 'hierarchy of the deserving' of state recognition and assistance (Kent 2010: 194). In contrast, a member of civil society argued that many Timorese people do not want to be classified as 'victims', but instead see themselves as 'heroes' because 'we fought for our independence and we won'. He suggested that the language of 'victimhood' has been promoted by international NGOs, which have adopted the international language of human rights and transitional justice, but which does not necessarily resonate in the Timorese context. Interview with a member of Timorese civil society, 1/10/2010.
37   Interview with a member of parliament, 27/9/2010.

Politicisation

This suggests that the cash payment schemes may be politicised and used to appease certain groups, which could lead to the allocation of revenues in ways that do not advance the country's overall development, welfare and security. There is a perception that the government has sought to use the payment schemes to create a 'moral and political binding'—a sort of clientelist loyalty between recipients and government (Fundasaun Mahein 2011).[38] Cash payments might also reflect Prime Minister Gusmão's rather paternalistic approach to government spending.[39] In fact, several times a year Gusmão magnanimously hands out (his own) cash to people on the steps of his home.

Cash payments to veterans run the greatest risk of politicisation. Veterans represented a valuable political constituency for former Prime Minister Xanana Gusmão, who used the issue of pensions during election campaigns and expanded their benefits several times since he took office (*La'o Hamutuk* 2013).[40] Certain veteran groups have also assumed a vocal role in state affairs, and exercise considerable influence in parliament, including by advocating for larger veterans pensions (ICG 2011).[41] Indeed, since their introduction in 2008, the veterans' pensions and Survivor Pension have expanded dramatically. In response to lobbying from veteran groups (March 2008), in 2009 cash payments were made to veterans who 'took part on a full-time basis in the struggle for national independence for a period of four to seven years'. The amount of the payment was US$1,380, which corresponded to 12 months of the civil service minimum wage (of US$115 per month).[42] In 2009, the government also made a payment to cover cases where there was no immediate relative eligible to receive the survivor pension. This payment went to 'relatives up to a fourth degree in collateral line' of a deceased veteran, provided these relatives 'suffered torture, deportation or imprisonment as a consequence of the militancy of their … relative'. The government also began to provide a limited number of scholarships to orphans of deceased veterans and to children of those veterans who receive the Special Subsistence or Special Retirement Pensions.[43] This raises

---

38 Interview with a member of parliament, 28/9/2010; interview with a member of Timorese civil society, 26/9/2010; interview with a member of Timorese civil society (a), 27/9/2010.
39 Interview with a member of Timorese civil society (b), 27/9/2010; interview with a member of Parliament (a), 30/9/2010.
40 Interview with a member of Timorese civil society, 1/10/2010.
41 Interview with a member of parliament, 27/9/2010; interview with a member of parliament (b), 30/9/2010.
42 Statute of the National Liberation Combatants.
43 Statute of the National Liberation Combatants; Decree Law on the Pensions of the Combatants and Martyrs; Decree Law on the Regime of Awarding Scholarships to the Children of Combatants and Martyrs of the National Liberation no. 8/2009.

a risk that the veterans' pensions may entrench a perception that veterans (and their families) are a privileged social group, particularly as the Survivor Pensions and scholarships may embed intergenerational advantage (Wallis 2013).

Economically sustainable?

The expansion of the veterans' pensions raises questions concerning whether the cash payment schemes are economically sustainable, especially given that oil and gas resources are finite. These questions feed into a broader debate about whether Timor-Leste should save or spend in order to advance its development, and if it opts to spend, what that spending should be on.

While the IDPs' recovery packages and the payments to the petitioners are finished, the number of recipients of the elderly and disabled support allowance and *Bolsa da Mãe* program has risen, largely because administrative improvements have facilitated the identification of more recipients. There are also proposals to make payments to clandestine resistance; estimates of their numbers run as high as 70,000.[44] The proposed Reparations Law could potentially lead to payments for the 'vulnerable victims'. Each expansion of the cash payment schemes places additional strain on the state budget.

However, the veterans' pensions remain by far the largest cash payment scheme, largely because the value of the veterans' pensions and the number of veteran recipients has increased. In the US$1.7 billion 2013 budget, US$239 million was allocated for cash payment schemes, of which US$84.8 million was for veterans (RDTL 2013: 45). The lowest veterans' pension of US$276 per month is many times higher than the average Timorese income; in 2010, 41 per cent of the population lived on less than US$38 per month (UN 2010). Despite these large amounts, there is a widespread view that 'the state should pay attention to veterans because they fought for independence. Even if the country was poor, it would pay them.'[45]

The World Bank noted that the size of the veterans' pensions 'are relatively high compared to other post-conflict countries, particularly as a percentage of Timor-Leste's non-oil GDP' (World Bank 2008: 27). Timor-Leste could face a challenge similar to Guinea-Bissau, where 'commitments to veterans have impeded the government's ability to address other social issues' (World Bank 2008: 27). However, one international official noted that Timor-Leste is still in 'short-term mode' following the 2006–07 security crisis during which it needs to respond to stability needs first, and economic sustainability second.[46]

---

44   Interview with a member of parliament, 27/9/2010.
45   Interview with a government official (a), 27/9/2010.
46   Interview with an international development adviser, 30/9/2010.

Alternatives?

The size of the cash payment schemes suggests that it is necessary to assess whether they advance development, particularly in the long term, or whether alternatives should be considered. While payments to the elderly, disabled and vulnerable female-headed households appear to advance social protection aims, it is less clear that payments to the IDPs, petitioners or veterans are targeted based on need or that they advance the development of their recipients.

Although there has not been a formal study that tracks the spending patterns of cash payment recipients, there is anecdotal evidence that many IDPs invested in their homes, started small businesses or engaged in consumption valuable to the local economy.[47] Studies of programs similar to the elderly and disabled support allowance and *Bolsa da Mae* in countries such as Brazil and Mexico suggest that cash payments to poor households have a strong poverty reduction effect. Buying basic goods like food and clothing represent investments in human capital, and the extra income (especially if tied to school attendance) can increase the family's incentive to have their children in school rather than working (Moss 2011).

However, there is also anecdotal evidence that some recipients spend their cash payments on luxury items, parties or traditional gambling and cockfighting.[48] Similarly, cash payments bear other economic risks, such as elevating prices of non-traded goods and inflation (Corden and Neary 1982)—risks emphasised by the World Bank (World Bank 2009). There is scepticism that the cash payment schemes will lead to long-term improvements in livelihoods, given the lack of a savings culture cultivated by the fact many people have lost their houses and belongings several times during the Indonesian invasion, occupation and subsequent conflicts.[49] There are also concerns about 'dependency', with parallels drawn to Indonesia's provision of rice and other handouts in order to control the population.[50] One village chief noted that the cash payments have made some people 'lazy', which has led to people failing to work their fields and then later facing food shortages.[51]

---

47 Interview with an international humanitarian worker, 27/9/2010; interview with an international humanitarian worker, 28/9/2010.
48 Interview with a member of parliament, 27/9/2010; interview with a member of parliament (b), 30/9/2010; interview with a member of Timorese civil society, 26/9/2010.
49 Interview with a member of Timorese civil society (b), 27/9/2010.
50 Interview with an international humanitarian worker, 27/9/2010.
51 Interview with a village chief, 28/9/2010.

Consequently, alternatives such as social housing, income-generation projects (such as small shops, fuel stations, and livestock and transport co-operatives), microcredit schemes, tourism facilities, or infrastructure investments might produce more lasting development results. In this regard, the *Hamutuk Hari'i Economia Sosial* (Together Building Social Economy) pillar of the National Recovery Strategy aims to create livelihood opportunities and employment-generation schemes. Infrastructure projects are perceived as particularly useful as they benefit communities as a whole, especially since resource shortages were a source of tension during the security crisis.

However, Timor-Leste is a very young state, in which administrative, planning, logistical, accountability and oversight capacity is still being developed. While infrastructure investments might offer much greater returns than cash payments, without adequate state capacity, infrastructure projects can be poorly planned, difficult to implement, and prone to corruption. Even if well executed, years can pass before welfare benefits accrue to the population. In contrast, cash payment schemes can be implemented quickly, and can provide a direct economic benefit to the population, particularly in rural areas where state services and public goods are often limited. Cash payments also offer administrative 'simplicity', as they 'cut out layers of bureaucracy and cut back problems of logistics and corruption'.[52]

While cash payment schemes might represent a relatively effective way to distribute state resources, questions need to be raised concerning the way they are targeted. In a very poor population that receives insufficient social services, it appears that most of the cash payment budget does not target the neediest households. While the schemes could be expanded, the finite nature of Timor-Leste's resources appears to militate against this. Instead, it might be better to reallocate the cash payment budget so that it is more finely targeted at those in need. However, such a move might be politically difficult, as it would probably involve moving resources from the veterans' pensions.

Conclusion

Overall, it appears that the cash payment schemes have improved many Timorese people's lives by providing funds to build and repair houses, helping them to buy basic necessities, or supplementing their income. The schemes facilitated peace-building in the aftermath of the security crisis, and provide citizens with an immediate and direct benefit from the oil and gas revenues. However, the implementation of the schemes poses challenges, and their impact highlights

---

52 Interview with an international humanitarian worker, 27/9/2010.

the risks of politicisation and questions over their economic sustainability. Most significantly, there are questions over whether the schemes target those most in need, as opposed to members of certain social groups. If Timor-Leste is serious about advancing development and lifting its population out of poverty, this suggests that the schemes could be redesigned so that they target recipients who are most in need of social protection.

References

Conflict, Security and Development Group 2003. *A Review of Peace Operations: A Case for a Change*. London, King's College.

Corden, W.M. and J.P. Neary 1982. Booming sector and de-industrialisation in a small open economy. *Economic Journal* 92:825–48.

Fundasaun Mahein 2011. *Veterans in Timor-Leste since the Crisis of 2006*. Dili: Fundasaun Mahein.

ICG (International Crisis Group) 2009. Timor-Leste: No Time for Complacency. *Asia Briefing no. 87*. Dili: ICG.

ICG 2011. *Timor-Leste's Veterans: An Unfinished Struggle?* Dili and Jakarta: ICG.

Impact Alliance 2010. Timor-Leste: Development for Social Reintegration of the Internally Displaced in a Post Conflict Environment. Case Story. www.impactalliance.org/.

IOM (2008a) *IOM Community-Based Data Collect and Analysis for Sustainable Return: July–August 2008 Results*, Dili: International Organisation for Migration, http://mac.iom.int/jahia/webdav/shared/shared/mainsite/activities/countries/docs/timor-leste/return-monitoring-reports/round-1/Round1-IOM-Phase-I-Return-Monitoring-Results.pdf, accessed 11 August 2015.

IOM (2008b) *IOM September–November 2008 Monitoring Report: Chefes de Aldeias Surveys*, Dili: International Organisation for Migration, http://mac.iom.int/jahia/webdav/shared/shared/mainsite/activities/countries/docs/timor-leste/return-monitoring-reports/round-2/IOM-second-return-monitoring-report.pdf, accessed 11 August 2015.

IOM (2008c) *IOM October–November 2008 Monitoring Report: Community and IDP Surveys*, Dili: International Organisation for Migration, http://mac.iom.int/jahia/webdav/shared/shared/mainsite/activities/countries/docs/timor-leste/return-monitoring-reports/round-2/Community-and-IDP-Report-Round-2.pdf, accessed 11 August 2015.

IOM (2009a) *IOM December 2008–February 2009 Monitoring Report: Chefes de Aldeias Surveys*, Dili: International Organisation for Migration, http://mac.iom.int/jahia/webdav/shared/shared/mainsite/activities/countries/docs/timor-leste/return-monitoring-reports/round-3/Third-round-monitoring-Chefe-de-Aldeia-surveys.pdf, accessed 11 August 2015.

IOM (2009b) *IOM Return Monitoring Report: Community and Former IDP Household Surveys (January–March 2009)*, Dili: International Organisation for Migration, http://mac.iom.int/jahia/webdav/shared/shared/mainsite/activities/countries/docs/timor-leste/return-monitoring-reports/round-3/Round-three-monitoring-Community-and-returned-IDP-report.pdf, accessed 11 August 2015.

Kent, L. 2010. The Politics of Remembrance and Victims' Rights in East Timor. In M. Leach et al. (eds). *Understanding Timor Leste*. Hawthorn: Swinburne Press.

La'o Hamutuk 5/3/2013. The National Impact of Benefits for Former Combatants. Presentation to Belun. www.laohamutuk.org/econ/pension/VetPension6Mar2013en.pdf.

La'o Hamutuk 2014. Timor-Leste Petroleum Fund. www.laohamutuk.org/Oil/PetFund/05PFIndex.htm.

Lopes, I. 2009. Land and Displacement in Timor-Leste. *Humanitarian Exchange Magazine* 43:June. www.odihpn.org/report.asp?id=3007.

March, S. 11/9/2008. E Timor's Resistance Fighters Call for Pension. ABC Radio Australia.

Moss, T. 2011. *Oil to Cash: Fighting the Resource Curse through Cash Transfers*. Washington DC: Center for Global Development.

OVPMRDTL (Office of the Vice Prime-Minister of the Democratic Republic of Timor-Leste) 19/12/2007. *Hamutuk Hari'i Futuru: A National Recovery Strategy*. Media Release, Dili.

RDTL (*República Democrática de Timor-Leste*; Democratic Republic of Timor-Leste) 2013. *2013 State Budget. Book 1*. Dili: RDTL.

RDTLMSS (Ministry of Social Solidarity) 2008. Minister of Social Solidarity Provides Update on Work of MSS during 2008. Press Release, Ministry of Social Solidarity.

RDTLMSS 2009. Timor Minister of Social Solidarity Provides Update on Work of MSS during 2009. Press Release, Ministry of Social Solidarity.

UN (United Nations) 2010. Report of the Secretary-General on the United Nations Integrated Mission in Timor-Leste (For the Period from 21 January to 20 September 2010). UN Doc. S/2010/522. Geneva: UN.

UNDP (United Nations Development Programme) 2013. *Human Development Report 2013: The Rise of the South: Human Progress in a Diverse World.* New York: UNDP.

UNDP 2014. Timor-Leste Human Development Indicators. hdr.undp.org/en/countries/profiles/TLS.

UNESCAP (United Nations Economic and Social Commission for Asia and the Pacific) and UNDP 2003. *Exploring Timor-Leste: Mineral and Hydrocarbon Potential.* New York: United Nations.

Wallis, J. 2013. Victors, Villains and Victims: Capitalizing on Memory in Timor-Leste. *Ethnopolitics* 12(2):133–60.

World Bank 2008. *Defining Heroes: Key Lessons from the Creation of Veterans Policy in Timor-Leste.* Dili and Sydney: World Bank.

World Bank 2009. Interim Strategy Note for the Democratic Republic of Timor-Leste FY 2010–2011. Sydney and Dili: World Bank.

CHAPTER 17

Displacement and Informal Repatriation in a Rural Timorese Village

Pyone Myat Thu

Introduction

On 30 August 1999, a UN-led referendum was held to determine if Timor-Leste (better known then as East Timor) should remain a part of Indonesia or become an independent nation-state. The result was that 78.5 per cent of East Timorese favoured separation from the occupying regime. However, their choice was met with intimidation, violence and forced displacement by members of the Indonesian security forces and pro-integration militia (CAVR 2006: 134). The *Comissão de Acolhimento, Verdade e Reconciliação de Timor Leste* (CAVR; Timor-Leste Commission for Reception, Truth and Reconciliation) found that the Indonesian military and police were complicit in forming, supporting and funding pro-integration militia groups as early as late 1998 (CAVR 2006: 124). The militia threatened and attacked pro-independence supporters in the months leading up to the ballot, which culminated in the massacres in Dili and Liquisa. Violence broke out again following voting, leading to the torture, mutilation and death of nearly 1,000 East Timorese across the territory. Upon withdrawing from East Timor, the Indonesian military's 'scorched earth' campaign destroyed 70 per cent of existing infrastructure (CAVR 2006: 145). Over half of the population—550,000 people—were displaced during this troubled period, including 250,000 who fled independently out of fear, or were forcibly removed by land, sea and air to Indonesia (Achmad 2003: 193;

CAVR 2006: 145). While a large number of refugees who supported integration with Indonesia have resettled there, a small but steady informal process of repatriation to Timor-Leste carries on.

Among those forcibly displaced into West Timor, part of Indonesia's East Nusa Tenggara province, were residents of Caicua village in Baucau district (see Figure 17.1). Following nearly 13 years of resettlement in Naibonat village in Kupang district, Caicua residents are choosing to return to Timor-Leste. On 23 September 2012, I followed a local East Timorese non-government organisation (NGO), *Fila Hikas Knua* (Working Group to Bring Families Back), to the Mota Ain border crossing post to receive six returnee families (totalling 18 individuals) as they made the long journey towards their origin village of Caicua. In August 2013, I retraced these families in Caicua and carried out in depth interviews to learn about their initial flight and how they were restoring their livelihoods after repatriation. I also took the opportunity to interview other returnees who repatriated through their own means, as well as Caicua residents who did not leave the country in 1999. In this chapter, I highlight the displacement experiences of six returned families and their eventual repatriation to Caicua in 2012 to draw attention to how lives are rebuilt in rural communities that continue to confront the realities of post-conflict society. I argue that in the case of Caicua, repatriation has yet to provide a 'durable solution' in itself, since returnees have received little official recognition and social assistance from the Timor-Leste state. Community-level reconciliation is, moreover, stalled as Caicua residents continue to anticipate the return of their remaining relatives in Naibonat. Notwithstanding the lack of a permanent resolution, translocal circulations established between Caicua and Naibonat challenge the securitisation of the Indonesia–Timor-Leste border and call forth the need to broaden existing notions of 'durable solutions' to displacement.

17. Displacement and Informal Repatriation in a Rural Timorese Village

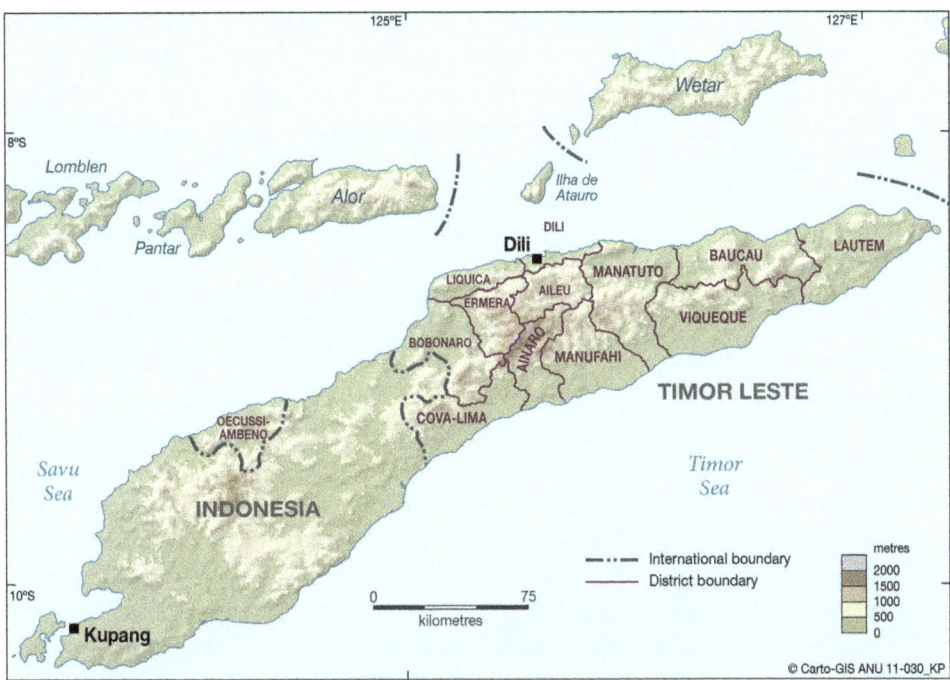

Figure 17.1 Map of Timor Island showing the districts in Timor-Leste and Kupang, the capital of West Timor.
Source: CartoGIS, College of Asia and the Pacific, The Australian National University.

Leaving Caicua

A large proportion of residents in the rice-growing, Wai'mua-speaking coastal village of Caicua in the eastern district of Baucau fled their homes following the announcement of the 1999 ballot results. On 9 September, respondents in this study, fearing a violent backlash, joined family members who worked in some capacity for the Indonesian security forces as they prepared to leave the country. At the time of flight, respondents took only minimal possessions with them. Aderito and his wife, Rita, together with their five-year-old son followed Aderito's brother—an officer in the Indonesian army. Rita recalled the moment of flight: 'I did not know where we were heading. Cuba? Portugal? We did not bring anything. We just went.' They were flown out on military aircraft from Baucau and transported to Kupang district in West Timor. Fear of violence drove people to abandon their homes. An elderly man who worked as a helper for the Indonesian police explained why he chose to leave: '[I] was afraid that's why I ran. Not because of experiencing difficult sorts of things. Not because [I] do not love [East] Timor. [I was] afraid to die. [I had] to hide in order to survive.'

In a study on resettled East Timorese in West Timor, Damaledo (2009: 24) highlights the liminal space occupied by civilian refugees, describing this category of refugees as 'guilty by association' since they were not members of the militia, or the Indonesian army or police, but rather were vulnerable to incrimination by virtue of being closely related to Indonesian loyalists. The remaining residents of Caicua escaped into the hills further inland. The whole community in Caicua was thus affected by forced displacement, even those who did not flee abroad.

The majority of East Timorese refugees were transported across the border into West Timor, where they were sheltered in refugee camps in Kupang, Atambua and selected areas of the Belu district. As the numbers of refugees soared, many people could not be accommodated in the camps, and they resettled in the surrounding areas in the open fields, schools and parishes. The United Nations High Commissioner for Refugees (UNHCR), the International Red Cross, the Catholic and Protestant Churches, and NGOs supported the local provincial government to provide emergency aid relief in the camps. Upon arrival in Kupang, a number of Caicua residents were taken by trucks to the Tuapukan refugee camp. Rosa, a female respondent then aged 12, recalled the dire situation among refugees: 'We lived opposite the Tuapukan Church. Every day we could see the dead being carried past. Maybe five people each day.' At the time of flight, Rosa was separated from her father, who was an Indonesian military officer. While her father joined the troops in Manatuto, Rosa, her mother and her younger brother fled into the hills. They emerged a day later to join her uncle on the flight out of Baucau. They were later reunited with her father in the Tuapukan camp. Some families from Caicua were resettled in *asrama* (Indonesian term meaning 'lodgings') in military stations, where temporary shelters were constructed by the Indonesian military to house the combatants of the 743, 744 and 745 battalions, who mainly originated from Baucau and Lautem districts. A number of respondents resided in an area popularly called Sosia, which was in the vicinity of a youth centre built by the Indonesian Ministry of Social Affairs.

Unsurprisingly, the crowded conditions in the West Timor refugee camps gave rise to severe health issues, starvation and death. Some camps flooded during the rainy season and access to clean water was limited. Moreover, humanitarian agencies and their workers faced security challenges posed by East Timorese militia refugees who obstructed relief efforts for the repatriation of civilian refugees (CAVR 2006: 140; UNHCR 2002: 26). Indeed, some respondents were reluctant to share more details of camp life. Their apprehension hints at the widely reported misinformation, intimidation and violence carried out by fellow militia refugees and community leaders, who subsequently chose to take up Indonesian citizenship.

When official aid relief ceased, most respondents gained access to the state's welfare system—for instance, *Rumah dinas* (public housing) in Naibonat. Their relatives who were Indonesian public servants were moreover entitled to state pension schemes. In subsequent years, the refugees camps were closed, forcing the 'former refugees' to relocate into state resettlement sites or elsewhere independently. In numerous cases, poor accessibility and weak integration with the local community led some to return to the camp areas. To date, over 500 East Timorese households from Baucau and Lautem continue to reside in Naibonat.

Meanwhile in Timor-Leste, Caicua residents who escaped to the relative safety of the hills faced similar hardships. 'We dug for *kombili* [wild yam] in the forest. We didn't carry any food since we had already eaten our harvested rice', a young female respondent explained, recounting her experience of foraging food and living in the forests for nearly two months, before returning to Caicua. Even when residents emerged from the hills, they were too afraid to resume everyday activities. Consequently, food supplies ran short. It was not until 2001 that residents gradually recommenced cultivating their gardens and rice fields.

The UNHCR's Framework for Durable Solutions for Refugees and Persons of Concern (2003) puts forward voluntary repatriation, local integration or resettlement in a third country as a global set of standards to address situations of forced displacement. In accordance with this framework, a formal repatriation program for East Timorese refugees began in October 1999 under the flagship of the UNTAET, and in co-ordination with the UNHCR, the International Organization for Migration, the peacekeeping International Force for East Timor, and the Indonesian security forces. To encourage return, video messages were exchanged between separated families, and family reunions were organised at the border (*Jakarta Post* 5/1/2002). Refugee returns peaked prior to the restoration of national independence of Timor-Leste in May 2002, and ahead of the UN cessation of refugee status for the East Timorese on 31 December 2002. In 2005, official humanitarian assistance from the Indonesian state ended for East Timorese refugees, and these populations were given the opportunity to become new citizens. To date, there are little reliable statistics on the actual size of the resettled population of East Timorese origin who have become Indonesian citizens. Estimates suggest the population to be close to 100,000 in 2010 (see ICG 2011 for more discussion). A decade since the repatriation program ended, there continues to be a small but steady stream of East Timorese who are informally and voluntarily heading back to their former homes.

Returning to Caicua

On 23 September 2012, six families from Caicua were repatriated with the assistance of two humanitarian NGOs. CIS-Timor (Centre for Internally Displaced People's Service) in West Timor has been actively assisting former East Timorese refugees since 1999, while *Fila Hikas Knua* (Working Group to Bring Families Back) was formed in 2010 in Timor-Leste through volunteers coming from the civil society networks. The two organisations have worked collaboratively since 2010 to support Timorese families separated by the '99 conflict. Building on The Frontiers' (an international NGO) messenger programme, which connects dispersed family members affected by conflict through letters and video messages, CIS-Timor and *Fila Hikas Knua* started a voluntary repatriation programme for former East Timorese refugees. Both NGOs work with minimal funding from the Timor-Leste and Indonesian governments. Each repatriation trip can be costly; adding up to US$3,000 for rental vehicles, fuel and food for returnees and volunteers. Returnees must surrender their Indonesian citizenship, which CIS-Timor takes to the West Timor district and provincial authorities for approval. Correspondingly, *Fila Hikas Knua* requests of the village chiefs in Timor-Leste who receive the returnees to endorse an official statement acknowledging their return and guaranteeing their safety upon reintegration into the village. The repatriation process is thus managed foremost by local level authorities and civil society. To date, over 180 East Timorese have been repatriated through this informal process, and there were plans for nearly 200 people to return after the Indonesian Presidential election in July 2014. There are also undocumented former East Timorese refugees who have returned illegally either through bribing border patrol officers or taking risky paths to evade arrest.

Caicua returnees decided to repatriate after reconnecting with family members through the messenger programme, which encouraged them to make subsequent trips to their origin village. A number of respondents took the opportunity in 2001 to obtain Indonesian passports, which enabled them to travel more freely across the border. The homeward journey for returnees was drawn out over two days; they were accompanied by CIS-Timor as they left Naibonat to travel to Atambua where they stayed overnight in the CIS-Timor office. The following morning, they continued to the border at Mota Ain. At the border crossing, CIS-Timor and *Fila Hikas Knua* managed the immigration process while returnees unloaded their belongings from the first truck onto a second truck that would take them to Caicua. Akin to the day they fled Timor-Leste, returnees had to leave behind most of their belongings and those who had livestock reluctantly sold them prior to moving. Other returnees are known to have taken their livestock illegally to the bordering villages and then picked them up after repatriation.

Due to limited funding, the two NGOs could only hire one truck for each phase of the journey, and returnees were restricted to take only what they deemed necessary.

Respondents cited a number of reasons for deciding to repatriate. These included the desire to reunite with family members; to secure better access to land and resources; and to return to one's birthplace. Jaco, who returned with his wife and four children, highlighted his duty as a son to care for his ageing parents: 'My parents are growing older. They have goats and other livestock. My brother doesn't plan on returning so I chose to.' Jaco's brother, like many retired Indonesian civil servants received a pension and preferred to remain in Naibonat. Abel, a returnee in his 40s, shared a similar story. Abel followed his brother to Kupang where they lived in the 743 battalion lodging before resettling in public housing. Unlike his brother who worked for the Indonesian military, Abel worked as a cook and a tailor when he was not occupied with his garden. He later married a West Timorese woman and now has two children. Abel first returned to Caicua in 2002 to visit his mother, and then again in 2010. He decided to return permanently to be a carer for his ailing mother who died five months after he repatriated.

After residing in the refugee camps and in the 743 and 744 battalion lodging, a number of respondents were given housing assistance by the Indonesian government. Some respondents moved onto private land owned by West Timor residents where they paid rent or were given access to land in kind through established social ties. The neighbourhood of Naibonat began to re-emplace the origin community of Caicua among other refugee communities as families and friends clustered near one another—particularly social groups originating from the eastern districts of Timor-Leste. Jaco and other respondents described everyday life in Naibonat as resembling Caicua, 'even the environment, the flat land, and the climate were similar', they stressed. They engaged in subsistence agriculture: cultivating gardens and rice paddies, rearing livestock, and relying heavily on the land as the primary source of livelihood. The only difference, they contended, was that they had access to smaller parcels of land (typically less than one hectare) and they were residing on someone else's land. As one respondent described, 'our livelihoods were the same in Naibonat. We eat from the land. But over there we were not living on our land. We are free now living on our land.'

Respondents further highlighted some tensions with local landowners that resulted in poor integration in Naibonat. Rosa was quick to acknowledge that the newly arrived East Timorese refugees were partly at fault: 'oh, we had troubles everyday! [East] Timor wants something, [East] Timor will get it.' When asked why the West Timorese were fearful of the East Timorese, Rosa continued, 'you know, we left here because of a crisis. So when we arrived, they knew our attitudes (*jeitu*). Some [East Timorese] killed people's animals, and they [West Timorese] couldn't raise their voice. There were too many of us.' Indeed, as reported in the media, the large influx of East Timorese migrants often provoked tension and conflict with local residents particularly concerning land access (see, for example, IRIN News 2010).

At the time of their repatriation, in 2012, *Fila Hikas Knua* provided food rations for Caicua returnees. This was supplemented by food rations from the Timor-Leste Ministry of Social Solidarity (MSS), which included two *karong* of rice (approximately 15 kilograms) for each individual. Returnees were told that MSS would return in the several months to replenish food rations, but this had not eventuated a year later when I was in residence in Caicua. The village chief of Caicua, together with the relatives of returnees, were central in helping to rebuild returnees' livelihoods. As the food supplies diminished, the village chief, who is also a member of kin, bought returnees more household provisions. While returnees were in West Timor, their relatives looked after their land and properties in Caicua. Upon return, respondents began to cultivate gardens and rice paddies on family land, however, most of them were still reliant on their kin group for food and economic assistance during the first year. The village chief moreover assisted returnees to obtain Timor-Leste electoral and identification cards. A number of individuals and families returned in the previous years from West Timor through their own means. Similarly, they received no state assistance and turned to their kin networks to rebuild livelihoods.

The dead are also among those repatriated. In 2012, the six returnee families brought with them a small coffin containing the corpse of an elderly man who passed away in Naibonat in 2009. His body was exhumed to be reburied in Caicua—his birthplace—in accordance to Wai'mua mortuary ritual practice. Respondents explained that there were more bodies to come across the border, however, their return must be preceded by staged negotiations and payment exchanges within the kin and affinal groups, which was a difficult feat to organise among the geographically dispersed families. As Senhor Supriano, A former FALINTIL (*Forças Armadas da Libertação Nacional de Timor-Leste*; Armed Forces for the National Liberation of East Timor) combatant elaborated: 'my brother-in-law is buried there. His family [residing in Naibonat] refuse to hand [him] over.' The village chief suggested that they might exhume and repatriate all the bodies of Caicua residents in West Timor in one occasion in order to save costs on logistics.

Caicua–Naibonat flows

Between 30 and 60 former residents of Caicua remain in Indonesia. Some individuals have married local West Timor residents, while others have married fellow East Timorese who were also displaced in 1999. Still others have migrated elsewhere in Indonesia. However, there is a sustained movement of people, goods, money and information between Indonesia and Timor-Leste, more specifically, a circulation between the two localities of Naibonat and Caicua. Family relatives from Naibonat may stay up to two weeks or a month in Caicua, while visitors from Caicua who travel across the border stay a similar length of time in Naibonat. Their visits are typically related to marriage or mortuary negotiations. School holidays and the end of agricultural cycles are coupled with visitations between the two sites. These transnational circulations, which can also be described as translocal, have created geographically extended social spaces. These spaces challenge the attempts by the Timor-Leste and Indonesian governments to clearly demarcate and 'secure' the border and also raise questions about what constitutes 'durable solutions' for displaced populations.

The refugee and forced displacement literatures (with notable exceptions, for example, Wise 2006 and Elmhirst 2012) tend not to adopt a 'translocal' perspective, however, I see translocality as a useful analytical framework to problematise the dichotomous notions of thinking of people as either 'displaced' or 'emplaced'. Studies of translocality stress that as people move their affiliations to specific places, along with the social ties embedded in place, may not necessarily diminish but rather become extended, multi-layered and plural (Appadurai 1996; Conradson and McKay 2007; Brickell and Datta 2011). Building on this, paying attention to translocal social relations can cast light on the enduring yet dynamic place-based connections established by returnees, non-returnees and other family members between the resettlement areas and the places of origin.

Since the colonial days, the two halves of Timor Island have had distinct histories despite the populations sharing linguistic and cultural characteristics. West Timor was ruled by the Dutch and East Timor by the Portuguese. With the departure of the Dutch, West Timor became a part of the Republic of Indonesia. When Indonesia proceeded to occupy the eastern half, it kept East Timor as a separate province from East Nusa Tenggara. In spite of security concerns within the occupied territory, border crossing in certain areas, such as Oecussi, became relatively easier. Since the independence of Timor-Leste, the Indonesian and Timor-Leste governments have taken steps to accommodate the high rates of cross-border movement. For instance, in 2002, the long-standing cultural and trade links between the border areas of the two countries were officially recognised under the arrangement on 'Traditional Border Crossings and Regulated Markets', which enables residents in the recognised border areas to obtain a Border Crossing Pass permitting free border crossing for 10 days (KBRI 2002).

This official cross-border scheme does not, however, comprise residents who originate from places beyond the recognised border areas, such as Caicua. As such, it is common for Caicua residents who travel to Naibonat, and residents in Naibonat who travel to Caicua, to tread along the 'rat trails' (translated from the Indonesian phrase *jalan tikus* as drawn on extensively by respondents), especially since they cannot afford to apply for a passport and pay the visa fees. One respondent humorously described the perils of crossing the border illegally and fearing capture by border security forces, 'the local landowners don't mind. They actually warn us, "walk quickly otherwise the military will catch you!"' Notwithstanding the political demarcation of national borders, there is much permeability on the ground where local populations on both sides seem empathetic to trespassers.

During social exchanges with non-returnees, returnees and other relatives in Caicua often encouraged them to repatriate. Senhor Supriano relayed that he did not hold any animosity towards his relatives residing in Indonesia, 'we have received those who returned with both hands. Some of us were angry initially, but it has been such a long time. I said to them this is your land, your birthplace.' Those who have not returned were typically benefiting from Indonesian state pension and welfare schemes. To date, formal community-level reconciliation processes/ceremonies have not been initiated in Caicua. Respondents emphasised that this delay was intentional, without everyone present to ensure that individuals' narratives were consistent with one another, there could be potential for misunderstandings to occur. In line with this view, the village chief suggested holding a community-wide reconciliation process only with the presence of all those concerned. The flow of people, material and cultural exchanges between Naibonat and Caicua nonetheless suggest that social division within this community is likely to be minimal.

Conclusion

More than a decade has passed since the East Timorese chose to separate from the occupying powers of Indonesia. Nevertheless, members of the West Timor refugee diaspora (or 'new citizens' as they are now referred to in Indonesia) are continuing to search for long-term stability in their lives. Caicua village is exemplary of the many communities that are overcoming the legacy of the 1999 conflict. Livelihoods and social life among returnees are independently rebuilt with social and economic assistance from NGOs and local kin networks filling the void left by the Timor-Leste state. At the national level, the Timor-Leste political leaders have publicly encouraged the return of its refugee diaspora, but they have not formally embarked on assisting voluntary repatriation since 2002. The repatriation of former pro-integration leaders and militia members presents a politically sensitive issue, particularly at the local level where disquiet persists among former pro-independence veterans and victims, about the fact that perpetrators of violence and crimes have not been brought to justice. Former civilian refugees are inevitably entangled in these broader politics, perpetuating the vulnerable positions in which they find themselves. They occupy a liminal space where they receive few benefits in Indonesia, but are likely to receive even less state assistance upon repatriation to Timor-Leste. At the international level, East Timorese returnees are technically Indonesian citizens and, as such, they have received little assistance from international humanitarian agencies.

For the community of Caicua, the repatriation of former residents in itself has yet to provide a 'durable solution' to the impacts of the 1999 conflict. Rather, there should be more state assistance provided for returnees in the immediate months following repatriation. There also needs to be recognition of, and allowances made for, the mobility involved in maintaining kinship ties and spiritual commitments between non-returnees in Naibonat and the origin community. The temporal dimension of repatriation must also be acknowledged here since the returnees chose not to repatriate in the early years when official assistance was provided. A related question then is, would returnees' reintegration in Caicua have been any different if they had returned much earlier when 'wounds' were fresh?

As refugees resettle in a second country, the living conditions in their new country or origin country might transform, leading some people to reconsider repatriation. Considering West Timor is situated in one of the poorest Indonesian provinces, along with everyday pressures over land, and unemployment, informal repatriation will likely continue to Timor-Leste if it remains politically stable, and makes progress in social and economic development (ICG 2011). The translocal and transnational circulations between West Timor and Timor-Leste highlight the ability to move across the border as an important mechanism for accessing resources and securing livelihoods for the East Timorese refugee diaspora (cf. van Hear 2006; Long 2010). This demonstrates the need to think more creatively about what constitutes 'durable solutions' and to take into account the dynamism of migrants' lives.

Acknowledgements

I am grateful to the residents of Caicua village for accommodating me, particularly Senor Geraldo da Costa. I sincerely thank the volunteers of *Fila Hikas Knua* who generously gave me the opportunity to observe the repatriation process, notably Sister Monica Nakamura of The Congregation of the Sacred Heart of Jesus (Japan), and Charles Meluk from The Frontiers. I also thank Charles for his patience and providing research assistance in Caicua village.

References

Achmad, J. 2003. East Timorese refugees in West Timor. In J.J. Fox and D.B. Soares (eds). *Out of the Ashes: Deconstruction and Reconstruction of East Timor*. Canberra: ANU E Press, 190–206.

Appadurai, A. 1996. *Modernity at Large: Cultural Dimensions of Globalization*. Minneapolis: University of Minnesota.

Brickell, K. and A. Datta (eds) 2011. *Translocal Geographies: Spaces, Places, Connections*. London: Ashgate.

CAVR 2006. *Chega! The Report of the Commission for Reception, Truth and Reconciliation of Timor-Leste*. Dili: CAVR.

Conradson, D. and D. McKay 2007. Translocal Subjectivities: Mobility, Connection, Emotion. *Mobilities* 2(2):167–74.

Damaledo, A.Y. 2009. From Refugee to Citizen: An examination of the identity of the ex-East Timorese Refugees in Indonesia. Masters of Development Practice (Advanced) thesis, University of Queensland.

Elmhirst, R. 2012. *Displacement, Resettlement, and Multi-Local Livelihoods: Positioning Migrant Legitimacy in Lampung, Indonesia. Critical Asian Studies* 44(1):131–52.

ICG (International Crisis Group) 2011. Timor-Leste: Reconciliation and Return from Indonesia. *Asia Briefing* no.122. Dili/Jakarta/Brussels: ICG.

IRIN News 2010. Indonesia: Land Tensions flare for Former Refugees. www.irinnews.org/report/91329/indonesia-land-tensions-flare-for-former-refugees.

Jakarta Post 5/1/2002. Many East Timorese Refugees Remain at Camps in W. Timor. www.thejakartapost.com/news/2002/01/05/many-east-timorese-refugees-remain-camps-w-timor.html.

Kedutaan Besar Republik Indonesia (KBRI) 2002. 'Arrangement between The Republic of Indonesia and the Democratic Republic of Timor-Leste on Traditional Border Crossings and Regulated Markets'. treaty.kemlu.go.id/uploads-pub/4284_TLS-2003-0003.pdf.

Long, K. 2010. Home Alone? A Review of the Relationship Between Repatriation, Mobility and Durable Solutions for Refugees. United Nations High Commissioner for Refugees Policy Development and Evaluation Service. PDES/2010/02. Geneva: UNHCR. www.unhcr.org/4b97afc49.html.

UNHCR (United Nations High Commissioner for Refugees) 2002. East Timorese Refugees in West Timor. In *UNHCR 2002 Global Appeal. Addendum*. Geneva: UNHCR, 25–33. www.unhcr.org/3e1a9fc00.html.

UNHCR 2003. Framework for Durable Solutions for Refugees and Persons of Concern. Geneva: UNHCR. www.unhcr.org/3f1408764.html.

van Hear, N. 2006. Refugees in Diaspora: From Durable Solutions to Transnational Relations. *Refuge* 23(1):9–14.

Wise, A. 2006. *Exile and Return Among the East Timorese*. Philadelphia: University of Pennsylvania Press.

www.ingramcontent.com/pod-product-compliance
Lightning Source LLC
Chambersburg PA
CBHW040313240426
43666CB00030B/2924